CW00801991

ABERFORD CHURCH OF ENGLAND SCHOOL
1716 TO 2016

MAROLYN PIPER

APS Books
Yorkshire

APS Books,
The Stables, Field Lane
Aberford, West Yorkshire,
LS25 3AE

APS Books is a subsidiary of the APS Publications imprint

www.andrewsparke.com

Front and rear covers: Ceramic Shield and Plaque created by Aberford
School children to commemorate the year 2000.

First published worldwide by APS Books in 2024

CONTENTS

INTRODUCTION

This book is an amalgamation of two volumes printed in 2009. I never obtained an ISBN back then as that printing was just sold around the village and raised £350 for school funds. I have decided to make this History more widely available – as 15 years have passed and many new people have moved into the village who may be unaware of the amazing connection of our school with Oriel College.

There have been slight amendments due to a little extra information being discovered

When you walk up the little lane to Aberford village school, you are not alone. You are walking in the company of many teachers and hundreds and hundreds of children if you could only see them. Some of the children are as young as 3 and some will reach 15.

Aberford teachers and children have walked up and down this lane in snowy winter and summer sunshine. Many children walked with their brothers or sisters. Many children's children and grandchildren took this path. On their first day some children approached in cheerful anticipation and some in tearful apprehension of what they would find. The school which helped to shape these ghostly boys and girls has been witness to all of human emotions – much like the Church close to which it stands.

There are very few schools which were founded as early as Aberford School. There are none with such a unique connection to Oriel College, Oxford. Very few records specific to Aberford School have been found but, by reference to material about other similarly early schools, I have tried to give an idea of how things may have been. The early school can only be glimpsed 'darkly', through drawing together the little information which could be found about the (Head) Masters of the day, and through describing aspects of the village at that time. Events in the village and outside world which would be known to the children have also been described as I move forward in time, to try to give a flavour of the school and village history.

Later Headmasters 'speak for themselves', through the series of Log Books they all kept, with just a little help from me.

So, I hope you enjoy this 300 year-old story of Aberford School and village .... and forgive any errors ....

Marolyn Piper
Aberford 2024

Chapter One
THE ORIEL COLLEGE CONNECTION

Some people, with ancestors in the village, know there is a connection between Aberford School and Oriel College, Oxford but perhaps don't know that this goes right back to the very founding of Oriel College itself. So what is that connection?

Oriel College was founded by a man called Adam de Brome – he was an almoner to King Edward II. He carried out many varied tasks such as, in 1297, collecting food supplies in Dorset. In 1299 he was in charge of the Assize of Corn and Wine. In 1305 he was auditing accounts of the Papal Tithes. Early in Edward II's reign he was one of the Clerks of Chancery. He had also been ordained a priest in 1301 and held several religious posts in different parts of the country, including Rector of Handsworth, Yorkshire between 1313 and 1316.

De Brome was Rector of St Mary the Virgin Church, Oxford from 1320 to 1326 and, in 1324, he purchased two properties in Oxford and the advowson of a church in Aberford. There would have been land – and possibly property – forming the advowson all of which produced income from rents. Presumably De Brome must have thought these purchases a good investment.

In this same year De Brome obtained a licence from the King to found a College of Scholars and he made over the Oxford properties and Aberford advowson to the newly formed College. (The name Oriel came about because the College received, by way of Royal Grant, a large house known as La Oriole for it had an 'oriel' window and stood on the site of what is now First Quad.)

Adam de Brome was the first Provost of Oriel College and St Mary the Virgin Church is used by Oxford University for official functions to the present time, which gives the College a constitutional importance in Oxford. Adam de Brome died in 1332 and was buried in St Mary's Church and he is depicted in a stained glass window in the Hall of Oriel College.

The advowson of Aberford Church would have produced income for the College from rents which accrued to the holder of it, maintaining that invisible thread which joined the two distant communities. In addition, the position of Vicar of Aberford Church was (and remains) in the gift of Oriel College if they choose to exercise that right.

For some centuries, whilst the education of some lucky young men was taking place in Oxford, there was no education for ordinary people in Aberford; as was the case throughout the country. Universal education, well into the 1800s, was not held to be necessary – or indeed desirable - for it was felt that the Church could supply all the guidance necessary and salvation was not dependent on the power to read. There was a belief that 'the poor' should remain in that condition and that the different levels of society should not be disturbed. Industry and domestic life were laborious with most of the population spending their lives in simple and heavy work so that a minority could live in comfort.

It was to be almost 400 years after the founding of Oriel College before a charity school was created in far-away Aberford. In 1716, when Aberford Charity School was created, it typified the sort of limited and rare schools which had started up across the country. These schools were supported by a mixture of endowments, private charity and church collections. Often the school was founded and maintained by the local clergyman who might do the teaching himself. Sometimes the Master was supplied by a man who held some existing office like that of Clerk to the Parish.

It was a lucky child who had a Master or Mistress who liked children and who had sufficient education themselves to be able to teach the basic '3 Rs'. Unlucky children could find themselves, at best, with a kindly well-meaning but barely literate man or woman, or even an elderly tyrant who had only taken the job to get a little money.

What was taught varied widely – usually reading, which would be from the bible or other religious tracts. There might be singing of psalms, writing and simple arithmetic. In some places there would be skills such as navigation taught (as at a school in Greenwich so that the boys could be apprenticed to ships).

Children were taught in a huge variety of buildings ranging from a spare room above a shop to the undercroft in a church, with all manner of totally unsuitable premises being used. It was quite usual for children to stand for the whole of the time – perhaps sharing in the use of the small amount of furniture. We cannot know what our early Aberford School was exactly like but we can try to glimpse it.

(See, for interest, Appendix I for the Lady Elizabeth Hastings/Queens College, Oxford connection to Aberford village dating back to 1739).

Chapter Two
HOW, WHO AND WHERE!

From an early book (i) we can get a good idea of what was going on in the country. This book said that the local minister sometimes proposed a school, sometimes some gentlemen or merchants or local landowners got together. They would ask others to subscribe, then they would agree upon what kind of man should be the Master and under what terms and what should be taught in the school. Aberford School was not mentioned in this book but one or two were already established in the area and these are set out below for interest.

Spofforth: a school with a house adjoining to it for the Master, formerly built by one of the Earls of Northumberland and repaired by the inhabitants of this town. A person of quality has given 5/- per annum for teaching 10 poor children of Spofforth and Linton. 5/- was given by the late Rector deceased for the like number. 5 are likewise gratis taught by the Schoolmaster of Spofforth in consideration of his being chosen Clerk of the Parish. All the children are daily taught to sing Psalms. ¾ of the Offertory are appropriated towards supplying the poor children with books and cloathed and binding them out apprentice. Some collections are made yearly in every Township throughout the Parish for the same uses, after a sermon preached on this occasion, at Spofforth and Wetherby.

Kirk Deighton: £7 p.a. given by 3 persons for a school there.

Leeds: a school for 28 boys and 12 girls, the fund is about £208p.a. namely £20p.a. out of the collection at the communion, £20 p.a. from the Feoffees, for clothing the poor of the town. And the rest is made by subscription of the Magistrates and the inhabitants. The Corporation gave a large house for the school and for the repairing and fitting it up. A gentleman intends to settle on it £6 p.a. for ever. A Merchant has given £50 and another gentleman £50 which has purchased £8 per annum and another Merchant £100. A Dissenter lately gave to it £10 by Will.

Skipton: a school called "the song school" where all the boys of the town are taught to sing Psalms by the Parish Clerk, who has a salary for that purpose besides his Parish dues. He is obliged also to teach all the children of the town to read and their Catechism. 12 of the children are cloathed by a private gentleman.

Aberford village was very fortunate in having some residents who came together to found the first school at such an early date and who were prepared to create a dedicated building to house the children. Rev. David Dawson was the vicar in 1716 and he was one of the group of men. The names of the Aberford men and their subscriptions are listed in Appendix II. (Note: Lady Elisabeth Hastings was not found as a subscriber, although Rev. Bentham in 1764, stated 'the school was set on foot anno 1716 at the instance of R.H.Lady Elisabeth Hastings'. She may indeed have taken part in discussions and made a contribution as it would have been in keeping with her charitable and generous nature).

Also in Appendix II is a copy of the letter sent to Oriel College asking for the use of an old Tythe Barn – which was to be taken down and the materials reused. The list of costs for building the school are also shown. There is quite a large gap in the subscriptions raised and the total cost but how this gap was dealt with is not known.

(There may have been a little schooling going on in the village prior to this for some notes have been found which state: "payment was made to Widow Cullingworth for a year and eight weeks for her house for the boys from Oct. 1715 to Christmas 1716.")

The position of the old Tythe Barn in the centre of the widespread village and next to the Church was a lucky and well-chosen one. Happily situated right in the heart of Aberford it was to become an important institution in the village. If the founders had been able to look forward in time, how pleased they would have been at the way the school prospered.

There are no records of how the Master was chosen but it is likely that the requirements would be very similar to those listed in the early book referred to (i):

1. A member of the Church of England of a sober life and conversation and not under 25 years of age.

2. One that frequents the Holy Communion

3. One that hath a good Government of himself and his passions.

4. One of a meek Temper and humble Behaviour.

5. One who understands well the grounds and principles of the Christian religion and is able to give a good Account thereof to the Minister of the Parish, or Ordinary, on examination.

6. One of a good Genius for Teaching.

7. One who can write a good Hand and who understands the Grounds of Arithmetic.

8. One who is approved by the Minister of the Parish (being a subscriber) before he be presented to be licenced by the Ordinary.

9. One who keeps good orders in his Family.

A good long list! In addition there was advice that the newly elected Master should consult with some experienced Masters who could "communicate ... the divers methods of teaching and governing their scholars, according to the different capacities, tempers and inclinations of the children". (i) So, even in these early days, there was recognition that one size didn't fit all!

The Master's duties were quite onerous for they probably included:

"Catechism .. he shall first teach them to pronounce distinctly and plainly and then, in order to practice, shall explain it to the meanest capacity by some good exposition approved of by the Minister and this shall be done constantly twice a week that everything in the catechism may be the more perfectly repeated and understood.   ... take particular care of the manners and behaviour .... correct the beginnings of vice and particularly lying, smearing, cuffing, taking God's name in vain.... minding them whereof those things are mentioned as forbidden by God ......". (i) When the children had sufficiently learned their catechism they would be catechised in

Church and when they could read fairly well they would be taught to write "a fair legible hand with the true spelling of words and definition of syllables with the points and stops." (i) The children should be brought to Church twice every Lords Day and Holy Day and have their Bibles with them.

The Master was to keep an account of the children's attendance and of their faults together with the weekly bills to put before the Subscribers or Trustees. The Master should not receive money from anyone " but shall content himself with his salary upon pain of forfeiting his place". (i) The following chapters try to glimpse the early days of Aberford School.

Chapter Three
JAMES WILSON
(October 1716 – February 1717)

It was during this early first year or so that the old Tythe Barn was being remodelled to form the first building for the school. There were many and varied expenses incurred and there must have been much activity around the site. The whole community must have been interested in the building works but whether the children who would attend the school looked forward to the completion we cannot know. Sketch 1 shows the basic footprint c1716 of the Tythe Barn together with the 1717 small extension. (This undated sketch by an unknown person was found amongst papers from Aberford School and shows three views of the first school as it developed. The basic footprint of the Tythe Barn looks to have had a small extension added when it was developed into the schoolroom c1717.)

In this early time Sir Edward Gascoigne was the 6th Baronet and he married in November 1726 – his bride was Mary the daughter and heiress of Sir Francis Hungate of Huddlestone Hall. He was to remain at Parlington for some 17 years and four of his children were born there. Much of the Gascoigne's wealth came from mining interests and one of their early pits was in Parlington Hollins – today totally erased and planted with trees. Some fathers in the village would have been miners as, perhaps, would some of the boys though much employment would have been in agriculture.

James Wilson may have acted as the first, short-lived, Master. If so, then he only served from 17th October 1716 until the Candlemas (February) following. (ii) From the Parish Registers there was a baptism of a John Wilson, the son of a Christopher Wilson, on 16th March 1678 and several more children followed to this same father. No James was found but as James was a common alternative for John it may well be that this was the man who was referred to.

We do know (iii) the school was for fifteen boys and fifteen girls at that time so these numbers may have applied from the start of the school. We also know something of what the Master was to teach the children from the previous Chapter, but there could have been expectations of the children. The recommendation was that certain things should be carried over into the home life of the children: "pray at home ... and to use Graces before and after Meat." (i)

We know that caps and aprons were worn (ii) and parents should "take care to send their children to school and keep them at home on no pretence except in case of sickness ...correct their children for such faults as they commit at home ... send their children clean washed and combed ..... the Subscribers will take due care that the children shall suffer no injuries by their Master's correction which is only designed for their good.." (i) The latter statement must have been a comfort to the children in those times of liberal use of corporal punishment!

There was a happy occasion in 1725 for Rev. David Dawson who had been one of the prime movers in helping to found the school – he was married on the 6th May to Mrs Mary Baxter at Selby. Presumably this lady had been married previously but she was described in the Parish Register as "spinster".

Chapter Four
THOMAS BLOOM(E)
(February 1717 – 1763)

Amongst the Diocesan papers (iv) was a letter, signed by David Dawson Vicar, Robert Potter, George Rhodes and Vall. Priestman, which is reproduced here:

"We whose names are hereunto subscribed being the Trustees for the Charity School at Abberford, do hereby certify that Thomas Bloome made choice of (by) us to be the Schoolmaster, is also by the Vicar of the aforesaid parish to be Clerk, as a man of an honest and sober conversation well schooled in reading writing and arithmetick and comfortable to the doctrine and discipline of the Church as by law established. In testimony whereof we have hereunto set our hands this day 19th January 1718".

It is possible that Thomas Bloome lived in the house next to the Arabian Horse which stands to the present time - ".... was a long-fronted building having a blank wall at the back with only a small window on the top landing. A very pleasant room inside and in the kitchen was a force-pump to pump water to a tank in the roof. In the garden, which adjoined the river, was a very good puzzle walk. Mr Dixon was tenant and the Bloom family were the owners". (xii)

This man became Headmaster from February 1717 in the first building dedicated solely as Aberford School and he probably served some 46 years. From the Town Book (iv) in the accounts of Thos Walker (Constable) c1753/4, there was a note: "N.B. Thos Bloome not paid for writing the Land Tax and Window duplicates the last 2 years as appears by Henry Clarkson and Thos. Walker's accounts due. 20.11.1755 – paid by Wm Hick 3/-". No doubt Thomas Bloome was one of the few who could write at this time and therefore held more than one position of importance in the village. It seems he was Headmaster until c1763. Retirement was unknown in these early days.

There were agreed charges that the Master could take for every boy and these were less for those boys whose parents had contributed to the creation of the school. For learning English per quarter there was a charge of 2/- (2/6 for non-subscribers), for Writing per quarter 3/- and for Latin or Arithmetic 3/-. (ii) Equal opportunities came early to Aberford School for in March of 1717 Mrs Sarah Shillito (wife of Richard Shillito) was elected Mistress for fifteen girls at a salary of £7 per annum. She seems also to have been a long-serving teacher for it was recorded that she was succeeded in 1752 by Betty Jackson (wife of Joshua Jackson) who was paid initially £6 per annum for thirteen girls. In 1764 this salary was raised to £6.10s. – a gap of 12 years without any increase for inflation! (ii)

We know (v) that Joshua and Betty Jackson were buried in Aberford Churchyard for a gravestone there has the following inscription: "Here lies the body of Joshua Jackson, son of Hyllam (Hillam) Mill who departed this life 25.2.1759 age 63. Also here lies the wife of Joshua Jackson 28.10.1775 aged 87". Betty lived to a good age and must have been over 60 when she started teaching. Hillam Mill was in an area now part of Leyfield Farm on the Aberford/Barwick road and the only vestige now to be seen is the goit through which the water was channelled to power the waterwheel.

Rev John Harris was Vicar at this time and had been from 1733 to 1738. He was followed by Rev Thomas Bentham in 1738 and it was this man who was the vicar mentioned in the Trust Deed of Lady Elizabeth Hastings (Appendix I). He was to use her bequest of £30 towards rebuilding the Vicarage which was the old house featured in the photograph reproduced below. Which property had previously been the Vicarage is not known but perhaps it stood on the same site and was just enhanced at this time. (This photograph previously appeared in the book 'Aberford in Times Past').

Some 7 years later the year of 1745 was a tumultuous one throughout the country for it was the year of the second Jacobite Rising and with Aberford situated on such a major road, everyone would have been very worried. Every traveller was no doubt asked for news in this time before television, radio and newspapers. No-one knew the exact positions of the opposing forces and whether fighting would touch the village. This period was not a happy time for Catholics as there was much anti-Catholic feeling in the country and Sir Edward Gascoigne, in 1743, took his whole family to Cambrai in France. The Gascoignes had very strong ties to the Catholic faith at this time with several members of the family having become monks, priests and nuns over the years. Catholics had to pay financial "taxes" on their holdings and there were other sanctions such as being prevented from holding public office like Justice of the Peace. In fact Sir Edward died in France in 1750 and was buried in the cemetery of the monastery at Cambrai.

According to Parish Registers, Thomas Bloome married Ann Priestman in 1745 and a son was born to the couple in 1747 and baptised in June, named after his father who was given as "SM and PC" – Schoolmaster and Parish Clerk. Further children followed: Matthew baptised 23.9.1750, James baptised 31.5.1753 and Jane baptised 31.5.1764 when the entry of Parish Clerk was made against the father's name. We know that, at this time, there was a bridge over Cock Beck in the centre of the village since it was repaired in 1749. There was also a ford, vestiges of which remain to the present day.

In June 1758 Margaret Jackson was elected Mistress for thirteen girls at £6 per annum. In 1764 her salary advanced to £6.10s. (ii) Perhaps Margaret was a relative of Betty Jackson who had been Schoolmistress. There was a happy occasion when Thomas Bloome was a witness at a wedding when, on 8th May 1763, Miles Jackson married Jane Pool of Bramham. This Miles Jackson was buried in the same grave as Joshua and Betty Jackson. (v) Miles held various positions of importance in the village during the 1700s. (iv)

Some research has been done to try to trace forward the Bloome family which was once a prominent one in Aberford. This was helped by the unusual last name! As of 2008 it looks as if Thomas may have been the father of Matthew Bloome who held various Parish jobs during the 1700s (iv). In 1783 Matthew was a 'Collector'. In 1784 he was an 'Assessor'. In 1786 was a 'Surveyor'. In 1787/1788 he was the 'Parish Constable'. In 1791/1792/1793 and 1794 he was the 'Parish Overseer'. In 1796/1797 and 1798 he was again 'Constable' – additionally in 1797 he was also 'Overseer'. More than a hundred years later, the Bloome family were still represented in Aberford as we can see from the following:

"There is in the keeping of Matthew Bloome Esq. Of Aberford, a document bearing date 2.6.1694 being a marriage settlement of Valentine Priestman with the widow of Rev James Watter, Clerk, Vicar of Aberford and which document I have this day seen – 10.3.1862 – C.P.E."(v) *(Charles Eden was Vicar at this time).*

Since the earlier Matthew Bloome married Ann Priestman, presumably this is why this later Matthew was in possession of a document relating to Valentine Priestman.

Chapter Five
MATTHEW MALHAM
(1763 – July 1778)

This man became Headmaster (and he was also the Parish Clerk) in 1763. It seems he succeeded Mr Bloome who had been Headmaster virtually from the start in 1717. When the long-serving Mr Bloome resigned (surely because of old age) the Master taught fifteen boys at £9 per annum and the charges were increased for the first time since the school started some 46 years previously. Each boy would now pay per quarter 2/6 for English, 4/- for Writing and 5/- for Latin or Arithmetic. It is not known what the girls paid. The following year it seems that Matthew must have requested an increase in salary for he received an increase of £1 per annum "on account of the dearness of provisions." (ii)

Matthew must have married in this year for there is a note of "Banns" being called, in the Parish Register, on 3 occasions in 1763: 31st July, 7th and 14th August. He married Jane Tinsley of Ripon and presumably the couple married there. No doubt Matthew's securing the salaried post of Headmaster at Aberford played a part in the couple being able to marry.

Just a year earlier, in 1762, Sir Thomas Gascoigne had inherited his family's extensive estates around Aberford on the death of his elder brother. He was only 19 and living with a tutor in Paris and remained abroad for many years with the estates managed by trustees. He had lived with his father Sir Edward at Cambrai and had no strong ties to his Yorkshire roots. Sir Edward had taken his family to Cambrai perhaps to live more freely as Catholics. Catholics were banned from many aspects of life in England which were open to Protestant families of commensurate wealth and education. He visited occasionally but did not settle in Parlington until 1779. Thereafter he became an ardent agriculturalist running two of his farms as 'models' to his tenants and established extensive paddocks for racehorses. Whether he played any part, or took any interest, in the little school is not known but he was a benefactor to the district in many ways.

In May of 1764 a daughter was born to the Malhams and baptised on the 31st May with her father being listed as Parish Clerk. It was a busy year for Matthew for he was a witness at two weddings this year in Aberford: on 31st July William Brayfit of Spofforth married Elisabeth Lockwood of Aberford and on 13th August William Barker married Frances Robinson both being from Aberford.

In 1764, (iii) Rev.Thomas Bentham (instituted in June of 1738) stated:

"We have one charity school for 15 boys and 13 girls who are all taught to read and write and some learn arithmetic. The girls are, moreover, employed in sewing and knitting and, to inure the boys to labour, they have occasional leave of absence for such work in the husbandry way as they are fit for. None of the children are clothed or maintained. The master of the boys, whose salary is £9 per annum, is Matthew Malham the Parish clerk; the mistress of the girls (is) Margaret Jackson, her salary is £6 per annum. They are both very diligent in instructing the children in religious principles as the canon requires. The school was set on foot anno 1716 at the instance of the late R.H.Lady Elisabeth Hastings and by the generous contribution of her Ladyship and other neighbouring gentry and of the inhabitants. Her Ladyship, by her deed of estates settled in trust for charitable uses dated 18 December 1738, gave 5 guineas per annum towards the support of the said school forever; and her sister the R.H.Lady Margaret Ingham lately gave £100 for the same purpose which is placed out upon a mortgage at 4.1/2 percent. This is all the certain revenue belonging to the said school: the rest is supplied by the voluntary contributions of the inhabitants and neighbouring gentry and a small collection after a charity sermon preached on the first Sunday after Trinity in every year."

Reverend Bentham also stated: "My custom is to catechise the children of the school (for none or very few others will submit to that exercise) on most Sundays from the beginning of Lent to the end of October. The children on the foundation do all learn Lewis's catechism besides. Alternately with Lewis's exposition I read a lecture on some part of the church catechism". In addition Reverend Bentham reported: "There are besides 2 petty schools in the parish, one in Abberford taught by Elisabeth Gill, a dissenter, the other by Frances Hunter in Parlington". These two small 'schools' have not been traced.

In 1766 some 25 caps for the boys cost £1.7s.0d and their hair was cut 4 times at a cost of 2s.0d. Maybe this was an early attempt to have a smart and uniform look which was reinforced by the boys having their untidy hair made more presentable! In 1767 more caps: materials for 20 boys' caps together with 18 aprons for girls which came to £1.13s.11d.The caps cost 11s.0d to make and £3.1s.10.1/2d was spent on books from the Society for Christian Knowledge. Mary Jackson (late Mistress) was paid £2.7s.6d, Hannah Hollins taught to midsummer at a cost of £1.2s.6d and Eliz. Sampson taught for half a year at a cost of £3.5s.0d. (ii) It may be that Mary Jackson had either died or become unable to teach and that two other women had taken over for the rest of the year.

In 1770 a new vicar was appointed – Rev Edward Carne who was also Vicar of Thorner and Prebend of York and Ripon. This man must have been quite senior in the Church to have held the appointment of Prebend (Canon).

In 1773 the Master's salary was £12. and that of the Mistress £6.10s. Various items were purchased, some being: 7 bibles, 6 spelling books, three different entries for 4/4/3 bibles, 7 "readings made easy" and 9 Common Prayer books.(ii)

Several children were born to the Malhams during his time as Headmaster and their baptisms were recorded in the Parish Registers: 6.10.1765 Matthew, 19.3.1767 Ann, 17.3.1768 George, 3.3.1771 Mary, 25.3.1773 Ann, 27.7.1777 Edward and 14.4.1779 Robert. Matthew Malham was the Schoolmaster for some fifteen years but it seems his tenure ended under something of a cloud. He was actually dismissed in July 1778 by the Vicar Rev Carne (vi) for "irregularities" which may have been monetary, and for "neglect" – presumably in his application to teaching the children.

Research has been done to try to trace forward the Malham family and on the 1841 census, records showed a Mary Malham age 21 living in Aberford – possibly helping a William Eastwood age 80 an Agricultural Labourer, whose name appeared directly above. There was also a Thomas Malham age 15 who appeared to be living in the household of a local farmer and his occupation was listed by the initials "M.S." which is thought to be 'man servant'. Whether these two people were descended from Matthew Malham is not known but certainly research on later census records show some Malhams living in and around Aberford down through the 1901 census, who may be related to the early Schoolmaster.

Chapter Six
EDMUND SHAW
(July 1778 – c1792)

Rev Edward Carne dismissed Matthew Malham and appointed Edmund Shaw as Master. Very little information has been discovered about Edmund Shaw. However, from 'guesswork', using various data bases, it may be that Edmund Shaw was a Garforth man. There was a marriage record in Garforth Parish Registers of an Edmund Shaw and Hannah Fletcher dated 2nd August 1778. They were married by the Curate Thomas Carr and the witnesses were John Robinson and Josa Vevers. It is possible that this last witness was a member of the Vevers family of Aberford – maybe it was with their influence Edmund Shaw obtained his appointment. Certainly there are Vevers buried in Aberford churchyard. Here is an inscription recorded on a gravestone in poor repair c1862 (v):

"Here lieth interred the body of Elizabeth wife of Geo. Vevers of Leayfield, who departed 12?/10/1741 in 30th year of her age . Also here lieth the body of Martha daughter of Geo Vevers by Elizabeth his wife who departed this life 5.8.1750 in the 21st year of her age, Also here lieth the body of Geo Vevers who departed this life 29.8.1762 aged 51 years, Also Sarah wife of Matthew Hall 5.7.177(1?) age 25, Also Ann wife of Geo Vevers who died 11.4.1774, age 62."

A separate gravestone to a Mary Vevers may be seen at the back of Aberford Church dated 1779.

It is possible that Hannah was a witness at the wedding of a relative for there was a marriage of Robert Johnson of Pontefract to Frances Fletcher of Garforth on 13th June 1790 and one of the witnesses was Hannah Shaw – which would have been her last name if she was married by this time. Further evidence for these two women being sisters: there was a Garforth baptism record for Hannah daughter of William Fletcher dated 12th April 1762 and one for a Fanny (Frances?) daughter of William Fletcher dated 14th October 1764.

Hannah was only 16 when she married Edmund Shaw, not unusual for those days. The marriage of Edmund and Hannah in August 1778 would have coincided with his appointment as Master of Aberford School in July of that year – perhaps his settled circumstances made it possible for Edmund and Hannah to marry.

The prospect of being sent to the Workhouse was always present in these times for poor or sick people. Every Parish raised a rate to be spent on supporting the very poor and here is how one Overseer spent the money available to him (iv). In 1787, Tim Bainbridge was Overseer, which was one of many terms of office/positions this man held during the latter half of the 18th century. He had a lot of trouble with one particular woman and the entries appear here:

Catherine Waite's expenses at Workhouse: May/June/July/Aug/Sept
£ 1.12s.9d

To E Cullingworth for delivering C.Waite of bastard	5/-
Churching	1/-
Butter, Sugar, Tea etc for laying in	7/-
Cloth for shifts	6d
Shoes	9s.8d
Mary Birks for nursing C.Waite's child	7s.6d
Wine and attendance for C.Waite's child when ill	2s.9d
C.Waite's child's funeral	9s.6d
Warrant for C. Waite	2/-
Expenses	2s.6d
Commitment to House of Correction	2/-
Myself and Bailiff expenses	2s.6d
Justices order for conveying C.Waite to Wakefield	7s.6d
Given to C. Waite at her departure	2s.6d
To Barwick Constable for horse hire and Expenses in conveying C. Waite to House Of Correction	7/-
Own expenses	2s.6d
For horse hay and corn	1s.6d
Liberation of C. Waite from House of Correction	2/-
Conveying the Liberation to Mr Waugh and expenses	2s.6d
At Barwick for C.Waite after her return from Wakefield	10s.6d.

The total amount spent from Parish funds on Catherine Waite was £6.16s.5d which must have been a considerable sum in those times. The following is an attempt to interpret the story behind the entries.

Catherine Waite was perhaps sent to the Workhouse in the first place (probably the one in Barwick) because it was discovered she was pregnant and unmarried. Perhaps her family cast her out. In any event the Parish paid for someone – perhaps the woman who was recognised as the village Midwife – to attend her when the child was born. Midwives were licensed by the Church authorities. Perhaps the 'E. Cullingworth' was related to John or James Cullingworth who held Parish posts at this time.

Sometime after the birth the woman – perhaps with her child – was 'churched'. This was an old ceremony often carried out on the 40th day after childbirth. The mother might attend Church veiled and sit on a special seat. It was a kind of purification ritual.

During the period immediately after the child's birth, some extra provisions were supplied to the new mother together with some cloth for clothes – maybe for her and the baby or just for the baby – and some shoes. A woman helped to nurse the child (whether this was a 'wet nurse' or just a helper is not clear). When the child became ill then more was paid and, when it died, the funeral expenses were met.

The reason for a Warrant being issued against Catherine Waite was probably because of her having a child and being unmarried which was considered to merit punishment in those times. In any event she was taken to Wakefield House of Correction which sounded a harsh punishment indeed, especially as her child had died. It might have eased matters a little when she was given 2s 6d on her departure for the House of Correction.

However she could not have languished there long for, within the same year, there were entries showing she was liberated for the sum of 2/- and brought back to Barwick, perhaps to the Workhouse again, where the story ended.

All in all it seems that the unfortunate Catherine Waite was dealt with in as caring a manner as the morals and customs of the times allowed. No doubt her circumstances would have been well known to all in the village and probably provided much gossip!

Tim Bainbridge died in 1816 and was buried with his wife Mary in Aberford churchyard on the left-hand side of the small path going up from the main road. The words recorded on their gravestone surely reflect the man: "Useful and active in his station, He lived respected and died sincere lamented, His judgement was sound, his heart was kind, His faith and his practice were Christian, The love of his relatives pours sorrow upon his tomb, Their hope – follow him to Heaven".

In great contrast to the story of Catherine Waite was what was happening in the life of one of the local gentry. It was in 1779 that Sir Thomas Gascoigne returned from France and travelling extensively on the continent to settle at Parlington. In partnership with Thomas Stapleton of Carlton Towers (a Catholic) Sir Thomas won the first St Leger with Hollondaise in 1778. This must have been a great talking point in the village and surely amongst the children of the village school. The following year Thomas Stapleton won the race with his own horse.

At some time between 1779 and 1784 Sir Thomas Gascoigne recanted his Catholic faith. This decision by Sir Thomas must have been of tremendous importance to the Gascoigne family – so many of whose ancestors had held to their faith down the centuries. *(Recommended reading: 'Catholicism, Identity and Politics in the Age of Enlightenment: The Life and Career of Sir Thomas Gascoigne 1745 - 1810 by Alexander Lock)*

Some of them had been persecuted and some had taken Holy Orders. They were members of the local Catholic 'aristocracy' like the Vavasours and one wonders what local people made of this decision. Did he feel a genuine calling to join the Church of England or was it an act of expediency. Together with his Catholic friend, Charles Howard, Earl of Surrey of would have to make a public act of recanting in front of the Archbishop of Canterbury at

Lambeth Palace. However, Sir Thomas continued to have strong connections to Catholicism, with many Catholic tenants, many acts of monetary support in the area and continuing friendship to Catholic priests in northern England. In 1784 he married Mary the daughter of James Shuttleworth (a widow with three children) and his change to the established Church enabled him to hold public office, first becoming M.P. for Thirsk. This was followed by becoming M.P. first for Malton and then by 1795 for Arundel.

The Triumphal Arch built for Sir Thomas Gascoigne was erected 1784/1785 which was some years after the American War of Independence and it is said that the Prince Regent aborted his visit to Parlington in 1790 when he read the inscription on the Arch. Of course it still stands today, a relic of the one-time magnificent parklands surrounding the old Parlington Hall. At this time the road to Leeds was along the present-day bridleway which Aberfordians know as 'The Fly Line'.

It was around this time of 1780 that William Markham, who had been Private Secretary to Warren Hastings the Governor of India, built his 'new' Becca Hall around the basis of an older dwelling. William's father – also called William – was Archbishop of York from 1777 until 1808. Perhaps this building work gave employment to some people in the village and certainly the children would have been well aware of it for the old Aberford/Thorner road passed very close to Becca Hall. This track today exists as a well used bridleway, familiar to Aberfordians.

In 1786 a son was born to Sir Thomas Gascoigne but his wife died within a month of the birth. Despite Sir Thomas having become a member of the established Church he gave some land at this time at the south end of the village for a Catholic church to be built there. This Church was known as 'St Wilfrid's' and was a 'barn church' as it resembled a barn prior to a later priest installing stained glass windows in the building. During the years of persecution of Catholics it was prudent to disguise such buildings so that their use might not be suspected. The first priest was Fr Jerome Marsh and he, like later priests, was drawn from the monks of Ampleforth Abbey. St Wilfrid's was once mother church to St Joseph's (later St

Benedict's) in Garforth but St Wilfrid's declined in importance over the years. At the present time in 2008 it forms part of a private house.

(During 1809, whilst John Wilks was Master, the young Gascoigne heir was killed in a hunting accident at the age of only 23. A truly unlucky Friday the 13th of October! This must have been shocking news throughout the village. He was buried in Barwick churchyard on the 28th of October and, according to newspaper reports of the time, over 2000 people attended with around 400 of them being tenants of the Gascoigne family.

Just a year later Sir Thomas himself died and his estates were left to his step daughter's husband, Richard Oliver, who took the last name of Gascoigne. The Oliver family had extensive Irish estates).

A familiar scene to children at this time would have been the sight of animals being driven through the village to various markets. Sometimes these herds must have stopped for a few days to rest and feed and the Leeds Intelligencer of 1789 carried a report about an associated incident. It seems some drovers agreed with a local farmer to pay 40/- to him for pasturing their animals provided the number did not exceed a certain figure. However the figure was exceeded considerably and the beasts destroyed a neighbouring field so the farmer asked for an extra 20/-. A fight broke out between farmer and drovers, they made off, he pursued them down the Great North Road and eventually the farmer managed to bring the drovers before a magistrate. The drovers agreed to give the farmer some more money but what a trouble they'd been to him! It was common for drovers to understate the number of their beasts in this way so perhaps the Aberfordians of that day kept a careful watch on them.

A man called Ephraim Sanderson was of interest as, according to the Universal Directory dated 1793, he was also teaching in the village. A Mr Alan Sanderson contacted the Aberford website to say that his ancestor was Ephraim Sanderson who had run a small private school in the village. Mr Sanderson stated " (He) ..... opened a private school in Aberford in 1787. He was obviously well educated and well in with Sir John Goodricke of Bramham. He taught mathematics, navigation, land surveying and book-keeping etc. and lived at St. Johns. He is reputed to have had 22 children although I have only found 14! He was buried in Aberford in 1822." In the Baine's Directory and Gazetteer of 1822 Ephraim Sanderson was described as a Gentleman living at St Johns House and there was also a William Sanderson described as hording (sic) school. It seems likely that the elder man had handed the private boarding school over to his son by this time. (Mrs Mary Thompson was listed as running a day school.) Information about other positions of importance held by Ephraim Sanderson has been found (iv): in 1790 he was 'Assessor', in1798 he was 'Parish Constable, Assessor and Surveyor', in 1799 he was the 'Overseer and Surveyor'.

In addition at this time Richard Hewitt was listed as 'Parish Clerk and Vagrant Officer' and there seemed some chance he had been Schoolmaster of Aberford School, as the two jobs of Clerk and Schoolmaster were often carried out by the same person. This proved not to be the case.

Some Hewitts were found in the census records who may have been related to this man.

In the census for 1841 there was a George Hewitt age 40 a Bookkeeper and a Sarah age 50 – perhaps his sister or wife – their address was Garforth Road. In the same area there was a Matthew Hewitt age 70 a Labourer and Ann age 30. There was an Emma Hewitt whose address was Aberford, age 70 and of Independent Means. Lastly there was a Mary Hewitt, living next door to William Carnell the Schoolmaster, her age was 75 and she was of Independent Means. With her were Hannah Storey age 23 and Mary Smith age 12.

There was a Garforth burial record for a Hannah, wife of Edmund Shaw 'Schoolmaster' from Thorn, aged 37 years, dated 26th October 1799. This short entry seemed to give weight to the widower being Edmund Shaw, Master of Aberford School. The notation "from Thorn" may be a reference to Edmund Shaw originating from Thorn(e) near Doncaster.

Edmund Shaw remained as Master of Aberford School from 1778 to sometime after the death of his wife. The only certainty at the time of writing is that a John Wilks was known to be the School Master in 1809. (See later chapter) It should be remembered that pensions were not an option in these early days and people worked for as long as they were physically and mentally able.

Chapter Seven
RE JOHN WILKS/JOHN PRITT

At the bottom of the first page of the old 'Account Book' there was an intriguing short list of twelve names, five of whom were definitely known as having been Headmasters:

The order in which these names were written was: Wilks, Pritt, Carnell, Barker, King, Swanwick, Finch, Spencer, Todd, Hardcastle. [Then the Headmasters for whom Log Books exist: Freeborn and Rayson.] Further research was done to see if some, or all, of these men had been Headmasters.

Between Edmund Shaw, from c1792? to c1829 when William Carnell took over, there may have been two other men – John Wilks and John Pritt.

John Wilks

There was a John Wilks, who married Jane Morris in Aberford Church, in 1792 and the couple had four children between the years of 1798 and 1808. This John Wilks may have been the Linen Draper, at an earlier time in his life, as a man of this name was mentioned in the Universal British Directory of 1791. He was possibly a member of the Wilks family of Bramham. If John Wilks was, at one time, a Linen Draper then he might have had a change of a career, for it is known that, in 1817, John Bradley (stone mason of Bramham) purchased a piece of land from William Wilks (yeoman of Bramham), John Wilks (school master of Aberford) and John Scrivens tallow chandler of Aberford). The price was £44. The land was described as being: part of the Dodgson Garth, lying north against Town Street.
Reference:www.historicBramham.org.uk/archive

Certainly a John Wilks was mentioned in the account book in 1809: "to Mr Wilks for book for girls £0.6.6d". Again there was a receipt signed by Mr Wilks and dated 26th July 1811 for half a year's salary and books. A loose paper listed various expenses incurred by Mr Wilks during 1814 in the sum of £0.13.10d and he was finally mentioned in 1819 as being paid £9.11.6d for salary, subscriptions and collection in the church. It looks fairly certain that a John Wilks was Headmaster, therefore, from possibly 1792 to sometime around 1819.

It was certainly at this time, whilst John Wilks was Headmaster, that the school was brought within "The National Society" (1816) and the building enhanced and expanded. This must have been a very exciting time for the Headmaster of the day.

James Landon was the Vicar (from 1805) and an old account book (vii) listed some items this Vicar brought to the Vicarage to provide some 'home comforts'! The date was May 1807.

Dining room:
    Scarlet and Black Scotch carpet binding   £8. 8.0d
    Scarlet Curtain for Window   £2. 7.6d
    Bell Pulls   6.0d
Drawing Room:
    Curtains with 2 draperia fringe   £4.19.0d
    Sopha cover/chair cover   17.8d
    6 Chairs painted   £3.12.0d
    Wilton carpet   £17.10.9d

John Pritt c1819 to c1829

John Pritt was not mentioned in the account book – many entries merely stated: "Master's salary". However, as his name appeared between 'Wilks' and 'Carnell', it seems likely he had a period as Headmaster from sometime possibly c1819 to 1829 when William Carnell was listed in Pigot's Directory as 'Master of the National School'.

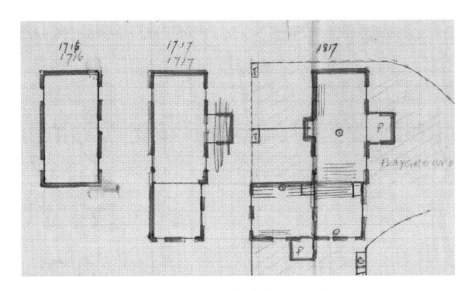

SKETCH ONE

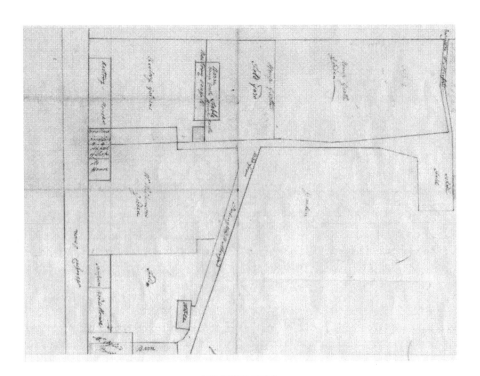

SKETCH TWO

30

Chapter Eight
INCORPORATION OF SCHOOL WITH THE NATIONAL SOCIETY AND ENLARGEMENT c1816:

British Schools were introduced in 1810 by a non-denominational organization called the 'British and Foreign Schools Society' to promote the work of the Quaker teacher Joseph Lancaster. The schools made use of the 'monitorial' system where older children taught younger ones under the supervision of paid staff. In this way many children could be taught by only one master/mistress and could be educated quite cheaply.

Members of the Church of England, seeing the success of Lancaster's schools, decided to set up a similar system for themselves with teaching centred on the Church Liturgy and Catechism. 'The National Society for the Education of the Poor in the Principles of the Established Church' was formed in 1811. They invited a Dr Andrew Bell, another proponent of the monitorial system, to organise the creation of the National Schools system, which by 1851 numbered 17,000 schools.

The Society became highly active in many aspects of education, from the publishing of books and the provision of equipment to the training of teachers. The mission of the Society was to found a Church school in every parish in England and Wales. By offering grants to prospective founders, on condition that development was fostered on chosen lines, the Society funded the construction, enlarging and fitting-up of schoolrooms. It was involved with the foundation of the majority of Church of England and Church in Wales schools, which were originally known as National Schools.

It seems likely that, during the time either John Wilks or John Pritt was Headmaster, around 1815, there must have been discussions between the Vicar/Managers/Subscribers and the National Society about bringing the school within the mission and aims of the National Society. It was at this time that the school was greatly rebuilt and enhanced. Rev. James Landon collected money from various sources, including £20 given by the York Diocesan Committee and £30 by the parent National Society in London.

Sketch 2 dates from prior to 1815 and shows the area where the Oriel cottages were built. The area was previously Hemp Garth Fold and Garden. School Lane is clearly marked as 'road from Parlington to Aberford'. The original small school building is just seen shaded at the very top of the sketch. The word 'vicar...' can be seen extreme right and is taken to indicate the position of the old Vicarage, built 1739 and demolished 1861.

In the archives at the Borthwick Institute there was a document (viii) which was an account of money received from Rev. Landon by Thomas Simpson "on account of erecting the National School at Aberford". Some of the items are interesting:

During August of 1816 cash was received from Rev Landon being his subscription of £20, Mr Pavers gave a cheque, drawn on Leathams Company's Bank for £10, Mr Gascoigne gave a cheque drawn on the same Bank for £50 and on the same day two £5 York notes. At this time currency notes were issued by many provincial Banks. On the back of the document was a further list showing what appeared to be more donations: Mr Gascoigne £50, ? Mr W.R.? £30, Lady Hastings £10, Mr Wilkinson £5, Mr Markham £5, National Society £30, Diocesan £20, Rev Landon £20, Mr Bain £15.

In 1817 a cheque drawn upon Rapers Bank in January for £50 was paid out for unlisted purposes. In June a cheque for timber was issued to Robert Harrison for £62 and £60 cash was paid to Leonard Overend, a Slater, in December. Some of the local people who were involved in bringing materials to the school were:

Mr Morris	stone from Hook Moor
	twice to Leeds for slate and brick
Mr Ellerton —	sand and twice to Leeds for brick
Mr Harrison Wood	stone from Hook Moor once flags
	from Leeds : back carriage
Mr Gascoigne	teams and sand – 3 days load each day
	leading rubbish – 1 day
	Thorner for window sills

Mr Cockrem	1 day flags from Leeds	
Joshua Wilkinson	flags: back carriage from Leeds twice	
	stone	

During this time research indicated that either Edmund Shaw or William Carnell was Master of the School. Although it must have been very disruptive whilst the building work was going on, it must have been greatly appreciated by the Master of the day when all was finished.

The total cost of building works came to £376.15s.5.1/2d.and included some interesting items:

Thos Bradley	Mason work	£82. 2s.10d
Barker & Wood	Joiner/Carpenter	£70.12s. 1.1/2d
Leo Overend	Slater	£53.17s. 3d
Dvd Jennings	Plaister	£16. 9s. 9.3/4d
Thos Wilkes	Plumber	£33.19s. 6d
John Batty	Lime	£11.12s 9d
Walters	Ironwork	£ 5.15s. 8d
Wm Braithwait	Leading	£ 3. 5s
John Smith Leeds for timber	Tolls/Expenses at	£ 10s.
Rob Lennox	Tolls/Expenses at Leeds for bricks	£ 6s. 4d
Geo Wilson	Tolls at Aberford For sand	£ 7s
Rob Atkins	For Hair	£ 1.
Harrison	For Lime	£ 62.15s. 6d
Wm King	For Gating stone	£ 7. 7s.11d
Jas Nelson	For Iron	£ 12. 1s. 1/2d
Martin Cawood 6.1/2d	Recasting Bell	£ 13s.
Adam Barker	Spouts & Blocks	£ 8.14s. 1/2d
John Nicol	Lead for Spout	£ 12s. 7d
Thos Bradley		£ 8s. 0d

Chapter Nine
WILLIAM CARNELL
(c.1829 – c.1857)

From Baine's Directory of 1822 there was a William Carnell listed as a Boot and Shoe Maker – a profession it seems he was to return to towards the end of his life. It may also be that he continued in this as well as Schoolmaster but perhaps unlikely. However, he must have been a man of some education for, from Pigot's Directory of 1829, this man was listed as Master of the National School with Mary Banks as Mistress and Elizabeth Wood (girls day). These two ladies may have taught the girls at the National School. Pigot's Directory of 1834 again listed William Carnell as Master and Mary Banks as Mistress with Elizabeth Wood separately listed which looks like the latter woman possibly ran a separate private school.

It is possible that William Carnell and his family were the first to live in one of the Oriel Cottages which had been built when the school was enhanced. They must have been considered unusual dwellings (a matching pair) at this time, compared to the houses in the village and in a very pleasant situation. However, we know from census returns some years in the future that the family lived in Main Street and perhaps never lived in one of the Oriel cottages. (Certainly in 1851 the cottages were leased to Thomas Flint and Sarah Lawson.)

William must have considered himself very fortunate indeed to have secured the Headship together with (possibly) a fine house. The houses would have appeared very much as the Photograph 2 taken when Mr Freeman lived there except, of course, the garden areas would be less mature. Today one has been extended and one has a lot of white render on the exterior. The railings no longer exist but the pleasant garden areas are still enjoyed by the current owners of both cottages.

In the village at this time were many artisans, some of these: Saddler, Boot and Shoemaker, Draper, Keeper of the Tollbar, Teazle Dealer, Wheelwright/Pony Gig Maker/Tea Dealer,

Plumber/Glazier/Dealer in silvered glass for mirrors, Chimney Sweep.

The village bustled with horse traffic. The "Ebor" coach went to and from York and Sheffield via the Swan Hotel. Going to Sheffield it called every afternoon except for Sunday at 3p.m. and going to York it called every morning at 11a.m. In addition there were various Carriers all of them returning the same evening:

To Leeds,   John Brown, from his house, every Tuesday morning
               James Seanor, from his house, every Tuesday and Saturday morning
               William Wood, from the Red Lion, every Tuesday and Saturday morning.
To York,   John Brown, from his house, every Tuesday morning
               James Seanor, from his house, every Thursday morning.

There was also mail going to and from the Post Office: in a morning letters arrived from and were despatched to Wetherby and at teatime letters arrived from and were despatched to Ferrybridge. The Royal Mail coach changed horses at the Swan Inn and the horses were stabled on the opposite side of the road in the tall building still standing there. The stables behind the Inn were for about six pairs of 'post' horses. These horses, together with their riders, would be hired by coach proprietors (and private carriage owners) to pull the coach to the next stage. The 'Post Boy' would ride one horse and lead the second, or there might be a team of 4 horses required. (A hugely interesting account of coaching times can be found in an old book "Old Coaching Days in Yorkshire" by Tom Bradley.) At times the Aberford school children must have found it quite as difficult to cross the busy main street as children of a later time would find when motor traffic roared through.

A popular Sunday afternoon entertainment in summer was for people to gather at the north end of the village by the farmhouse at the crossroads of the A1/A64 to see the Hudson's stagecoach go by. There would have been a team of fresh horses drawing it, having been changed at the Fox and Grapes a short distance back towards Leeds and by the time they reached the crossroads the driver would have had his team up to speed on the level road. What a sight that must have been with a full load up and the hornblower sounding his 'yard of tin' to warn other traffic of their approach as they dashed onwards to York!

In 1820 there was an incident in the village which must have provided much gossip for adults and children alike. In a report in the Sporting Magazine it seems a young man called Richard Coverdale, a Gamekeeper, had been involved in a quarrel with some other young men from Sherburn whilst drinking in one of the ale houses of that time in Aberford. Later in the evening as he made his way home, the young men confronted him and he drew a pistol from his pocket and shot Richard Hawkins dead! Perhaps Richard Coverdale had been a pupil at Aberford School.

The Master's salary at this time was £30 per annum with that of the Mistress being £4.4s.

The sum paid out for coal was not much less than the Mistress's salary, being £3.14s. and many candles must have been used at a cost of £3.2s.(ii)

At this time Reverend Landon's niece, Letitia Elizabeth Landon, came to stay with her uncle and family for Christmas of 1825. She became very well known in her day as a poet and novelist under her initials L.E.L. and was joint editor of the Literary Gazette at one time. Perhaps there was gossip in the village about 'the London Authoress' staying with Reverend Landon! What a long journey from London and how 'provincial' she must have found Aberford. In 1829, the accounts show "in debt to Vicar (accumulated) £60.8s.4.1/2d" (ii) which was a very considerable sum for that time and it seemed as if the Vicar heavily underwrote the expenses of the school himself.

The small market 'town' of Aberford in the 1830s had five fairs during the year and a regular Wednesday market. The total population of the three 'townships' of Aberford, Lotherton and Parlington was around 1300 in 1831. The fairs were sited at the junction of Cattle Lane with the main street and there would have been much hustle and bustle. The Scottish cattle herds would sometimes be seen journeying southwards. These herds could be huge at certain times of the year, perhaps filling the road up to a mile in length as they passed through and must have caused a great disruption to other traffic.

There were Toll Bars operating at both ends of the village and a notice in the Leeds Intelligencer of September 1832 advertised these, together with the Wetherby Bar, for letting by auction. The tolls produced from the Aberford and Bramham Bars in the previous year were £650 above the expenses of collection. The winning bidder had to pay one month's rent in advance and provide proof of their ability to meet the monthly rental.

It was around 1837 that the rail line was opened to connect Aberford with the line passing through Garforth. This was principally for coal to be conveyed but passengers were also being carried soon after the line opened. (The story of the Aberford Railway can be read within an excellent book "The Aberford Railway and the History of the Garforth Collieries" by Graham S.Hudson.) At first the motive power was supplied by horse for the short uphill section but then the little train freewheeled down the long gradient to Aberford and it was christened "The High Flyer" – causing the line eventually to be called "The Fly Line" by Aberfordians.

This year was also significant in that King William IV died in June and Victoria was crowned Queen in June of the following year. So began the Victorian age. In 1840 Victoria married her cousin Albert and a child was born in November of that year.

There were many more village inns/taverns at this time – Bay Horse, Fox and Hounds, Fox, Gascoigne's Arms, New Inn, Red Lion, Rose and Crown, Royal Oak, Swan Inn, Travellers and White Hart. There were also many other small alehouses such as that at North End Cottage. Plenty of choice for the thirsty traveller!

On the 1841 census William Carnell was listed as Schoolmaster and age 45 having been born in Grantham Lincolnshire. He was married to Abigail age 40 who was born in Bishopthorpe York. There were three sons at this time – Henry, John and Thomas.

In 1842 a sum of 4/- was spent on a bell and £1.5s. on a clock with a sum of £2.12s. "John Gray for attending Sunday school as assistant".(ii) From the 1841 census there was a John Gray Jnr, an agricultural labourer, aged 35 listed very close to the entry for Mr Carnell so he probably lived close by. He was aged 35, married with five children. In what capacity he assisted is unknown.

It may have been that Mrs Elizabeth Hollings was teaching the girls for Reverend Eden, in his notebook (v) when he was writing about some gravestones, recorded : "On both were verses written by Mrs Elizabeth Hollings 'the Schoolmistress' who was buried 25.8.1859".

From White's Directory of 1837 there was a Mrs Elizabeth Hollings shown as a "Midwife". However, this would not preclude her also teaching at Aberford School, or in a private capacity. She may have been teaching skills like sewing, not necessarily academic lessons. Reverend Eden must have considered that her primary role was a Schoolmistress or he would not have described her in those terms. It would be interesting to trace the gravestones referred to and read the verses.

On the 1851 census Elizabeth Hollings was shown as age 68 and "Wheelwright" but this probably referred to her late husband's profession for on the previous census William Hollings was 61 and a Carpenter and Elizabeth was shown age 58 and there were three adult children, Caroline, George and Hannah, 35, 30 and 20 respectively. However she must have died in the summer of 1859, she was certainly buried in August of that year. (v)

There was also a John Thompson listed as Schoolmaster, age 35, wife Mary age 35 and two children Mary age 7 and Arthur 6 months. John Thompson possibly ran a private school for in Baine's Directory of 1822 there was a Mrs Mary Thompson listed as running a "Day School" and it seems likely husband and wife were teaching.

Field House was named with John Moreland , age 30, Schoolmaster , Ann his wife age 36, children John age 9, Isabella 8, Richard 5, Edgar 1. There were eleven Boy boarders and two female and one male servants. Possibly John Jnr. went on to become Headmaster of

Barwick school when he would have been aged about 26 (x) during the years 1861-1864.

William Carnell was not just Schoolmaster at Aberford School for, certainly on the 1851 census he was listed as Schoolmaster/Parish Clerk. The addition of this second responsibility was no doubt due to him being an educated man. His wife was listed with him together with sons Henry age 22 a Carpenter, John age 19 a School Assistant and Thomas age 11 a scholar. Almost certainly John was assisting his father by teaching in the school.

In 1844 the Aberford Almshouses were built by the Gascoigne sisters towards the south end of the village – this must have been a huge talking point in the village and we may imagine the children taking a big interest in the massive building. Richard Oliver Gascoigne died in this year and the Almshouses were in part a memorial to him. The Architect was George Fowler Jones – a Scot – who designed the Baronial Castle Oliver in County Limerick for the two sisters at the same time as the Almshouses. This Architect was responsible for a number of new churches and other buildings around the Aberford area, including St Mary's Church, Garforth and the chancel from the old church was re-erected in Parlington Park as a 'folly'.

Jones' eldest son was named Gascoigne in honour of his patrons – which is hardly surprising since he must have had a huge financial boost from his extensive work for them! He was a keen photographer and some of his photographs dating back to 1851 can be found in the York libraries and archives.

It was during this year that Reverend Landon's daughter, Barbara, got married to a T.D.F. Tatham at Aberford Church. This may have been a 'big do' and one can imagine lots of villagers and children going to watch.

Another example of school expenses (ii) at this time :

New Partition	£2.13.9d
2 Stoves & Pipes	£2.11s.0d
Mr Williamson,	

Singing Master	£5.
Books,Sheet Lessons	£1.10s.0d
Paid for charity,copy	
Books,stationery,	
Firemoney,cleaning	
School brushes	£5.17s.0d

A search of the 1851 Aberford census was done to look for children listed as scholars and, whilst accuracy is not guaranteed, it is likely that all the children so described attended Aberford School at this time. In total there were 138 of which 72 were boys and 66 girls. There was 1 four year-old girl and 1 three year-old and 1 four year-old boy but their description as 'scholars' may not have been strictly correct. In total there were 18 five year-olds, 10 six year-olds, 16 seven year-olds, 15 eight year-olds, 14 ten year-olds, 17 eleven year-olds, 12 twelve year-olds, 7 thirteen year-olds. 4 girls were fourteen years old and 2 boys were fifteen years old.

There were only 16 boys between age 5 and 15 who were not described as scholars, the majority were sons of Labourers who perhaps could not afford to pay a small contribution or needed the income from the boys' work. Two boys were the sons of a Blacksmith, one a Farmer's son, one a Tailor's son and may have been employed helping their fathers and learning their trade.

There were only 6 girls between 5 and 15 not described as scholars. One was a Basket Maker's daughter, one a Farmer's daughter, one a Coal Miner's daughter, one a Farm Labourer's daughter, two whose father was a Tailor.

The records for Parlington and Lotherton were not examined, but an assumption was made that the above figures reflect that roughly ten per cent of children were not going to school at this date, but may have gone at some point and overall the majority of Aberford children were receiving some schooling to a good age for the time. The numbers "on the roll" appear to be 138 for Aberford alone so, together with those from Parlington and Lotherton, may well have been similar to the number of 200 recorded by Mr Freeborn some 45 years in the future.

This reflected a good emphasis on education within Aberford at this early time.

On the 1851 census John Thompson was again listed as a Schoolmaster with his wife and two children. There was an entry which it is thought refers to Field House again but there is a John Peacock now listed as Master with his wife Janet age 58, his Brother in Law John Wright Schoolmaster and his wife Sarah, age 39, Sarah Cooper age 19, single, School Governess, two female and two male servants and a Washerwoman, 18 Boy Boarder/Scholars. Also in the village a Fanny Wright – Head (Widow) age 56, Schoolmistress with her two sons – John age 19 and William age 7 both scholars. Maybe she was related to John Wright above?

There was also an Elizabeth Howcroft listed on this date at the Almshouse Lodge, she was age 26, a Schoolmistress, and single and there with her father Robert age 67, an Agricultural Labourer and niece age 12 a scholar. Also there was John, her brother age 34 a married Agricultural Labourer and William her nephew age 12 a scholar.

At the Almshouses, Mary Brooke was Matron and had a female servant to help her. There were four elderly men and four elderly women 'inmates' as at census date. At the Hook Moor Toll Bar, Valentine Raby was the Toll Collector. He was elderly – 74 – and born in Kippax. He lived with his wife.

At Parlington Hall Frederick Trench was in residence with his wife Mary Isabella (he did not style himself "Gascoigne" on the census return). The couple had been married the previous year. Elisabeth Gascoigne was staying with them and there were numerous servants, fourteen in all, including a Housekeeper, Under Butler and Ladies Maid. Elisabeth Gascoigne married Frederick Trench's cousin – Baron Ashtown – the following year.

There must have been lots of activity up at Hazlewood Castle at this census time for Sir William Vavasour was in residence with his wife The Hon. Constancia who had just had a baby. The couple, aged 29 and 26 respectively, had three older children – (possibly twins) Henry and William aged 4, and Oswald aged 2. There were two visitors – George and Mary Clifford and nineteen servants, including Nurses.

There was a change of Vicar in this year – Rev. Charles Page Eden who was 44 and unmarried and he had a Curate with him on this date – James Moore age 26 and a Cook and Housemaid. This man seems to have been fairly important in Church circles being a Fellow of Oriel College and having been Vicar of St Mary the Virgin Oxford from 1843 – 1850 (the Oriel College Church). He was Prebend of Riccall in 1870. He had been an Examiner in Lit.Hum. Oxford 1840-1842 etc. From the "Guide to Aberford Church" we see that "he married the daughter of the previous Vicar" and a marriage has been found between him and Isabella Jane Landon which took place in the December quarter of 1852 reference Tadcaster 9 c 773. Presumably the couple met through the church connection. Isabella was much younger – as her own mother had been much younger than her father.

By 1852 the Master's salary had risen to £37.5s.0d and "many repairs" had amounted to £73.0.0d (ii) – a large sum. Around this time c1857 the following holidays were kept at the school. For Christmas there were two weeks, a half day for Shrove Tuesday, two days at Easter, one week at Whitsuntide, five weeks were set aside for the harvest time, one day for Aberford Fair and one day for "statute fair".(ii) This was not a great deal less than the holidays kept c2008. Children at this date would help to get in the harvest either working directly in the fields or looking after younger siblings and helping in the home.

From two sources (ix) and (xii): " At Nip Scaup, or Nut Hill, by the side of the ridge, is an old farm where the family of Noverleys have dwelt for hundreds of years. Report says they came in the train of the first Vavasour and were huntsmen for that House when most of the land hereabouts was wild moor, fen and forest." One source (xii) almost certainly refers to two of the same extended family members but calls them Moverley which is the name shown on the 1861 census.

On the 1861 census there has been a drastic change for William Carnell – it looks as if he had relinquished his position at this time for he was listed as living in Main Street Aberford and his occupation at age 66 was "Cordwainer". His wife Abigail was still alive and his son John age 29 was with them also a Cordwainer. This was a 'Shoe Maker' so it seems that he had returned to his old profession.

In Main Street – possibly the large house called "Field House" – there was a John Wright age 38 a Schoolmaster with his wife Sarah 46 and his sister Elizabeth age 49 as Housekeeper. There was his son John age 8 and Ann ? age 22 a Governess. There were also two male Teachers and two Housemaids and a Cook. There were 43 scholars listed. There is a large memorial, surmounted by a cross, in Aberford churchyard to this man. It is opposite the entrance door and bears the following words: "By former pupils now resident in various parts of the world, this monument is erected to the memory of their Preceptor, in token of their grateful sense of his kindness of heart and of his ability as a Teacher in giving a sound practical education".

Also in Main Street there was a Mary Ryder who was age 32 and single, she was alone on census date and listed as a Schoolmistress. There was a Sarah Pearson age 22 and single, who lived with her family and was a Schoolmistress. There was a Mary Thompson who was single, age 25, living with her father a widower and potato merchant age 55 – she was listed as a Schoolteacher.

In the Lotherton census of this date, a Police Constable was mentioned – Robert Huckle. There was also a Police Constable in the Aberford census of 1861 – Elijah Fowler. Also, for the first time, Father Atkinson, the Priest of St Wilfrid's Chapel Presbytery was mentioned, together with a Housekeeper and Servant, aged 37/13 respectively.

At the Almshouses a Mary Brooke was Matron and she was a Widow and a female servant helped her. There were four elderly men living there, one having previously been a Butler – presumably for the Gascoignes. There was only one woman 'inmate' as at census date, age 63.

The Reverend Charles Eden at this date lived with his wife and two sons and a daughter together with a Cook and three Housemaids. Also lodging in the village was the Curate – Wm Whitting. This year was a very important one for Aberford Church as it was in April that the foundation stone was laid for the alterations to the old Church. Some information has been found in a publication (xi) and here are some extracts. This huge undertaking must have been very interesting to everyone in Aberford – especially the children with their school so close to the Church.

Master Gascoigne did the honours of laying the foundation stone as his parents had "chiefly contributed towards defraying the expenses of the work" (xi). The 'great and the good' and parishioners gave towards the costs. The alterations revealed the antiquity of the Church "which had probably been standing between seven and eight hundred years" (xi) (at this time).

The opportunity was taken to move the Vicarage: "a large addition was made to the burial ground by the site and garden of the old vicarage, which it was necessary to remove, a new one having been built by the present vicar". (xi) This new vicarage was the large house sited beyond the school and no longer a vicarage but a private house. Some cottages fronting the main road were demolished to make way for the steps, trees and grass to the churchyard.

"Some of the Parlington men (and at their head old Henry Lock, then for more than 60 years a servant on the estate) had been employed for some weeks previous in levelling the churchyard and preparing it for seed".(xi) Henry was 83/84 at this time – a good age! When it was re-opened and consecrated in April of 1862 there was a huge attendance at the ceremony. At the evening service nearly 100 candidates were 'confirmed'.

The ancient connection of church, school and village to Oriel College Oxford was apparent when "Rev. Dr Hawkins, Provost of Oriel College ... was asked to occupy the pulpit on this, his first visit to Aberford, and he preached a most appropriate sermon .." (xi) Perhaps the Provost also paid a visit to the nearby school.

All the notable persons present were entertained to lunch by the Gascoignes. The girls of Ledsham Orphanage, who had formed the choir, were given a substantial dinner "provided by Mrs Gascoigne's kindness, by Mrs Pawson (wife of the Parish Clerk)". This was served "in a suitable and convenient room near the Depot, where Mr Pawson, as Coal agent, resides".(xi)

Joseph Pawson was buried in Aberford churchyard, to the rear on the left-hand side next to the large monument to Isabella Gascoigne (died 1891). His gravestone is inscribed 'Clerk of this Parish' and dated 1864.

Chapter Ten
BARKER/KING/SWANWICK/FINCH
(c.1853 - 1861)

Between William Carnell and Benjamin Spencer the four names above were listed amongst the twelve names at the bottom of the account book. William Carnell possibly ceased teaching in 1853 as there were two men listed in that year giving temporary help – J. Green who was paid £1.2.6d and E. Ramsden who was paid £2.8.0d. "Candidates' travelling expenses" were mentioned as if a new Headmaster was being sought. Indeed there was a short entry in this same year "Sundries, through A. King, schoolmaster - £1.6.0d". Certainly it seems Alfred King was the Headmaster for a short period around this time.

Between 1853 and 1860 no name of Headmaster was listed, but in 1860 there was an entry "Expenses of candidates - £2.0.0d" which indicated a new Headmaster was being sought. This was to be Benjamin Spencer, listed on the 1861 census records as a teacher.

It may be that Thomas Barker, A. King, Samuel Swanwick and George Finch were Headmasters during the period 1853 to c1861 but no further information about them has been traced.

Chapter Eleven
BENJAMIN SPENCER
(c.1861 – c.1867)

The next Master of Aberford school may have been the first to have been through more formal training to become a Master – See Appendix III. In addition, many reports and surveys on the state of education throughout the country had been done during the preceding decades. The result was an Education Act of 1870 which established limited elementary schooling for all children.

The only man listed in the 1861 census records as a teacher, apart from John Wright, was Benjamin Spencer age 25 and unmarried, who was lodging with a widow Hannah Hewitt. Corroborating evidence was gathered to try to prove this man was the Schoolmaster of Aberford School for the time between William Carnell and James Todd.

Going back to the 1851 census, Benjamin was living with his family in School Street, Manningham, Bradford where he was listed as age 15 and a Pupil Teacher at a National School. On this census his father Abraham was age 45 and Woollen Cloth Maker, his mother Ann was 40. There were siblings Joseph age 22 a Leather Shoemaker, Martha age 20 a Spinner in a cotton factory, James age 18 an Apprentice Blacksmith, Samuel age 12, Robert age 6, Crossfield age 3.

By the 1871 census this man had married and moved back to 17 Paul Street, Manningham, Bradford. He was listed as a Schoolteacher and his wife Alice was 35 and they had five girls and a boy who had just been born at this time, being 5 months old. The eldest child, age 8, was born in Manningham but the next two, age 7 and 5, were both born in Aberford. The next two children, age 4 and 2, were both born back in Manningham.

It seems then that Benjamin Spencer married shortly after the 1861 census, but why his first child was born in Manningham is speculation. However the fact that his next two children were born in Aberford indicated that he was settled in the village for a while. His tenure could have lasted from sometime around 1861 to around 1867 when his 4 year-old was born in Manningham. A replacement Master may have been sought as early as 1852 for an extract from the accounts read "candidates travelling expenses £1.15s" (ii) which may refer to those coming for interview for the post of Headmaster.

Another extract from the accounts (ii) mentioned a "John Grey" or "Gray" receiving £2.12s.0d in 1855. Research revealed a man of this name who was a Labourer age 72 who was with his wife and two grown-up sons on 1851 census date. Perhaps he had done some jobs around the school but this may not be the man mentioned. An Arthur Cockrem was mentioned as helping and paid 3/- for this – perhaps "William" who was mentioned on the 1851 census aged 13 at that time and a scholar.

Over the two years of 1860/61 we learn from items in the accounts (ii) that slates, pencils and pens were in use in the school, together with maps and geography books of some kind. An easel was purchased for 1s. 6d and there were "prizes at inspection" costing 4s.0d. Another extract mentioned an item in 1861 "Henry Wood intended as pupil teacher - £4.15s". This was almost certainly the son of a William Wood a Farm Bailiff who was aged 33 and lived with his wife and son Henry aged 17 and daughter Louisa aged 11 in Aberford at this time.

We cannot be certain that this man ever lived in one of the Oriel Cottages for, according to the Oriel College Archivist, there was a lease for those cottages, granted by Rev Eden, to two other people dated 1851. They may still have been leasing the cottages during the time Benjamin Spencer perhaps was Headmaster.

During 1863 we know the 'monitorial' system must have been in use for in this year Monitors were paid 5s.2d. A Register was purchased for 2s.8d and small repairs and sweeping of school cost 13s.7d. J Ward was paid 10s.2d for "lighting fire" and this may have been James, shown on the 1861 census as living with his father Thomas and mother Fanny in the Lotherton census district. There were three other children in the family and, if James was able to earn a little money for his duties, it would have been a welcome addition to the family finances.

Chapter Twelve
JAMES TODD
(c.1867 – c1880)

James Todd began as a Pupil Teacher in Barwick in Elmet School. On the 1861 census he was aged 16 and was living with his parents and brother John, sister Jane and training under John Morland the Headmaster of Barwick School. James Todd passed an examination to obtain a Queen's Scholarship enabling him to attend York Training College to study to become a Certificated Teacher. (x)

In this he must have succeeded for, by the 1871 census, he had become the Headmaster of Aberford School at the age of 26. It looks as if he may have been living in one of the Oriel Cottages, provided as a school house for the Master, as his entry appeared directly above that for the Vicarage (although no addresses were shown at this time) and his sister Jane age 28 was with him. She was listed as single and a School Mistress so perhaps she was also working at Aberford School in the capacity of Mistress to the girl pupils.

During 1869 it seemed as if three women acted as "Mistresses", one being a Miss Ryder to June 30th who was paid £12.10s.0d. Research indicated that this was a Mary Ryder, aged 40, who lived in the village. A Miss Moor(e) may have been Ellen, age 32, the unmarried daughter of George a Boot and Shoe Maker. The third woman mentioned was Miss Todd but she was not traced. A monitor helped out: William Ward who was paid £2.4s.0d. It looks as if this boy was the son of William Ward a Land Agent aged 66 and the family lived in Barwick. William Jnr. was shown on the 1871 census as a "Pupil Teacher" age 14 and he may have been the person in receipt of £8. that year shown as being paid to Pupil Teacher.

The Master's salary was £90 per annum with a further £8 per annum to a pupil teacher, £14 per annum for Assistant Mistress and £25 per annum to the Assistant Mistress Infants. Further expenses made up, what appeared to be, a total annual outlay of over £141 against an income of around £96 being school pence of c£42 and Government Grant of c£55. (ii)

At the Vicarage Reverend Charles Eden continued, now aged 64 and he employed two Maids. (The Curate Francis Inge, age 30, was lodging with a Grocer and family.)

It was during this year of 1871 that the Vicar sent out a letter (ii) asking for volunteers to become annual subscribers to the school as the income was insufficient to cover expenses. The alternative he stated was to have a school supported by "the rates". Some extracts from his letter are as follows, but the response from villagers is not known:

"... whether we shall have a school supported by voluntary contributions ....or by Rates. The advantages of the present system are that we may teach Christian doctrine in the school freely ... in a Rate supported school, on the contrary, no creed or catechism can be introduced......it is obvious also that, in an institution supported by Rates, a primary object will be the saving of money and there will be a continual temptation to find the cheapest schoolmaster rather than (what has hitherto been our object) the best.... but the Rate supported school .... release the Incumbent of the Parish from pecuniary responsibility; he pays his rate and then is free.....it has fallen to the Vicar to make up from his own means each year, deficits in the accounts.... has required from him an outlay of more than £500. This scale of outlay the Vicar is not able to continue..... perhaps after this statement some among the parishioners ..... will allow their names to be put down on the list of annual subscribers".

An event which took place in the village at this time, but it is not known for how long, was a Sheep Show. This show was for sheep coming solely from "the estate". This was held for a few years and a report taken from the British Farmers Magazine of 1863 tells of Lady Ashtown (Elizabeth Gascoigne) in full Highland costume, attending the 7th Show in May of this year and presenting a Silver Cup to Brady Nicholson of Stourton Grange. Some of the classes were: for 10 fat hogs – for 10 gimmer hogs – 5 single ewes and lambs.   The prize for clipping was won by the shepherd of J.

Rishforth. The show was well attended and maybe lots of families and children from the village went along to enjoy the sights. Some 60 persons to do with the show "club" had dinner at the White Swan the evening of the show and heard from J. Fowler of Leeds, a pioneer in steam cultivation. Members of "the club" decided to go along with Mr Fowler to view some farms using the new process

On the 1871 census, Greenhill Boarding School had come into existence. Listed there were a Jean P? Age 68, a widow and born in Switzerland with Jane, her daughter, age 36 and unmarried and born in London. There were two female Governesses age 24 and 20 and a female companion age 48 plus a general servant. The school had 16 girl scholars, one as young as 5 and one age 10 – most aged between 11 and 15.

At Field House there had been a change and the owner's name was the one associated with the school in subsequent years – still referred to by old Aberfordians c2008 as "Catley's". There was William Catley, age 28 a Schoolmaster. (From the 1861 census we know that William Catley's father had also been called William and was an Innkeeper. At this time young William was already, at 18, stated to be a School Teacher. There were two older brothers and one younger and a younger sister in 1861. The family lived in Kirkgate, Wakefield.) William's wife was Sarah age 30. There were also John Davidson, age 15, an Assistant Master and Henry H?ornby, age 32, an Assistant Master. There were 17 pupils – aged between 10 and 15 and a Cook and Housemaid.

At St Wilfrid's at this census date was Francis Williams the Priest aged 72 and in part of Church House was Ann Blake, a Visitor age 16, a Dressmaker.

In Lotherton Lane was Emma Robinson the wife of James a Hawker, she was age 47 and Schoolmistress born in Norfolk.

The Gas House appeared in this Census for the first time – John Barratt age 49 the Gas Maker with his wife Mary age 49 and children Thomas 13, Ben 7, Hannah 11. All the family were born in Billington Yorks. ".. up Windmill Lane was Aberford Gas Works who supplied a lot better gas than we get today and at a quarter the price." (xii)

There was no Vavasour at Hazlewood Castle on census date but several servants were there. Interestingly a Nut Hill School was recorded with a Monica Banks as Head, aged 66 and a widow together with her daughter Monica, aged 34 and a single Schoolmistress. Confirmation that there was a small school in that area came from the following description: "the other cottages were converted out of a school." (xii) That description dated from c1880 but on the 1881 census there was no mention of a Nut Hill School, but people were living in "Headley Bar Cottages" which may have been the new name for the converted cottages.

At this time there was also a Toll Bar in operation at the north end of the village for a Robert Moverley was at Headley Bar and he was a 34 year-old Toll Collector having been born in Hazlewood. He had a wife Mary and two children at this date, Jane aged 12 and James age 6.

An account (xii) tells us "…. the Toll Bar, a small stone lodge with one of the deepest wells in the village which had about 70 in under a mile and a half." This small building has been converted and c2008 is an attractive split-level house and perhaps the owners are enjoying the feature of their own well!

On the Parlington census return for 1871 the "Police Station" was listed and Elijah Fowler was the Constable, aged 52 and a widower. He had a domestic servant – a Maria Richmond age 57 and a widow. Up at the Almshouses a Delia Elsworth was Matron and her unmarried daughter no doubt helped her together with a 16 year-old domestic servant. There were four elderly widows living there, from Leeds, Lincoln, Wistow and Aberford originally. There were also three men, two of them elderly but one only 45 so perhaps he was incapacitated in some way. Two of the men had been labourers but one had been a Butler – presumably on the Gascoigne estate – and he was originally from Deal in Kent. Interestingly a "Page Boy" was found, called William Abbott, who lived with his family and his father was a gardener. Perhaps William worked for the Gascoignes but the family must have been away on census date for there are only servants listed at Parlington Hall – a Housekeeper, five maids, an under Butler and two grooms.

On the Gascoigne's 'Fly Line', locomotives were introduced around this time. The first two were named 'Mulciber' and 'Ignifer' and a third was to be introduced in 1897 called 'Empress'.

In 1877, during the time that James Todd was Headmaster, the "school pence" had increased a little from that recorded in 1871. It now amounted to £49.14s.4d with a "Government Grant" of £56.1s. The Master's salary was £96 per annum with four Assistants being paid various amounts. There was certainly a piano in school by 1878 for £2.10s.0d was paid out for tuning it.(ii) Only one Assistant has been found via the 1871 census and this was Mrs Emma Robinson, aged 53 in 1877, who was married to James a Hawker. The couple had three children as at 1871 – Elizabeth age 13, James age 6 and Mary age 4 and the family lived in Lotherton Lane. Emma Robinson was born in Grimston Norfolk and the family were certainly in the village on the previous 1861 census.

It was in 1879 that there was an incident of poaching from the Parlington Estate which resulted in the death of one of the Gamekeepers! Peter Hills, aged 51, died in May of that year as a result of blows from a poacher and several men were apprehended and punished. An account of this appeared in the Yorkshire Post and Leeds Intelligencer on the 14th May 1879 and one can imagine the incident causing a great stir in the village. There is also an account in The Barwicker issue 26. No doubt Gamekeepers had plenty to do keeping poachers away.

By the time of the 1881 census James Todd was on that date at 14 Wemyss Road, Lewisham, London with his brother Thomas and family. He was listed as married but no wife or family are there with him so it is not clear where he was then living and working. However, William Freeborn had certainly taken over as Schoolmaster at Aberford school at this date as he appears on the 1881 census in that capacity.

It appears that James Todd was Schoolmaster at Aberford from c1867 when he would have been 22 to March of 1880 when William Freeborn succeeded him.

Chapter Thirteen
SCHOOL AND VILLAGE LATE 19TH CENTURY

In 1871 William Catley lived at Field House (Catley's) with his wife and three children. They had a Cook and General and House Maids. There were sixteen boy scholars, the youngest 5, the oldest 15 but the youngest had an older brother. There was a male teaching assistant, James Robinson aged 16.

Greenhill Ladies 'Seminary' had acquired a grander name than in previous years and a change of proprietor; Joseph Mason, a retired Station Master, was there with his wife Elizabeth, daughter Mary Jane, a single Schoolmistress and daughter Elizabeth. There was a Music Mistress, an English Governess and a Pupil Governess. There were sixteen girl boarders/scholars, aged from 10 to 16. This establishment disappeared by the 1891 census.

On the Lotherton census Ellen Hankin was at the Catholic School house and she was the Schoolmistress, aged 20 and unmarried. On this date she had her niece Margaret with her and a female servant. In the Church House portion was Rev. George Fazakerley the Priest and his housekeeper Teresa Lennon.

On the Parlington census, Elizabeth Howcroft was still at the Almshouse Lodge but was now 'late Schoolmistress' so she must have retired. At the Almshouses a Sarah Bacchus had taken over as Matron but was listed as 'Almoner' born in Worcester. There was a full complement of four men and four women living there. John Drennan was the Police Constable and he was from Salford. He was married and had four children with only the youngest of 7 months born in Aberford.

At Parlington Hall Frederick Trench Gascoigne was in residence with his wife and sixteen servants of various sorts. Sir William Vavasour was not in residence on census date – he was visiting Lulworth Castle. At Hazlewood Castle were a handful of servants and there was a Catholic priest 'of R.C. Church St Leonards, Hazlewood' together with a female servant.

Around this time a once-daily service for passengers was introduced on 'the Fly Line' coal train between Aberford and Garforth. It must have been well-known to Aberfordians of that time and a beautiful run through bluebell woods and crop-filled fields, with the occasional sighting of deer in the park area. Children, in particular, must have loved travelling on it.

A young man from the village was a Pupil Teacher at the school in 1881 – Richard Bulmer aged 17. (xii) The Bulmer family lived in Main Street and father Thomas was a Mole Catcher. There was mother Ann and an older brother William, an Agricultural Labourer, along with sister Emma and brother Thomas, both scholars.

By the 1891 census the Freeborn family had expanded – Amy and Edith now 14 and 11 respectively and two sons had been born. Edgar was 9 and Harold was 8 and a further daughter Florence was 6. All the children were scholars.

Field House was still in operation under Wm. Catley and his wife. Their son was 17, a Solicitor's Clerk, daughter aged 16. Father-in-law, a Retired Grocer, was there. There was a female servant but the number of boarding scholars had decreased - six boys and one girl. Perhaps the increased availability and quality of State education was cutting into private arrangements by this time.

At the Vicarage was Rev Barnes-Lawrence with a Cook and Parlour and Housemaids. At Hazlewood Castle there was no Vavasour but a Margaret Saunders was there as Housekeeper together with her son Edward aged 7. There was a Belgian priest in the priest's house there. At Nut Hill Farm Thomas Conaty was in residence with his wife and family: "..... Mr Conaty, usually buying his horses from the Leeds Tramway Company at £1 a leg. These made useful horses on the farm after years of work on the cobbled streets of Leeds". (xii) Nearby lived a Jane Moverley described as 'Head', a single woman, aged 73 and living on own means together with her brother Sam aged 68. "... Sam Moverley .. an old pensioner of Sir W. Vavasour. To eke out his pension he had permission to chop up windfall timber and cut pea-rods from the undergrowth. The firewood in bundles called "kids" were tied with a withe from either willow or hazel and sold per dozen and the pea-sticks were sold per bundle". (xii)

Britain at this time was hugely powerful and had an Empire stretching across the world. Queen Victoria had ruled from 1837, becoming Empress of India in 1876 and during the Victorian age there was significant social, economic and technological progress in Britain. Education had become free for every child from 1891. Society was very structured into three classes – the Church and aristocracy, the middle class and the working class. There was a large gap between the middle class and the working class which was divided itself into those who were working and 'the poor' receiving public charity. However, industrialisation began to change the class structure dramatically and social divisions gradually became blurred. The Edwardian age was dawning but this Victorian background must be kept in mind when reading Mr Freeborn's account.

Chapter Fourteen
WILLIAM FREEBORN

Part One : To the End of the Century

From the 1871 census, William Freeborn's family consisted of his father Joseph, a Cloth Tenterer, his mother Janet, sister Hannah a Dressmaker and sister Mary a Scholar. William was a Pupil Teacher at this time and the family lived in Spring Street, West Leeds. William progressed very well from being a Pupil Teacher at 18 to becoming Headmaster at Aberford by 1880.

The writer was contacted by William Freeborn's grandson, Eric Kilner, and learned that William had trained at Cheltenham Training College. He had spent a short while in charge of Aberford school for the first time in 1875, then spent five years teaching at Saxton school, before gaining the Headship of Aberford. By the 1881 census, William had married c1876, become the Master at Aberford school and moved with his wife Mary and family to one of the Oriel cottages referred to as 'School House'. These cottages (see Photograph 1) stand to the present time at the top of School Lane next to the school. Mary Hannah Freeborn was known in the family as 'Polly'.

The first Log Book was begun by the Headmaster on 30th November 1896. He had been Headmaster from the 28th March 1880 but there were no surviving Logs from that time. The entries were almost all in Mr Freeborn's handwriting, exceptions being when he was absent or when entries were made by visitors like Her Majesty's Inspectors, Vicar etc. The first breakdown of the teaching staff was given at the start of the new school year which was March in those days.

Mr Wm Freeborn	Certificated 1st Class	Headmaster
Miss Margaret Tate	Qualified as per Art 68	Standards I
and II		
Edith Freeborn	Pupil Teacher 4th yr	Standard III
Lucy Piercy	Pupil Teacher 4th yr	Standard IV
Lucy Wormald	Certificated 3rd Class	

It was usual for bright pupils to become, first of all, Monitors and then to progress to becoming Pupil Teachers. The Pupil Teachers would train under the supervision of the Headmaster and had to sit formal examinations each year. After four years the Pupil Teachers could sit for a Scholarship to attend a Training College to study to become a Certificated Teacher. Miss Tate was a part-qualified Teacher as, on the 13th December, she was absent all week at Scholarship examinations and Miss Freeborn taught Standards I and II in her absence.

Miss Freeborn was the Headmaster's daughter. Miss Piercy was a local girl. "She was the daughter of George and Martha Piercy, Village Saddlers". (xviii) On the 1881 census George (John) Piercy was a Saddler; no mention of his duties as a Constable was made. He lived with his wife Martha and children Miles 11, John 8, Margaret 6 and Lucy 3. John and Margaret both died in 1885. "John Piercy employed two men, whose main work other than for farmers, was making harnesses for pit ponies at Garforth Colliery. It was the rule that every new pony had to have a new set of gears. Repairs to other sets were sent from the colliery on a coal truck which brought coal to the depot. Mr Piercy was the village Constable long before we had a resident policeman. He had a coat, helmet and staff but I do not remember seeing the staff in use". (xii)

Amongst regular visitors to the school were the local Vicar Rev. Barnes-Lawrence, who was a frequent visitor to take scripture lessons and in his capacity as 'Corresponding Manager' (the link to the School Board of Managers), the Organisation Visitor, H.M. Inspectors, one or other of the Board of Managers and, from time to time, locally important people like Mrs Gascoigne.

Rev A.L. Barnes-Lawrence M.A. of Oriel College, Oxford had succeeded Canon C.P. Eden in 1886. Canon Eden died in December of 1885 at the good age for those days of 78. He left a wife and two sons and they are all buried in Aberford churchyard. He had come to Aberford in 1850 and had also been a School Manager. The strong connection between Oriel College and Aberford School and the Church was demonstrated at this time by the fact that Canon Eden had previously been Dean of Oriel College and Vicar of the University Church at Oxford. [The Vicarage]: "... a grand old stone building with large entrance hall. The study is on the left and, if you ever visit here, ask to see the picture in the study, it is well worth seeing. It represents 'Hell' at its worst. Through the windows you will see a fine lawn surrounded by a sunk fence. The staff were Cook, Kitchen Maid, two Housemaids and Groom/Gardener. Canon Eden, who then had the living, was a widower. His daughter, Alice, kept house for him. There was also a son, Charles Page Eden, he was at home only in holidays, being away at school and college". (xii)

Attendance figures always preoccupied the Headmaster as the annual grant of money was dependant on a satisfactory annual inspection and based on the numbers regularly attending. The first entry stated: "Good school present - 182. On books - 200". This figure is astonishing compared to the number of pupils today. Classes were much larger then and, although the number of households in the catchment area of the school would not have been greatly different to today, the number of children per family was much greater. There were many reasons for children being absent, with the older children doing seasonal work and/or helping out at home. There was frequent illness. Occasionally there were reasons arising from the poverty of some families.

On 1st December, two assistant H.M.I's visited the school. Their names were Mr Thackwray and Mr Bell. Mr Bell must have noted that afternoon recreation time had not been scheduled on the timetable, as required 'by the Code', and requested immediate observance. This was duly put into practice on 7th December. These early Inspectors seem to have been just as 'picky' as in the present day!

On the 10th December the Vicar took scripture in the Infants Room and it was recorded that the Pupil Teachers (P.Ts) results were to hand: "they have passed fairly with E Freeborn being mentioned in History". Great emphasis was placed on teachers being knowledgeable about scripture for the 2 P.Ts had to sit a five hour examination in scripture. They must have been pleased to learn on the 21st January that they had both obtained a First Class on the 3rd year papers.

The school was used for meetings of various sorts on a regular basis – the first mentioned on the 22nd December when the schoolroom was used for a concert promoted by the Cricket Club. Mr Freeborn was a prominent member of the Cricket Club during his younger years. There were also other clubs which used the school from time to time.

In 1896 the children would have seen much building work going on close to the ford and bridge in the centre of the village, for a plaque on the front wall of 'Bridge Cottages' gives the date 1896.

When school re-opened after Christmas there was good attendance during the first two weeks of 1897 and a Sunday school examination was held on the evening of the 15th January and again on the 18th for Infants Sunday School. On the 25th January the Rev Toovey's report on behalf of the Diocese of York, Rural Deanery of Pontefract, concerning religious instruction at the school read as follows: "the efficiency of the school is well maintained. The teaching is thorough and the children are interested in it. The singing is bright and pleasing. The Infants and Standard I have been very well taught and do their teacher much credit in every way".

There was steady attendance through February in spite of snow and rain and on the 12th a drawing exam was held which was taken by 68 boys out of 71 names on the schedule. The P.Ts were examined in model drawing. On the 20th a concert was given by the children, the proceeds going to school funds and this raised £8-15s-6d.

The new school year in March 1897 saw the Infants being brought to Standard I and the rest of the school advancing one Standard. Children were admitted and left throughout the year. The Vicar made one of his frequent visits on the 3rd (Ash Wednesday) and the children in Standards IV and VII were taken to church. By 17th March there was the first of many reasons for absence which made regular appearances in the Log Book. "Attendance diminished to 162 (on books 205) consequent upon sales by auction taking place in the village". What was being auctioned the HM did not say. On the 18th March the schoolroom was used for the annual Parish Council Elections and Parish Meeting. The 24th and 26th March saw attendance fall due to a sale at a farm and a sale of boots in the village. Towards the end of the month the P.T's passed their examination in model drawing and a report of 'Good' was given for those boys who had taken the drawing exam. This resulted in a grant of £4.13.0d with a further £1 P.Ts grant. The annual grant was shown as £162.4.6d.

On the 26th April the schoolroom was used for a concert by the Aberford Musical Society and, on the 30th April, a School Managers' meeting took place at 11.30 a.m.

HM recorded that Edith Duffin (Monitor, Infants) left the village, this being evidence that the monitorial system was being used in the school at this time.

In early May attendance slipped due to children potato planting and on the 5th May: "Vicar opened morning school after which he announced to the Standard children that every child who attended every time the school was open during the school year would receive a medal – and all making 400 or more attendances would receive an illuminated certificate. The gifts are offered to encourage the children to the formation of habits of punctuality, regularity and all that assists in the building up of character". Despite the Vicar's efforts, attendance did not radically improve. The 24th May brought the first reference to the children being photographed during the afternoon, in six groups. This must have been an exciting and interesting event for all the children although HM made only the brief comment that they were photographed. As no prior Logs exist we cannot know if this was the first time for them. Photography was in its infancy.

Another exciting event for the children took place on the 17th June. The Log book entry read: "Half day holiday. Children met at the school 2.30p.m. Marched to Church 2.45p.m. Short service. From thence went to Becca Park where the children were entertained to tea, sports and fireworks in commemoration of the Queen's Jubilee, through the kindness of A.J. Schreiber Esq one of the School Managers". (Mr Arthur Schreiber was living at Becca Hall, which he rented from the Trustees of the Markham family, On the 1891 census he was there with his wife Elizabeth who was born in Ledsham. Their daughter Evelyn aged 16 was with them and she had a Governess from Scotland. The family had several servants although Mr Schreiber's profession was not stated – merely 'living on own means'. After his death his wife lived there until she died in 1907. In Aberford church, at the entry into the chancel, is a brass lectern which was given in memory of Arthur Schreiber).

In July of this year there was an outbreak of mumps, something which was to occur regularly over the years. Attendance was reduced by this and by the annual occurrence of 'pea pulling'. During the summer break the village children would have enjoyed the beauty of the surrounding area. The centre of the village at Cock Beck is not much changed even today c2008 "on the left is a ford over the river but the stepping stones were removed after the bridge was built and, looking up the river from the bridge, you could often see kingfishers fly swiftly just above the surface of the water. Waterhens were a common sight". (xii)

After the summer holidays, blackberry picking began to reduce attendance together with 'leading' and 'gleaning' followed shortly by potato gathering, despite the Headmaster appealing to parents via notes home.

The 7th October saw the start of fires being lit to warm the school and regular deliveries of wood and coal were obtained for this purpose. From the modern-day perspective it sounds rather cosy and homely to imagine a fire glowing in a corner, however the reality may have been something of a disappointment with only those nearest the fire getting any benefit of warmth from it!

No Headmaster today would write as per the next entry on the 8th October (even if he thought this in private). "Master taken Standard IV – the boys of this Standard are mentally deficient in several cases. I find them difficult to deal with for the want of intelligence. I notice that, with their Teacher, there is a tendency to sheer indifference as she is giving the routine of lessons".

A comment a few days later gave another flavour of the Headmaster. On 18th October: " 2 children withdrawn to the R. Catholic school because I punished the boy and detained him at the close of school for wilful disobedience, obstinacy and breaking his pen. The mother came in great fury with a procession of children just leaving school and neighbours. I closed the door 'til she cooled and grew rational. After a time she knocked politely and I showed her the evil effect of her passion and example and asked her to withdraw the boy from the school. He has been a source of much trouble continually to all his Teachers".

Periodically there were entries which showed the HM wary and indignant about 'poaching' of pupils during the time the Catholic school was open. Typical is the one on the 4th November of this year when he wrote: "4 children left this school and were admitted to the R. Catholic School. I visited the parent to find they had gone unknown to her on the enticement of another girl who was a scholar at this school but withdrawn by her father because she had been reported for very bad attendance". November 5th: "the children returned today". The school was closed in an effort to contain an outbreak of measles from mid November until over Christmas. However, the P.Ts continued to study daily with HM and took a scripture exam on the 4th December in the Vicarage – this exam was in two sessions from 9.30 to 12a.m. and from 2.00 to 4.30p.m.

The new year of 1898 began with good results in the Scripture exams and on the 14th February there was an interesting snippet: "Headmaster added a pair of buckles to the museum found on Towton battlefield". The school must have had a small museum of objects to interest the children. Perhaps these buckles had been ploughed up by a local farmer and donated to the school. What happened to them is unknown but perhaps some Aberfordian still has them? The school was used for prize-giving to Sunday scholars on the 21st February and this was followed by a Lantern Exhibition: "Scenes in the Life of Our Blessed Lord – Parents invited".

By February and early March the entries showed that both P.Ts. had completed their four year training and they became Assistant Teachers – they both passed their Scholarship exams getting Second Class with Miss Freeborn being placed 3250 and Miss Piercy placed 3597 in a list of 5912 pupils examined. HM noted there were 211 pupils on the Register and recorded the staff being distributed as follows for the new school year:

Headmaster	Standards	V – VIII
Miss Tate ex P.T.	Standard	IV
Miss Piercy	Standard	III
Miss Smith ex P.T.	Standards	II and I
Miss Wormald take the sewing	Infants Class	Misses Tate and Smith

Periodically children left on reaching the official school leaving age, which was 12 until 1899, and others joined. Sometimes 'migrant' children are recorded as attending for short periods.

An entry on the 20th May showed a softer side to HM: "I was very pleased today with the Infants Class. They had a tea party - milk and biscuits. Children taught how to lay a cloth, set table, handle cups, pass food, eat and clear away". For the many poor children attending the school, this very 'middle class' tea ceremony would be something they did not perhaps experience at home. This lesson seems to have been continued over the years: "Aberford Church of England School is where I first started school. My first teacher was Miss Piercy and, for the first month, you played with sand and things like that. She used to buy some alphabetical biscuits and she used to say 'you nibble a bit and then put your lips together and chew as if you're chewing something but you must keep your mouth closed'. Then, after, you started to learn to count and to learn to read". (xiii)

There were several occasions throughout the year when children would be taken to Church, not just at major Festivals like Easter and Christmas – any who had notes from parents were allowed to remain in school under the supervision of a Teacher. Two such visits occurred in June, one on the 24th for St John the Baptist Day and one on the 29th for St Peter's Day. On the 1st July the children had a Sunday School treat in the afternoon – following a short service they were taken to the Park (presumably Parlington).

Attendance, as often happened in the summer, dropped away amongst the older pupils due to seasonal demands for labour. In July HM recorded: "wretched attendance in 1st class. Marked 7 present, 23 on books. Girls quite as bad. Kept at home until mother worked in hayfield". Turnip thinning, pea pulling and hay harvest made their regular appearance.

During the summer holidays the school was given the yearly more thorough clean together with any extra work which was needed. The entry read: "The schoolrooms have all been colour-washed. The board and stand-porch converted into lavatories, boys and girls separately with wooden partition. A large underground concreted tank dug out in the girls' yard with pipes to carry off the roof drainage, the two classroom windows replaced with lights double their size and improved ventilators, the old leaden-paned window in the classroom taken out and larger panes substituted; the classroom boarded round, stained and varnished and the infants' room completed similarly". Not quite all the work was completed during the holidays as the entry on the 9th September stated "school porch brought to the ground to make room for two porches double the present size".

In September a circus visited the Parish and attendance fell from 181 to 140 – a novel reason this time for poor attendance. On the

28th the classroom was used for a Bank inspection at 4.00p.m.when depositors brought their books to be checked. In October Miss Smith received permission to sit the forthcoming Scholarship exams and HM reported: "have introduced 'Magazine' Readers to upper classes with success. The children are interested in the reading of literature distinct from their ordinary school readers".

A new cupboard was placed in school to hold 250 books. This came via the Vicar from the Trustees of the late Parochial Lending Library for the use of scholars in the upper classes and their parents. Payment of 1/- per annum in advance allowed for one volume per week to be borrowed. The facility was opened on the 21st November and 11 children joined.

On 16th December a list was sent to Mrs Gascoigne (wife of Colonel Frederick Mason Trench Gascoigne of Lotherton Hall) of the numbers and ages of scholars as she proposed to give the children a Christmas Tree and tea at the Almshouses – this treat took place after Christmas on the 9th January. The entry read: "the scholars were marched from the school 3.45p.m. to the Institute (presumably Almshouses) where Mrs Gascoigne provided them with an excellent tea, followed by a Xmas tree. Each child received a very suitable gift and a present from the tree".

The new school year started as usual in March and some details about the subjects to be taught appeared in the Log:

List of Lessons Object Infants' Class 1899
Cow, Horse, Sheep, Cat, Dog;   Tea, Coffee, Sugar;
Elephant, Camel, Bear, Stag, Mole, Squirrel, Ostrich,
Silkworm, Stork, Post Office, Railway Station, a Tree
Materials for writing, Materials for Clothing
Orange, Apple, Lead, Coal, Sponge. The Seasons (4 lessons)
Lessons for Babies:
Bear, Cow, Horse, Sheep, Cat, Dog, Squirrel, Mole,
Ostrich, Tea, Coffee, Sugar, Orange, Apple, a Tree
Materials for Writing   The Seasons (4 lessons)
Elementary Science Stds I and II – see Master's book for the list approved and signed by Mr Howard, H.M.I. on his visit Feb 2nd.

History for Stds 5/6 "The Reign of Queen Victoria" – 30 lessons. 6 Biographies of leading men – see Std VI Record Book.
List of Recitations – "Alice Fell on Poverty" Std I / II Wordsworth "The Last of the Flock" Wordsworth Stds 3 + 4.
Elem. Science Stds III List of Lessons:

Moisture in Air, Draught in Room, ditto in winds, clouds, rain, dew, snow, -(here appears a curious entry - make of it what you will) - boys sucker and squirt, popgun, chalk and lime, a magnet, the compass, a river (2), the earthworm (2), beaks of birds (2), feet of birds (2), mouse compared with rat (2), the mole (2), a glass bottle.

Miss Tate and Miss Smith finished as Assistants on the 24th March and a new Teacher, Miss Dooks, from Bridlington Girls National School started on the 10th April. Miss Dooks was not to last long for she left at the end of June and HM recorded: "she neither liked the school, the scholars or the village"!

In April and May there was the usual spate of absences due to measles, potato setting and large numbers of girls in all Standards absent on Wednesdays (washing day). Ascension Day was celebrated as usual on 11th May by children attending Church – on the 16th May the Headmaster: "wrote special notes respecting absentee children of the colliers – with very indefinite verbal replies".

The weather after the Whitsuntide week holiday was good but there were some problems with placing children in the right Standard: "W and W.G. have been in Standard II two years. A.C. and J.W. ditto. F.G – recently returned from Roman Catholic school ditto. E.C. and S.Y. have attended school so very irregularly that they are unable to follow Standard IV work. I pointed out these cases to Mr Ingham (the Organising Visitor) but he was unable to solve the difficulty of placing them. They are big and old for Standard II, are dirty children coming from a home of 13 people resident in one house".

After the holidays, a Miss Verity joined, coming from Pateley Bridge. (From the 1891 census: Henrietta Verity came from a farming family – on that date she was aged 10, a scholar and living with her Grandmother also called Henrietta who was a Farmer at Bewerley near Pateley Bridge. There were two grown up daughters Mary aged 39 and Sara aged 36.)

Two cases of typhoid fever broke out on the 16th October this year and four children were reported absent for this reason by the 23rd. Whooping cough began to influence attendance and, on the 24th November, several boys were absent for the third consecutive week: "bush beating at Hazlewood".

A treat was in store for the children on the 2nd November: "Miss Schreiber married in Kent. Mr Schreiber invited all the scholars to an excellent tea in a marquee erected in the village at 3.30 p.m."

The 1st December was All Saints Day and children attended church, except for those who had notes from their parents that they were to be excused. On the 4th December the schoolroom was used in the evening for a meeting to form a house-to-house collecting committee for the War Fund (Widows and Orphans) – which presumably was the Boer War. On the 12th this committee was able to report that they had received £27.7s.6d. This second Boer War was fought between the British Empire and the two Boer Republics of the Orange Free State and the South African Republic. It lasted from October 1899 to May 1902 and was a bitter and hard-fought conflict, overshadowed by the two World Wars which followed years later.

Part Two: 1900 - 1914

Despite the fact that a new century was to begin, no special mention of this fact appeared in the Log Book. There was a good report of the Religious Instruction throughout the school and a list of "Object Lessons for the Infants Class" appeared on the 6th February as follows:

"Cow compared with Horse, Cat/Dog, Camel/Ostrich, Snow/Rain, Apple/Orange, Water/Milk, Lion/Tiger, Clouds/Sky, Cork/a Tree, Salt/Coal, Mole/Fox, Camel/Elephant, Stork/Raven, Cat/Owl, a Stag, A Garden compared in Spring, Summer, Winter, Materials in writing, Materials in clothing.

There was also a quite extensive list of things to be taught to other Standards, including:

Standard I & II Object lessons – Paws and Claws their uses – the Farm Yard its Buildings and their Contents – Elastic substances – things porous – Animals which sleep in Winter – Gold compared with Lead – fusible substances

Standard III - the moon and its phases – moisture in air – coal gas – a syringe – bees and bee keeping – a popgun – mouse compared with rat – traps, their make and use – water from limestone, chalk or iron compared with rain – building stone compared with marble and slate".

Some severe weather in mid February and a blizzard three days later saw the children sent home for the afternoon with them being told not to come the following day (Friday).

The new school year started on the 1st March with 210 on the books and on the 5th March HM "gave Miss Benson a hint about using crayons". This hint was obviously acted on by Miss Benson for the entry on the 20th March recorded "Infants Class commenced crayon work with 3/8" squares with good results". The first Log Book mention of corporal punishment was recorded on the 12th March and hinted at the very frequent use of such punishment in that day. "Cane not used in school this week – no punishments inflicted. The children have worked hard and well".

There was a good H.M.I.'s Report: "Mixed School – the children behave well and their attainments give proof of very careful teaching.Infants Class – Order is excellent. Considerable improvement has been effected in the attainment and the class is in a highly satisfactory condition. The highest variable grant is recommended".

There was an upset regarding a member of staff. Miss Lloyd had only joined as an Assistant on the 18th December. Towards the end of March she was absent for a day without reason and on the following day she sent word that she was ill. "The Vicar visited her lodgings and found she had been guilty of returning on the Monday evening under the influence of drink which caused her immediate suspension". It appears she may have been dismissed for, on the 3rd May it was recorded: "Miss Berry (Art 50) Barnard Castle National (School) was appointed Assistant Mistress Standards I and II".

More attendance problems on the 10th May: "Mr Evers (Attendance Office) called and I pointed out to him a case of six children being employed by a Parlington farmer who carts them daily to Saxton 3 miles away to sort and set potatoes and to shake manure in rows for mangold wurzels. He promised to give immediate attention". A further entry 19th July: "pea pulling at Cocksford nearly 5 miles away. Mrs Watson received a postcard giving date for pulling and invited to bring as many as she could".

The 27th August 're-classification' of the school gave an interesting breakdown of the class numbers and the size of the rooms they were then in. It seems to the writer that only the strict discipline of the times kept the children in order with so many packed in together.

Large Room 45' x 22' – 123 scholars	Master - 50 scholars
Class Room 20' x 20' - 50 scholars	Cert Asst - 60 scholars
Infants Room 30' x 20' - 75 scholars	2 ex P.Ts - 90 scholars

On the 28th August Miss Berry left and on the 1st October Miss Gray joined. (On the 1901 Census Jennie Gray was lodging on that date with the Todd family in Main Street within the Lotherton Parish area. Mr Todd was a Joiner and Undertaker and he had a son at home)

The 2nd November saw older boys being tempted away from school: "10 boys taken all day to beat the bushes in Hazlewood for a gentleman who takes the shooting. This kind of work lost many attendances last year to the school. Not one child has a Labour Certificate and only 1 was above 13 years of age". The School was used on the 16th November "for the annual sale of winter material in connection with the Aberford Provident Clothing Society". People would pay small amounts regularly into the Society so that they could buy their winter material.

December 3rd saw the first reference to the method of lighting in the school "wet weather daily, afternoons got very dark, gas required to be lit". The use of gas for lighting had become widespread right from the beginning of the 19th century. It was largely the province of private companies during the first half of the century but chiefly in the hands of Local Authorities from c1880. Aberford had its own gasworks at this time.

(Briefly, research has shown that a John Barratt was the Gas Maker at the time of the 1871 Lotherton census and he lived with his wife and three children in the Gas House. He had been a Labourer on the 1861 Parlington census so it is probable that the Gas Works came into existence in the intervening years. The 1881 census showed a Henry Abbott as the Gas Manager, living in the Gas House and he had been born in Barwick. He was married with three children and his brother George a bus driver was staying with the family on census night. There are files about the gas companies of Aberford held at the National Archive at Kew. There was also a private gasworks built sometime between 1847 and 1863 situated along Parlington Lane (the Fly Line) for the Gascoigne estate. The premises are now a private house).

On the 11th December the Vicar visited the sewing class and on the 13th the school was used for a sale of work on behalf of the bicentenary of the S.P.G. Society. Since initials were used, what this Society was for is not known.

On the 17th January 1901 "the recipients of the Parochial charities met the Vicar and Churchwardens in the school at 12.15 a.m. and received their sums of money". The 21st January saw HM complaining somewhat bitterly: "The Standard children are kept away on frivolous excuses. Butcher boys, washing days, one boy is away half his time taking telegrams, minding baby". However, there was some success with attendance amongst some children for the entry on the 4th March recorded: "presented Freda H with a solid silver medal for having made a perfect school attendance for the school year 1900-1. This is the first occasion during time here (21 years) that a child has succeeded in coming the whole year. 44 children have attended over 400 times. One child has been absent only once. One boy twice". HM made no mention of the death of Queen Victoria towards the end of January – she had reigned for some 64 years.

The 1901 census appeared in the Log Books via the following entry on 11th March: "Master gave a lesson on the advantages of a Census in place of a grammar lesson". Again, on the 15th March: " Master explained the columns of the census schedule as a lesson on Common Things". Maybe these lessons enabled the children to help their parents in filling in the forms. HM opened the school on the 1st April but was then away for the rest of the day acting as Enumerator for Census Returns and he wrote that Harold Freeborn, an ex P.T. took his place and Mildred Freeborn took Standard IV all day. It seems that (Florence) Mildred Freeborn went on to become a Teacher and possibly taught at Barwick School between 1905 and 1910. Certainly on this census date Edith Freeborn was training at Cheltenham Training College for Mistresses.

Field House was still in operation with Wm Catley, wife, son and brother. Emily aged 24 was now Schoolmistress. There were five boys and six girls boarders and two female servants. Francis Hickey was the priest at St Wilfrid's house with his housekeeper and at the Catholic School House there was Margaret Upton, Certificated Teacher, Joseph her son, a Railway Goods Clerk, Mary daughter aged 16, Charles aged 14 a scholar and Clara aged 11. HM was recorded at home with his wife Mary, sons William and Harold, aged 19 and 18 respectively, both Bank Clerks, Florence aged 16 with no occupation stated and Dorothy aged 6 a Scholar. (Both William and Harold became Bank Managers and had good careers and long retirements).

There was what appeared to be a reference to the Boer War on the 6th May: "Col. Gascoigne and friend visited the school this afternoon to hear the children sing the Ode of Welcome specially written for the home-coming of Lieut. Col. Gascoigne from the Front by the Vicar. He expressed himself as pleased and surprised with the singing". [Col. Gascoigne]: ".. he was a soldier born. I remember ... he went out to the Boer War and took six of his own horses and his rough rider Harry Heap with him. Harry told me when they both came back how the Colonel was admired abroad and how he came at night and helped him groom his horses on the picket lines and share his last piece of tobacco and dog biscuit with him". (xii)

Miss Wharton, an old subscriber to the school, visited with her companion Miss Comins on the afternoon of the 20th May. She had heard about the special hymn and wanted to hear the children sing it. Miss Mary Sarah Wharton lived at Aberford House opposite the Church and was 66 at this time. She had a 'companion' living with her, a single woman aged 39 from Devon. Miss Wharton also had four female servants and a male servant. She had lived with her family in the same house and her father was John J Wharton a Magistrate. Miss Wharton's brother was John Lloyd Wharton who had been an Eton scholar. He became a Barrister and by 1901 had become a Privy Councillor. " .. he walked most Sundays in summer to dine with his sister and walked back. He would not have his coachman out on Sundays". (xii)

Two children were withdrawn from the school on the 17th June to go to the Catholic school and we get a sense of how HM hated to lose any pupils to a competing school: "The stepmother asked to send a child 2yrs 8mnths to school. I wrote and told her that, by the rules of the school, we could not admit the child until it was 3 yrs old. She then asked the Mistress of the R.C. school who consented to take the child if she sent the rest of the family, hence the two children at our school were withdrawn".

HM was angry on the 17th October when he wrote: "Poor attendance all week due to potato gathering. Geo. Varley, a working man, takes up a contract with farmers to gather their potatoes at a given sum per acre. He simply takes any or every boy or girl to work who will go. I wrote a strong letter to him. He came to school and promised not to employ schoolchildren without a certificate. In two days he reverted to the old plan and sent for the children".

The new year of 1902 saw Mrs Gascoigne of Lotherton Hall visiting: "to adjudicate upon the darn specimens". She gave the first prize of a work box and the second prize of a silver thimble and also offered two additional prizes for the best 'gather' in Standard IV. Mrs Ellerton of Sydenham House also visited and examined the worked garments. Mrs Elizabeth Ellerton was a widow of 76 at this time and lived with her 'lady's companion' a single woman aged 34 from Howden and a female servant. Her husband John had been a Surgeon and was born in Park House, Parlington. His father had also been a surgeon according to the earliest reference to the family on the 1841 census.

On the 27th March there were continued attempts to encourage good attendance by awarding prizes: "Miss Wharton and Miss Comins visited the school accompanied by the Vicar. Miss Wharton distributed 11 silver medals and certificates of merit to as many children who had not been absent once during the school year. 15 certificates of merit were also given to children who had not been absent more than 10 times".

There was a day's holiday on the 3rd June for the Log stated: "Peace proclaimed S. African War. Vicar opened morning school. Children sang the doxology and National Anthem and were then dismissed for the day". On the 16th of July: "Primrose League fete in Parlington Park. Many children kept at home. Several boys away the following day watching a Military display in the Park".

On the 28th August this year HM recorded attending the funeral of Mr Schreiber of Becca Hall who had been a Manager of the school. The Teachers and scholars contributed £1 for a wreath bearing a card in their names.

The yearly lighting of fires in the school started on the 7th October this year and a new rule was introduced "no children to assemble in the school yard until the bell rings at each opening of the school".

In addition to entries about HM occasionally being called to play in Church, there was an entry on the 12th November where he was Assistant Overseer at the audit of the Parish accounts at Tadcaster. In fact Mr Freeborn was to be Organist and Choirmaster at the Church for over 40 years! He was also an Assistant Overseer for 26 years.

HM was not a brutal man and had a kindly side – on the 13th November: "Miss Benson impertinent today respecting the punishment of a little boy who was trembling with fear. I refused to use corporal punishment on several grounds". We have to guess at what lay behind this brief entry but it seems that HM felt Miss Benson had acted too severely by taking the little boy to him for punishment for something and the boy was obviously terrified at the prospect. We don't know what HM meant by "Miss Benson impertinent" but maybe he felt she was making his judgement for him and usurping his powers. The little chap must have been mightily relieved when the HM revealed his kindly side!

On the 19th November Mrs Gascoigne, accompanied by Miss Ponton, made one of her visits. She looked at the work being done in the lesson and was shown all of the needlework. She offered several prizes to be given at the end of the school year for needlework. A week of dull and rainy weather at the end of November saw the gas having to be lit on three afternoons which was an unusual occurrence. On the 12th December the tender for re-flooring of the school and classrooms was given to Mr Todd (Joiner) and this was completed over the Christmas holiday closure.

The new school year of 1903 began with 218 on the books and on the 10th March Mrs Gascoigne, together with Master Alvary, Miss Cynthia and Miss Ponton visited. Mrs Gascoigne adjudicated on the sewing and knitting and Miss Cynthia presented the prizes for darning, gathering, trimming and knitting.

A matter of fact entry on the 17th March recorded the death of a pupil. Occasionally there were such entries and they usually gave just the bare details – "Fred Smith Standard V died after 3 weeks illness." (He was not traced in the existing Registers) On the 19th – "1st class attended his funeral. Left school 3.30 and were marched to church where they sang a funeral hymn and gathered round the grave". One can only guess at the feelings of the boy's friends but the death of children was still relatively common at this time.

April saw Mrs Barnes Lawrence visiting to give medals and certificates for good attendance. Mrs Henry Parlington (not clear whether Parlington was her last name or that this Mrs Henry was from Parlington) was also present and: "the Vicar spoke in very kindly terms to the children on the true formation of character".

There must have been a cold Spring this year for fires were only discontinued on the 15th May. Much warmer weather followed and there was a case of scarlet fever on the 8th June and a measles outbreak in several parts of the village was recorded on the 22nd June. The weather was very hot and the HM decided not to take drill on the 9th July as a boy had fainted on the previous Wednesday in the lesson but drill with staves was taken on the 13th July.

There were two entries in September which showed HM's frustration and irritation about attendance, on 15th: "The children are in two distinct groups. Some do uniformly good work, others do badly. The cause is, either obvious dullness or real want of care for any education. The parental influence in so many cases is one of absolute indifference and the children roam the lanes at all hours regardless of order or behaviour. Some are under the eye of the Constable". On the 28th: "Children are kept away half days on various pretexts – running errands, washing day, gathering blackberries, lifting potatoes. Every care is taken by the teachers to encourage regularity. Parents are visited – notes sent – children spoken to privately by way of encouragement but with little success. The common notion is 'I got on without education – it's all nowt'.

Here is a glimpse of the school from a brief account by an unknown ex-pupil. Since the Teachers were listed in the account as Miss Benson, Miss Verity, Miss Braham and Mr and Mrs Freeborn (sewing day) the account dated from this time:

"Stoves in middle of rooms. Desks – long ones with wells in top. The boys played cricket and football in the 10 minutes break and the girls had their sports at the same time. That was the only sport there was but the dinner hour, games could be played in the school yard. Slates and pencils to start with. The infants started to learn their A.B.Cs as soon as they could make pot hooks. (Thought to mean 'question mark like' drawings). We had to respect our Teacher if we met them in the street we always saluted and called our schoolmaster 'Sir' and our Lady Teachers 'Miss'. If we stayed away a day the school board man used to be on our track, no dodging. We had to have exams and didn't go up in the classes unless we passed. On the Register there was about 204. There was a board hung on the wall and every day after the Register was called the number was put up".

Scarlet fever broke out in late October/early November and on 10th November HM heard from the Medical Officer of Health recommending that school be closed for four weeks – this was handed to the Vicar who consulted with the Managers and, after a meeting on the 11th, the school was duly closed. It reopened on the 29th December and the children gradually recovered from scarlet fever though the usual coughs and colds prevailed. The following year saw quite a big outbreak of measles in the village.

Miss Benson the Teacher of the Infants Class left on the 9th January and, by the 21st January, Miss Piercy was appointed Assistant in charge of the Infants at a salary of £75 per annum to commence duties 1st February. The Staff now comprised of Mr Freeborn, Miss Verity, Miss Piercy and Miss Grey with Alice Rhodes as Monitress. There was a single line entry on the 31st March recording that Mr Freeborn had now completed 25 years service but he was to continue for several more years.

The stoves came in for criticism from the HM Inspector early this year "Report on Premises – Mixed – in the main room the stove is placed in the middle of the room and the pipe is carried through the roof. The stove in the classroom has too much pipe. Infants – the stove is cracked, it gets red hot and the pipe is too long. The conditions under which stoves are approved are set forth in the Building Rules".

The condition of the stoves was referred to again when, on 5th April: "Miss Piercy absent Wed and Thurs and Frid morning owing to bad throat caused by sulphurous fumes from a very defective stove in school. She is under the Doctor". She was again absent for a bad throat on the 17th and the morning of the 18th. Miss Gray left on the 28th April after nearly five years service for she was to be married.

At this time it was not the practice to employ married women as Teachers.

During August the problem of the troublesome stoves was addressed. On the 22nd August the entry read: "Alterations made in School. Reconstruction of girls' closets and infants' urinal. Lavatory made for infants. Stoves taken away and 4 fireplaces built. Infants' west window enlarged". Workmen were in and about school the following week and a man visited to take measurements and consult Managers about the screen for the big room. (This partition was fixed in early December). Air grates were installed around the school walls and the drain to infants' lavatory.

The 17th October entry showed that our modern-day 'stress' was not unknown, albeit HM seems to have no time for it! "One boy marked left with Medical Certificate said to be suffering from nervous debility and is to run about freely for six months. He has been master of his parents for some time on the mother's own testimony. Arthur B. aged 5 years".

In the early part of 1906 the school was used for a political meeting and on the 19th January the classroom was used as a Polling Station for the General Election.

On the 2nd April HM had the satisfaction of admitting 19 children who had previously attended the Catholic School which had been closed: "closed by the W.R.C. Education Authority. I have placed each school child in the same place where he or she left off regardless of attainment on purpose to avoid conflict or irritation of parent on being almost, of necessity, compelled to send their child to this school. Some of the children are obviously dull and very backward, particularly in Standards 3 & 4 and one in Standard 2".

Research showed this school to have been in operation between 1877 and 1906. It may be of interest also to record a little about the long-serving priest Father George Fazackerly – he was certainly at St Wilfred's at the time of both the 1881 and 1891 censuses. "Father Fazackley the Priest was well thought of. He was one of the first to help with any distress in the village no matter what religion the people were". (xii)

On the 27th August Dr Abbott visited the school and presented a section of the first Atlantic cable to the school museum.

On the 15th November there was a nasty accident: "Willie N, a boy of 6 yrs of age, attempted to enter the Infants' Yard by climbing the fencing (iron) and became impaled. I hurried to the scene and found a serrated wound in his leg and at once procured the bath chair kept at Vicarage and got him to the Doctor". On the 24th November: "the Managers decided to cover the spiked railings in Infants' Playground with woodwork to prevent the possibility of any future accident. The work was completed today by the local joiner".

In January 1907 the school was used for a Girls Friendly Society tea and address by Mrs Hemsworth from Monk Fryston. Another 'matter of fact' entry appeared concerning the death of a pupil on the 17th January: "Joe Lawn Standard II buried today. Several "Brigade" boys attended the funeral and the children in his class subscribed a wreath – been ill 8 weeks". (Joe Lawn was not traced in the Registers).

The H.M.I's report of January drew attention to the following: "the two great needs for full efficiency are some competent assistance for the Teacher and better floor space for games and movement, especially for the younger children. One at least of the galleries might be spared?".

This comment was addressed by Mr R.J. Smith the Divisional Clerk when he visited the school on the 25th January: "after inspecting the Infants' Classroom he was in favour of removing the west gallery and turning the desks north/south, making the area for organised games etc. The result will be no seating accommodation for one class at all times. He suggested that the school Managers should send a recommendation to the District Sub-committee for their examination and approval in regard to the gallery and improved assistance for the school teacher". The 19th July saw an official notice sent to the school that the gallery must be taken away to be replaced with dual desks on the 27th.

In April four migrant children were admitted to school: "hopelessly backward" according to HM! Throughout the year there were various requisitions made for items such as coal and wood, inkwells, ink can and drawing materials, sewing materials, infants' crayoning materials, a cupboard for books and stock.

An attendance record was broken on the 21st June this year: "week end average 215.7 (record) 92.57 percent, on books 233". This was just beaten a few days later on the 28th when the average reached 217.3.

On the 9th October HM was supplied with a new Corporal Punishment Book and Temperature Charts to go with thermometers to be placed in every room.

There was a difficulty with the gas supply to the school on the 20th November: "time table suspended this afternoon after 2.00p.m. owing to the darkness of the school (fog) and the absence of gas owing to suspension pro tem of the Gas Works Co." However, on the 26th November, a new gas meter was supplied to the school and on the 5th December HM reported the gas lighting had been renewed that week. Each child received a small Christmas token from HM on the 20th December.

There was an example in February 1908 of a migratory family again passing through the village: "20th February – admitted a girl who lives in a van now located in Aberford". Perhaps this was a true Romany family like this description:

"... two very large caravans and between the wheel spaces were built large boxes like cases with wired front doors and sliding outside wood doors. One on the left and one on the right and one housed 6 poultry and the other a nanny goat. When the vans were in position ... a large tarpaulin was hooked up to 3 rails and pegged down at the bottom, the space between made a snug stable for 2 fine Cleveland horses they had. The top was also sheeted in bad weather. A manger was fixed to the middle rail at the back. Water was to be had from the 2 lodges (Hook Moor).....the 2 sons were sometimes employed per day, man and horse.... in their spare time they cut willows for making pegs and mats and small baskets...." (xii)

A simple entry on the 24th February recorded: "8 girls absent in the afternoon – bearers at a funeral". This was an intriguing entry for there was no pupil death recorded in the preceding few weeks. Would it have been unusual for girls to be bearers at a funeral? One would think so. A touching image comes to mind – an early instance of 'sisters' solidarity'?

In April the Vicar told HM that he was shortly leaving to go to another living. Later HM learned the W.R.C.C. had granted another uncertificated Asst. Teacher for the school. The Managers advertised the post in the 'Yorkshire Post' which resulted in Miss Braham joining.

There was an interesting entry on the 18th June recording HM absent all day as he accompanied his daughter to Liverpool to see her sail for America. Whether this was a pleasure trip, or for work, or to emigrate permanently was not recorded. In fact Edith Freeborn had married Henry Needham who had been an Engineer working on the Panama Canal and the couple were emigrating to America. This was perhaps a source of some sadness for HM and Mrs Freeborn – in these times it was not certain whether loved ones would ever be seen again when they settled so far away.

The H.M.I's report of June drew attention to the overcrowding: "Premises - the children, especially the older children at this time of year, are very inconveniently crowded and not seated so as to make it possible for the highest division to do any quiet independent study. This point calls for the serious attention of the Managers and the Local Education Authority. The possibility of providing a better playground and garden should also be considered. Work - the HM is very earnest and conscientious in his work and, with the advent of a new Assistant, may be able to raise the general level of attainments. At present the children are not well grounded when they come into his division and it has been quite impossible for him to do justice to sixty children in his own class, as well as supervise the rest of the school". This report was signed by the new Vicar, Rev Campion

Catley's school was mentioned on the 5th October – "Amos B left to go to Catleys Private School because the attendance officer has pressed for the boy's regular attendance!"

The H.M.I's report resulted in 3 Aldermen from the Education Committee calling on the 19th October. "They were unanimously of the opinion that a Classroom for Standards and a Babies' Room for Infants Class were urgently required with the numbers on the books. A new desk for HM was promised". Despite this it was to be several years before the school was extended. Several more officials met at the school on the 28th October – there were some from the Garforth sub-committee together with their clerk and the Vicar and Mr Broadbent from the School Managers – they discussed the closets, playground and enlargements etc. During the Christmas holidays the drains were reconstructed – a small but vital housekeeping job!

The new Vicar gave a lantern lecture on India on the 11th January. On the 24th he: "took 4 children to Leeds Infirmary to have their eyesight further tested as a result of the Medical Inspection and report of same in these cases. They are poor children whose parents have not the means to meet medical fees". On the 29th January "the 4 children taken again by Vicar to Leeds Infirmary. They were fitted with glasses which today have been received and the children commenced wearing them". Perhaps the costs were underwritten by the Vicar?

Miss Verity gave notice on the 30th April: "she proposed to qualify as a hospital nurse". This was quite a life-changing decision as she had been at the school as an Assistant for nearly 10 years. She left on the 28th May and Dr Abbott visited to make a presentation - "a very good writing case". Mr Broadbent and Mrs Lund from Becca Hall also attended the presentation "to bid goodbye to Miss Verity".

One wonders if Miss Verity qualified and what happened to her in the terrible war which came a few years later. Also during May – on the 3rd – two pupils left to go to Catleys private school "the parents are tradesmen and have been induced to withdraw the children to secure or continue trade given by Mr Catley"!

A simple entry on the 14th again recorded a death – "Mabel Addy buried on the 11th May, 4 yrs old". In the surviving Register there were brief records – Mabel was born 19.04.03 and started school 15.10.06 which was very young. Her father's name was Percy and "left for winter" was recorded so perhaps she had been kept at home during the months of poor weather – whether she had returned to school in the Spring is not known.

A lighter note was struck – literally – on the 21st and 24th May. On the 21st HM recorded he had taught the children a patriotic song in preparation for Empire Day. The song "Flag of Britain" was to be sung at the hoisting and saluting of the Union Jack. On the 24th there was a holiday in the afternoon for Empire Day and the children were given a badge and were marched to "Cow Pasture" portion of Parlington Park to witness the hoisting of the flag and to sing patriotic songs.

Miss Piercy had a lengthy absence in the summer suffering from rheumatism – from 11th June until after the August holidays. However, a new Assistant started on the 14th June – Miss Earnshaw – and the Infants Class was closed from the 24th June to the 24th July owing to an outbreak of whooping cough.

A simple entry on the 16th July recorded that Lottie N left for Ledsham Orphanage. (The records of the Lady Elizabeth Hastings Orphanage School can be found in the National Archives at Kew covering the years 1880-1905.) Lottie Nicholson was recorded in the Registers – her date of birth was 28.2.00 and she started at Aberford School 30.11.08 having previously attended Skelmanthorpe School, near Huddersfield. Her mother was listed as Mrs L.M. Nicholson with an address of Bunkers Hill. As father's names were usually listed in preference to mother's, it looks as if the father had already died, followed by the mother.

Another very short entry on the 23rd August was the first time HM mentioned Oriel College for he recorded "Visit of the Provost of Oriel College, Oxford – Vicar and Mr Broadbent showed him the buildings etc". On the 30th August HM had the satisfaction of readmitting 6 children from Catleys School which he recorded had closed.

Measles and sickness were prevalent amongst the infants and the M.O. asked for the section to be closed for 3 weeks from the 10th September. During the closure the room was thoroughly scrubbed out, the pictures taken down, walls swept, furniture washed with doors and windows kept open and a good fire going. The class remained closed until the 11th October. Another 'matter of fact' death – on the 26th October "Elizabeth Wharton died today". From the Register it appeared Elizabeth had two brothers who also attended Aberford School – Thomas and Harry. They all started on 24.10.06 but no birth date was given for Elizabeth (Thomas -.4.98, Harry 17.6.93). Their father was "David" with an address Main Street and the children had previously gone to school in Doncaster. Thomas left school 10.4.11 "left village", Harry left 30.11.08 "certificate labour", Elizabeth left 24.8.08 "gone to Bridlington". She had left school, therefore, some 14 months before she died.

On the 1st November HM had to investigate a complaint against one of the teaching staff: "Received two notes today complaining of Miss Earnshaw's treatment of children. On investigation, in the first case the mother said cane marks had been inflicted and were showing. When I asked for the girl to be produced that I might see the marks, which the teacher said would be the result of a hand slap on the child's arm, the parent withheld the child from observation. In the second case the mother had written in a temper on the information of her little children. When she saw her own child the facts were totally different".

An amusing incident was recounted by the HM on the 9th November – at least it is hoped the reader will find it amusing. "Mr Wordsworth (Vice-Chairman Garforth Education Sub Committee) called and examined books in the drawing lesson. He asked the first class the following question 'If a man went alone to live on an island what would he feel to be his first and chief necessity ?' – Each child was supplied with a slip of paper on which to place their answer, then collected and examined. 38 were in class. One answer was ' courage' one boy said 'corn' - 'God's help in all his wants through prayer' 'food and tools' 'box of matches' 'a companion' – and most of remainder 'food' or 'water'. The correct reply Mr Wordsworth wanted was "the bread of life". Mr Wordsworth ought to have realised that 'down to earth' Yorkshire lads and lasses would give him good solid practical answers!

HM had not been very satisfied with Miss Earnshaw's teaching and there were several entries over time but a typical one taken from the 10th November read: "HM examined Standard III and IV Arithmetic books – found seven boys in the habit of tearing leaves out of exercise book for scrap. Miss Earnshaw passively allowed it. I found no practical work in books. Teacher said weighing had been forming the lessons since my last examination of books. Examined Geog. Of Australia – result poor".

The year 1910 began with "10th January – marked Annie Braithwaite dead". Annie lived at Wakefield Lodge and she was 9 at this time. No name was recorded in the parents section of the Register. Extremely cold weather was experienced with 26 degrees of frost overnight on the 26th Jan and nine inches of snow on the 28th January resulting in very poor attendance. A thaw during early February saw the school lane in a wretched state and HM complained that, despite repeated warnings, the school cleaner was not cleaning out the fires properly. This resulted in debris being left in the grates so that the fires could not draw air in properly and produce a good heat.

A spot of bother occupied HM on three occasions in February – on the 10th: "Miss Whewell withheld and locked up in her cupboard a shuttlecock belonging to a child in her class for playing with it. The father visited the teacher's home, used violent language and threats and then came to me civilly, demanding his child's property. The girl told an untruth and when I fully heard the facts next morning and after going to visit the teacher at her home, I wrote the man stating my intention of reporting him and presented the facts to Mr R J Smith for the protection of the teacher publicly and the preservation of the privacy of her mother's home".

On the 14th: "Mr Smith (Divisional Clerk) wrote saying that the Managers in the first place must deal with the man who insulted Miss Whewell and asked if I had informed them. Miss Whewell reported the case the same evening to the Manager (corresponding) and next morning to me. I at once wrote the man stating I would report him for using abusive language and showed the Vicar the letter I wrote to Mr Smith. Mr Smith visited the school and he, I, Miss Whewell and the Vicar talked the matter over. The Vicar decided to write and ask the man to apologise to Miss Whewell". On the 21st Feb: "The man 'Jones' called at school to apologise to Miss Whewell which she accepted and the matter ended".

Miss Earnshaw received another unfavourable comment on the 4th March: "Miss Earnshaw's room very untidy – have noticed the same often". An entry on the 14th March reminds us that there was no safety net of a National Health Service: "A boy got his eye damaged with a gutta percha ball which a boy was throwing to another and who missed it. The ball rebounded from the floor and caught Cockrem who was playing at marbles. I sent a teacher at once with the boy to the Doctor whom I also saw afterwards. The mother came to see me and was anxious to know who was going to pay the Doctor's bill. I told her to wait patiently 'til we saw how the boy improved and referred her to the parish member on Garforth District Sub-committee".

HM made an entry on the 15th April 1910 which must have made him very proud indeed. He made a full description and it is reproduced here: "On Friday evening a purse of gold £30 and an aneroid barometer were presented to the Master on the completion of 30 yrs service as HM of the school. The presentation was made in the presence of all the Managers by Master Alvary Gascoigne. Colonel Gascoigne (Squire) was in the Chair and was supported by Mrs and Miss Cynthia Gascoigne. The school was crowded to overflowing. The gathering was interspersed with singing of glees and songs by the Garforth Glee Union who generously gave their service out of respect for the Master of the school. Several schoolmasters in the neighbourhood were present together with Mr R J Smith Divsnl Clerk who both spoke in the meeting and recited in the entertainment. Mr Wordsworth – Vice Chairman Garforth

District Sub Committee – and other friends [*were present*]. The teachers decorated the platform with beautiful flowers and plants and were responsible for all arrangements and the work leading up to the presentation".

The Premises Section of the HMI's report of the 27ᵗʰ April again drew attention to the lack of space: "the Babies will be more comfortable out of their present gallery and the Teachers in the Infants Room will have more opportunity for more effective work when the numbers in the room are lessened. The highest divisions are prevented from producing their most effective work by the fact that three classes are placed close together and crowd and disturb each other".

On the 10ᵗʰ May Miss Whewell took her class to Raper Hill for a geography lesson and the day was bright and warm. The area referred to is the high ground which can be seen from Field Lane, looking across the Cock Beck valley towards the A1 – the road off Field Lane on the lefthand side is called 'Raper View'. It is easy to picture a happy little band of children wending their way down Main Street, over the bridge, along Field Lane on the track which went straight through where the A1 now runs and then climbing the steep sides of Raper Hill. Later this same month the troublesome school yard was improved by having tarmac laid.

HM was very outspoken in his entry – believed to be about Miss Earnshaw as she was the teacher of Standard IV – on the 15ᵗʰ June: "Examined 4ᵗʰ Std exercise books at home with the following result. 1.Not a book without mistakes unmarked – bad spelling so marked by teacher that the child could not read the teacher's own writing and in two cases the teacher spelled words wrongly – 'polony' 'lettuce'. (How often have parents not been able to read a teacher's writing!) 2.The children are not shown errors in sentence forming, no idea of punctuation. Mistakes in dictation not written correctly and learnt. 3. General untidiness in the very marking by teacher and the writing of children going from bad to worse in 7 cases. This is the third occasion I have shown and begged the teacher's careful attention".

After the summer holiday there was a long entry concerning enlargement of the school dated the 19th August: "Visit of Mr R J Smith and Mr Wordsworth who met Mr Broadbent and Mr Prudent (Foundation Managers) and Dr Abbott W.R.C.C.Manager to discuss the plan for erecting two new classrooms, building of new offices and taking away present conveniences and lavatories to a more suitable place, also the enlargement of playground area for boys and girls".

HM recorded a personal entry on the 12th September when he left school at 11.30 a.m. to attend his son's wedding at Middleton near Leeds. The 20th saw HM at another wedding in the afternoon, this time in Aberford Church where he played the organ.

A Temperance Lesson was taken with Standards I and II on the 29th within the Citizenship Lesson and the same lesson was given to the other Standards. The boys and girls from the First Class were taken for separate lessons outside which sound very interesting: "First class girls taken with Miss Braham into the fields for observation lessons noticing trees, heights, colours of leaves, S aspect, N ditto, autumnal tints, undulating character of land, reason for pond in field, its position, how fed, growth in stagnant water etc. HM took boys and measured a field with chain, arrows and flags. Calculations made in school on return. Plan made on paper and measurements taken in field".

Very regular medical inspections were now a feature of the school year and the Church Cottage was used for these so that the school was not disrupted.

On the 28th October a further entry was made about Miss Earnshaw: "I have notified to Miss Earnshaw that I have noted in the Log Book she is 6 weeks behind in making notes of Lessons on Common Things and of the general untidy state of her room. Yesterday afternoon I fetched her from the playground and showed 7 arithmetic books throwing about on the floor open printed side downwards and a number of pens. One book had been trodden upon".

From the 8th November HM began to open the afternoon school at 1.00p.m. and close at 3.30p.m. "About 50 children attend from Becca, Lotherton, Hazlewood, Parlington and Hook Moor – distances varying from 1.1/4 and 2.1/4 miles. They will be able to get home before darkness sets in".

On the 17th and 29th November and the 6th December the different Standards had socials in school providing their own food and: "the teachers organised and assisted in making them happy during the evening 5.00p.m. to 8.00p.m."

There was a change of Vicars during December with Rev Walwyn – the new Vicar – calling with the Churchwarden on the 20th December. (Bernard Walwyn Shepheard Walwyn had attended Oxford University. He was the son of A.W. Shepheard Walwyn a J.P. in 1901 living with his family in a rural part of Cumberland. Bernard had 2 brothers at that date – Alfred aged 19 a Medical Student in Edinburgh and Richard aged 4. The family must have been 'well to do' having a Governess and four servants at that time.)

The new year of 1911 started with better news so far as Miss Earnshaw was concerned for the HM was able to report on the 31st January: "Miss Earnshaw is producing better results and carrying out suggestions made to her".

Another sad entry on the 6th March: "Nina Beasley died this morning (croup) Infants Class". Both a 'Mona' and a 'Norah May' appeared in the Registers but no 'Nina' could be identified. A boy was taken to hospital with scarlet fever. Another case of scarlet fever hit on the 20th March with another boy taken to hospital and HM had a few extra words to say about another death on the 3rd April – "Clarence Rush died of diphtheria today : was at school last Friday". It looks as if the boy must have died quite quickly after contracting the disease. He was not found in the Registers.

Healthcare via schools was growing at this time. There was an entry on the 12th April stating: "Mr Cressey called and left a specimen toothbrush and a number of circulars bearing on the teeth, to be distributed among children. I massed the classes, read the circular and sent one to each home by the children".

This year was the Coronation Year of King George V and there were several entries about this. On the 10th May the school was used for a public meeting in connection with Coronation festivities. Two Coronation hymns were taught to the children in the singing lesson. On the 16th June the school was closed for the whole Coronation week and on the 22nd some 200 children were entertained to tea in school followed by tea for everyone over 60 years of age.

It was in this May of 1911 that the first of the four sales of the Gascoigne's estates took place. In this sale there were some fourteen lots including Boston Spa Baths and Saline Spring and Well Timbered Pleasure Grounds, together with boating and fishing rights upon the River Wharfe. This showed how widespread the holdings of the family were. The sale must have been much discussed in the village and the children would no doubt hear their parents and others talking about it.

A new procedure was introduced in July concerning Fire Drill. On the 5th HM received notice of the Drill to be taught and he explained the signal and orders to the children on the 7th. A successful Drill was held on the 12th July but HM decided to make things more realistic at the next Drill by fastening one of the exits to see what the children would do. He was pleased to see that the children quickly headed for another exit and school was cleared within half a minute.

When school opened after the summer holidays HM reported on the 4th September "two jars have been purchased to hold water for drinking purposes and enamel mugs provided". On the 5^{th:} "received two jars for holding clean water with wooden taps. 4 enamel mugs. Arrangements have been made for one to stand in the boys' lavatory and one in the Infants – to be renewed daily with clean water". It seems that drinking plenty of water was felt to be a good thing then as now.

More 'rules and regulations' were beginning to gradually come into school life. On the 6th September the entry noted that a circular had been received about Teachers supervising the playground during break times. HM remarked that this was already the practice at

Aberford school: "to note correct conduct in language and act, repress the noisy ones and those inclined to bully or show a selfish spirit, organise a game, play with the children and generally to watch that their animal spirits are kept under control".

The difficulties of coping with the numbers of children were highlighted from time to time. Miss Braham was delegated to assist with Standards I and II at various times during the week and the HM noted "Std I should have a separate teacher and the infants a qualified assistant". A little movement on the enlargement of premises was shown by an entry on the 3rd October when Mr Brown of the W.R.C.C. and Mr Stewart an Architect, visited to inspect the building and examine the plans in connection with the building of classrooms. HM was informed on 27th October that the Managers were willing to purchase two kettles "for the use of children who wished to have a hot drink at noon – children from a distance who bring their dinners".

More visits to other schools and training courses were beginning to be brought in for teachers – an entry on the 1st November told of HM visiting Cross Flatts school for observations on the subject of Nature Study. Staff and museum cases were available to him and he stated he hoped to make out a scheme which would be of educational value to the children back at Aberford.

The First Class girls were taken to "the Institute" (probably the Almshouses) over the 27th and 29th November . They were given a lesson in bed making – there being two ambulance beds there and they had to get permission to use them. The same class also had a lesson in setting a dinner table and HM recorded: "the necessary articles being lent by the Master". Many poor children would never have experienced setting out a formal dinner table in their own homes for their families would not own the necessary items. Today it might be more of the case that many children have never experienced sitting down at a table to eat together – whether at breakfast, lunch or dinner !

Miss Piercy was absent all week just before Christmas for her brother had died but no cause was mentioned in the Log Book. HM attended the funeral on the 7th December: "Miles Piercy an old scholar". From the census records we know that Miles had worked in the family's business of Saddlers as a Book Keeper and he was only 41 when he died.

Early in 1912 HM decided to introduce some early 'show and tell' sessions for the children for he recorded on the 12th January: "Children this afternoon drawn together in big room. Each child who could recite, sing a melody, play any instrument or show any work executed at home was permitted to do so. We hope a spirit of emulation will result and children determined to spend their winter evenings profitably". This proved to be popular for, on the 16th February, HM recorded: "several children recited who have been very shy at speaking and answering in class".

Several children were allowed to leave school a little earlier than normal on the 27th February for the 'sod cutting ceremony' of the Wesleyan Chapel. The Wesleyan Chapel was built in a relatively short space of time – from the sod cutting ceremony on the 27th February to completion and opening on the 5th December – it had taken less than 10 months. Several children were absent on the 5th December for the opening ceremony at 3.00p.m. It replaced an earlier building.

A familiar one-line entry on the 18th March "Geo Nutton, infant, died today". He was not found in Registers.

Miss Margaret Magee began duties on the 1st April as a Supply teacher – her date of birth was 16th September 1887 and she came from Whingate Road School, Leeds.

The 26th April saw HM "determined to send specimens for exhibition at Knaresborough. Fossils (coal measures) in district, needlework specimens, grasses, plan of farm, pen and ink drawings, woodwork". This must have been an exhibition to be held at the Secondary School in Knaresborough for an entry on the 11th June talks of the items being sent there.

The first reference to the volume of traffic in Main Street at this time was on the 16th May when Dr Steadman enquired if there were any cases of sore throat amongst the children. HM stated: "I have replied and told him of the terrible nuisance endured daily of dust in the Main St lifted up in volumes by continual passage of motor cars". The number of cars passing through the village at this date would be small compared with those going through just before the village was by-passed!

Early in the new year of 1913 the children were given a talk by Mr Craven of the Yorks. Band of Hope Union – this lesson was related to 'temperance'. The children wrote compositions on the questions and these were sent for adjudication by him with the promise of illuminated certificates to be awarded to some of the best. The temperance message was reinforced to Stds VI and IV when the Vicar of Brodsworth gave them a very interesting lesson on the 30th January on "strong drink is dangerous". On the same day Mr Broadbent gave the school a number of good story books and a dolls house with some furniture for it to the Infants.

The first instance of early 'adult education' was recorded in the Log on the 14th March with the entry: "sent in a list of names of persons desirous of joining the Dressmaking class shortly to be commended by W.R.C.C. – 14 are married persons, remainder over 18 yrs of age". This class was started in school at 5.00 p.m. on the 7th April with twenty present.

The school lost a good friend in Mr Broadbent the 'Corresponding Manager' who was leaving the neighbourhood. On the 3rd April HM recorded: "Mr Broadbent … bid children goodbye … the Master presented him, on behalf of the teachers, with a very chaste, pearl-handled pocket knife. The intrinsic value was not taken into account - a simple memento from those who recognised Mr Broadbent's worth as a friend in sympathy with a teacher's life".

The long-awaited building alterations started on the 24th February. During building work Church Cottage was temporarily used as a classroom for Stds I and II. The Infants Class was transferred to the room vacated by these Standards and their class was to be altered "at once as per scheme". Work must have proceeded sufficiently for the Infants to return to their own room by the 19th May allowing the older Stds V, VI and VII to use Std I/II's room temporarily. Those who have had building work done on their houses whilst living in them will sympathise with HM when he recorded on the 19th May: "the noises created by workmen around the building are distracting to all classes in turn. Dust permeates all rooms. Teaching is conducted under difficulties". (At least there would not have been continuous playing of loud music whilst the men worked and endless cups of tea to be made for them as per these days!) The work continued to cause disruption and dirt for a while longer and continued through the school summer holidays – it was opened and re-dedicated on the 28th August.

A lengthy description of the extensive work carried was recorded in the Log Book:

"Main Room – an old building on the West side forming the lavatories for boys and girls pulled down. Conveniences boys and girls pulled down with stone boundary wall between the two yards. Three of the four windows raised to the eaves with new frames and larger panes. The fourth window taken bodily out and a new screen to take its place. The boys and girls cloakroom – partition wall taken out and the whole cloakroom now for use of boys only with lavatory. 4 basins and tank for their use. Gas meter moved from NW corner of room with boys cloakroom and a larger meter put in. The gas jets to be placed parallel to the side walls instead of two pendants hanging from the ceiling in the middle of the room. Two jets fixed to S. wall. Picture moulding put round room.

Class Room – The door in middle of W. wall opening into Infants Classroom built up and new door at S end of W wall.

Infants Room – Wall taken out and built 4ft forward with much larger window space – the gas pendant removed and jets put parallel to side walls – on the E side of the room a new wall built 9ft from present E wall – shortening the room by 5ft and making a space for new porch. A new board to come across this opening 9ft from N wall to be used as a store-room and space for teachers' hats and cloaks.

Pump and cistern for water to supply lavatories removed. Cistern filled up. Iron railings taken up and replaced in new school boundary. Present tank in infants yard for drainage to remain. Diversion of drains to the Vicar's drain in his walk. Old coal house pulled down and rebuilt in two parts – one for coal house, one for boiling water. Pump erected in this house and tank built outside for rainwater storage. 2 new classrooms built and additional playground space made. New conveniences built but in different positions. Alteration of infant boys' urinal. New cloakroom and lavatories for girls. New boundary wall on N side and entrance gate for ? purposes. New fireplace infants' classroom".

Here is some information about those who made donations to fund the alterations:

"Col and Mrs Gascoigne £200, Mr Lund £100, J Lloyd Wharton £100, E.O. Simpson £50, "Oriel Cottage" £50 (the Headmaster ?), Miss Wharton £50, Diocesan Society £50, Rev Campion £2.10/-, C.J. Ryder £50, Mrs Gascoigne 2nd donation £50, National Society £70, Diocesan £120, Bellons Charity £20, Managers' funds £50". (xiv)

As mentioned earlier, a Dedication service was held on the 28th August: "Invitations by circular sent out to friends. A fairly representative gathering took place at 6.00 p.m. Rev. Canon Atkinson, Rural Dean Darrington, chief speaker. Mr Broadbent – now of Ben Rhydding and to June 30th Correspondent of this School, also attended and spoke. The alterations and enlargements have cost £1260 and £17 only remains to be found".

There was a settling-in period over the next few weeks with hold-ups due to non-arrival or late arrival of desks etc. It must have been a trying time for HM having to cope with all the disruption and upheavals so perhaps it's no surprise that he recorded on the 8th September: "Master opened morning school but was obliged to retire owing to sudden attack of spasms – Doctor fetched and ordered me to remain quiet indoors for the day and take medicine as required". Or maybe HM had just eaten something that didn't agree with him!

On the 13th October HM introduced a system for 'ventilation' of the various rooms involving the taking of temperature and opening of windows if they had been closed overnight. Windows were also to be opened at play times and after school. Monitors in Standards VI and VII would take temperature readings and see that the windows were opened. The direction of the wind was to be taken into consideration before the large windows were opened.

The HM was in a very irate mood with a member of staff, judged by his entry on the 10th November: "Master took home Std 4 Ex books to examine during the weekend. I never saw a worse set, badly marked, careless work, dirty writing, no system of reproof. I told the teacher a standard of attainment and finished work should be aimed at and the teacher must not be satisfied until the class was raised to that standard. A fortnight ago I was compelled to bring Std III books before the Correspondent and stated that I could not further accept the responsibility for that class unless the teacher was seriously spoken to as she seems to take no steps to follow my suggestions".

Part Three : WW1 Years and Retirement

1914 was, of course, the year that WW1 broke out but the year began quietly enough – a Mr Harwood began to visit the school to do various artwork lessons. He took Stds V – VII on the 4th February for a class in printing the Roman alphabet. Later visits included the children being given a bluebell to draw and shade. A lesson by Mr Harwood on the 8th July was to bring a disparaging comment from HM: "Mr Harwood …. spent half an hour in talking of shading. 50 minutes in drawing the Church steeple with surrounding foliage. 42 children standing around watching". HM was more satisfied later in the month: "Mr Harwood took drawing again today with happy results. The time was well spent by the children who profited from the lesson".

Although perhaps unknown to HM, it was early in this year of 1914 that the school and land were conveyed to the Archdeacon of York, showing the link to Oriel College still existed for the signatories to the conveyance were the Archbishop of York, Cosmo Gordon and the Vicar of Aberford, Reverend Shepheard-Walwyn. The conveyance stated: "it is with the consent of the Provost and Fellows of Oriel College whose seal is affixed" (presumably to show proof of their assent). This transfer – at no cost – was perhaps to 'tidy up' the situation with regard to 'ownership' of the school and the land it stood on. An extract from this Deed (copy kindly provided by Oriel College Archivist) follows:

"All that plot of land situated at Aberford .. containing by admeasurement One thousand four hundred square yards ... also all that messuage, or School, with the outbuilding and conveniences thereto adjoining and belonging erected on the said plot ...to hold the same unto and to the use of the said Archdeacon of York and his successors for ever ... upon trust ... used as and for a School for the education of children or adults or children only of the labouring, manufacturing and other poorer classes in the Parish of Aberford aforesaid and for no other purpose such school to be always in union with and conducted upon the principles ... of the Incorporated National Society for promoting the education of the Poor in the principles of the Established Church .... said Archdeacon of York....may consent .. at the request of the National Society...grant or convey for educational purposes but not otherwise to any body, corporation or bodies corporate or person ... the estate or interest herby vested in them or any smaller interest in the said School ...".

The 24th March saw Father Turner beginning his regular visits to the school to take the Roman Catholic children in religious instruction and HM recorded on the 3rd April "the work of the school is going on smoothly". For some reason Father Turner was replaced by a Miss Richardson by the 30th June.

HM was not very pleased that, when Miss Braham left, (29th May) her place was not to be filled and this meant a reorganisation of classes. Miss Braham had been at the school almost 6 years and: "the teachers and scholars gave her a bracelet watch – the presentation being made by Mr Wordsworth the Chairman of the Garforth Dist. Sub Comm. accompanied by the Vicar". This meant that one of the classrooms would be empty by reason of having to organise the classes under the remaining teachers. Miss Piercy had the help of a pupil from top class from time to time as she had over

50 infants in her charge at times. With only three available teachers there was great difficulty if one was absent due to illness When Miss Magee was absent for most of June there was much juggling of pupils and these difficulties were to continue into July.

Although Miss Magee returned to work for a short time in mid-July her father died and she had to return home to Northern Ireland by the overnight mail boat on the 17th July. She did not return to school until after the summer holidays. It must have come as a relief when the school broke up for the summer holidays with HM sometimes having to take lessons like sewing and Mrs Freeborn also being pressed into service for sewing lessons.

School re-opened on the 1st September with Miss Magee returning in good health and on the 2nd Sept the first entry occurred connected (probably) with the outbreak of war: "distributed literature to all houses in the parish concerning gardens, small-holdings and poultry keeping". HM made no direct entry about the outbreak of war. Mr Harwood showed the top class how to paint a Union Jack on the 9th Sept and on the 23rd the lesson was painting or crayoning the flags of Belgium and Britain.

The 2nd October entry recorded "Sent 14s/6d teachers' contribution to War Fund, 1st month". Again on the 3rd November "Sent 16s/6d to Treas. of Army Distress Fund – Teachers' contributions for this month". It's not clear whether these were voluntary or compulsory contributions. The 10th October entry recorded: "2 Belgium refugees received" but this brief comment did not reveal the circumstances of the children becoming refugees. The work of the school continued quietly through the rest of the year.

1915 began with 190 children on the books - Miss Richardson continued to take the Catholic children for religious instruction She continued for a few weeks until, on the 18th March, HM recorded: "Miss Richardson taught the R.C. children. I showed her 5 obscene words written yesterday on a slate by one of the R.C. children. She promised to speak with Father Turner and see that the child was duly corrected and punished". (It seems doubtful the obscene words ran to anything more than the likes of 'bum' in those days. If HM

100

could hear the words commonly spoken by some children c2008 he would have fainted!) Father Turner resumed taking the Catholic children the following week.

The H.M.I's report this year seemed to hint at the changing methods gradually taking place in education. There had been H.M.I. visits on the 27th Sept. 1914 and the 18th March 1915. Some extracts: "… large amount of hard work that is done by the children. The discipline is of such a character as to develop grit and determination. While the value of these qualities – particularly at the present time – cannot be overlooked, it is felt that the children's progress would be smoother and quicker if knowledge were generally presented to them in a more attractive form and the lessons were given in a more sympathetic manner. In the oral lessons especially the teachers should endeavour to encourage spontaneity and individuality of expression, and their questions should rarely admit of collective answers. The attempt to make the whole class advance at a uniform pace in arithmetic for example, leads to waste of time….. Sectional and individual work should be easy to arrange now that new arithmetic books have been provided. Notwithstanding [the] level of development [of] children at top of the school is high.. The HM in addition to teaching a large class, supervises the work of his Assistants in a thorough and critical manner. … It is to be regretted that, owing to a reduction of the staff, one of the two new rooms cannot now be regularly used, and that owing to the absence of sufficient furniture it cannot even be profitably used for occasional lessons such as Drawing".

On the 18th June this year there was the first record of Nurse Cowen visiting school – HM had written to ask her to call and she visited: "the families of Chas D – one boy suffering in his left eye : rest very untidy and not well washed. G.G's two boys come habitually dirty. B's – a child has been absent months with ringworm". On the 22nd June HM: "sent her to see Grace B – ringworm case. Mrs G.G. dirty children and ragged and Mrs D who sends a little boy who has a discharge from his left eye. .. She promised to send a report of her visit". No outcome was recorded following her report but she was present at a Medical Inspection on the 25th October. It seems it was the case then, as now, that teachers picked up on possible neglect and abuse for an entry on the 28th October recorded: "Inspector N.S.P.C.C. called today to see W.C. He suffers with bad ear and his parents have long neglected seeing to its treatment. He got the boy's address and visited the home".

A further example of the HM's caring side – an entry on the 22nd November: "Fountain Wainwright fell in the yard when riding a boy on his back, just as the bell was being rung end of playtime. He complained of his leg. I took him to my home, laid him on his back, took away his trousers. He seemed to have sprained the muscles between thigh and kneecap left leg. My wife bathed the part and I sent for his Uncle who brought his pony and carriage and took the boy home to Hayton House". (It is doubtful any Headmaster would risk taking away a boy's trousers these days, no matter what the damage appeared to be!). Fountain Wainwright was born 28.1.09 and started school 19.4.15 He lived at Hayton House and his father's name was William. He had previously attended Sherburn school and he left 1.4.20 "to Tadcaster". He certainly had an unusual first name and one wonders how he came by it.

The Rev Moore, a Missionary from Japan gave the children "a very excellent address on the Japanese" on the 29th November "we were all sorry at the end of the time that he could not continue". Miss Earnshaw left the school on the 30th November and "teachers and scholars made her a presentation of books and Dr Abbott attended …. Beautifully bound volumes of Shakespeare, Dante, Modern Painters and Ruskin in volumes".

In December a collection was made for the Overseas Club for Soldiers and Sailors and £1 was sent. Attendance was bad – the weather and seasonal sickness affected children. The usual examination papers were worked by those children present to take home to show parents their progress as compared with the previous year. Christmas holidays were from the 23rd to the 5th January 1916. Sadly for Miss Magee, she received a telegram to tell her that her mother was dying and she was absent for several days so that she could help her sister nurse her. Her mother died on the 11th January.

Vandalism and 'yobbish' behaviour were not unknown in Mr Freeborn's day as the entry on the 19th January revealed: "Mr Powell visited the school and I drew his attention to the wilful breaking of pen nibs and points of lead pencils. For some time difficulties have arisen in and about the school by boys whom I have suspected but been unable to trace a positive case – five pieces of soap were found thrown into the water tank. Old carbide refuse has been put in ink pots, discolouring the ink and filling the well. A teacher's bicycle punctured with pins and another day screws of saddle all loosened. Whilst Mr Powell was speaking, the Policeman arrived at school with a man and asked to see 3 of the 4 boys whom I know behave badly. I asked him into the room to investigate a complaint I had just received from Mr Hawkes, who lives on the edge of the school playground, these boys jump his garden gate, have made a footpath across the garden, broken down a hedge and climb down a wall into the street. He investigated the whole matter. Before he had been gone a minute a complaint arrived that these same boys, during the noon hour, had been in Church, up the belfry to the clock, out on the tower and some higher up among the bells. I referred that to the Vicar. 3 boys had broken 17 panes of glass in the greenhouse of a market gardener which brought the Policeman to the school". (Surprisingly?) ... "Mr Powell spoke kindly to the boys, gave them good advice and also showed the penalty of their folly if the matter did not at once cease". HM did not record what he felt about this apparently lenient punishment but perhaps the Policeman was more severe with the boys in question!

It was bitterly cold during February and Miss Whewell terminated her service at the school on the 29th February (a Leap Year) after just over 10 years service. She was presented with a handbag – value 24s/6d.

Miss Braham started as an Assistant on the 12th March and the sun made an appearance for the first time in nearly 3 weeks on the 17th March, when HM received 60 Meal Record Cards. Miss Braham's appointment was to be short-lived for the entry on 21st July recorded "... Mrs Wormald was desirous of becoming an applicant for UA in Vacancy Schedule and Mrs Lock ditto for Std teacher in place of

Miss Braham resigning" and on 31st August after the summer holidays: "Miss Braham terminated her engagement at this school".

The new school year started on the 3rd April with 201 children on the books. On the 24th May, Empire Day, another collection was made for the Overseas Club with the money to be devoted to prisoners in Holland and Germany.

One or two entries began to appear in the Log Book which gave glimpses of the war that was raging in the world beyond the school gates. On the 19th June Mrs Wormald went, by arrangement, to visit her husband who was on leave from the fleet at Liverpool. On the 21st the Vicar called to say that Miss F Hawkes would start on the following Monday as an emergency teacher.

There was a happy occasion on the 4th August when "presentation made to Miss Magee who is to be married tomorrow – Fish Eaters and Silver Frame – the gift of scholars and staff" On the 28$^{th:}$ "Miss Magee was married but has received permission to continue her services during the period of the war. She is absent today as her soldier husband returns today and is expected to go abroad at once".

HM recorded a simple factual entry on the 19th September: "Alfred Storey, Willie Rhodes – two old boys killed in action. These two young men died just a few days apart. Rhodes held Commission Sec-d Lieut". This entry was researched and two sources were consulted to help to compile information on these men and others who were killed in this War. (xv) and (xvi)

The death of Alvara (Alfred) Storey was not recorded locally, which seemed strange given his strong local connections but it may be recorded closer to where his parents lived near Halifax. He was just 20 and a Private in the 1st/6th Battalion Duke of Wellington's West Riding Regiment having enlisted in Halifax. A small entry in the Yorkshire Post of 1916 read: ".... Son of H.S. Storey of Hazelwood, Tadcaster fell in action on September 3rd". He was buried in Connaught Cemetery, Thiepval. Research showed that Alvara's parents were Hubert and Mary Storey. Hubert had been a farmer at Nut Hill and Alvara's grandfather was William Storey, a farmer at Ledsham, for Alvara was staying with him on the night of the 1901 census when he was a little boy of 3 years old. The Registers did not go back far enough to record Alvara but it may be that he had a brother called Reginald who attended the school – there was a Reginald born in November 1901 with the address of Nut Hill Farm and no father's name recorded/no leaving date. There were also two other pupils with the names of Willie and Harold both of Nut Hill but Willie had no father's name recorded whereas Harold had 'Matthew' recorded. However both boys were recorded as leaving on the same date which looks as if they were brothers and possibly cousins of Alvara.

The death of William Rhodes was recorded on the Aberford War Memorial – he was a 2nd Lieutenant on the 4th Btn. Kings Own Yorkshire Light Infantry. He was 21 and an entry in the Yorkshire Post of 22nd September 1916 read: "2nd Lieut. William Rhodes, the third son of Mr F. Rhodes, Manager of Aberford Branch of Moon's Grocery establishment, was killed in action last Saturday morning, fell while leading a raiding party. He volunteered for the duty and was shot in the head whilst jumping on the enemy's parapet. Aged about 22 years, Lieut. Rhodes was a clerk in the office of Mr William Bateson, Solicitor, Albion Street, Leeds until joining the RAMC as a private immediately the war broke. Only recently he was given a commission in the KOYLI and came home from the front on a short leave a few months ago". He lies where he fell but is remembered on a Memorial to the missing in Thiepval.

Research showed that William was one of a large family having three brothers and five sisters as of 1901. None of them were recorded in the surviving Registers starting around August 1906 as the youngest child, Charles, was born in 1901 and would probably have just started school before the Register commences. Both Jarvis and Joseph (aged 26 and 22 in 1914 respectively) would have been old enough to have served in the War but it is not known if they did – if so they presumably survived. Charles would have been too young.

In early October the school was used by soldiers: "Staff Officer (Military) called at the school and stated it would be used next Monday the 9th to billet a number of soldiers (en route) for the night.

Wrote for 'order' for coal (2 tons) and load of logs (firewood)". 8th October: "Schoolroom used at night for 120 soldiers en route to Doncaster who slept on the floor and desks. The caretaker washed all the closets down and applied disinfectants. The men left 5.00a.m. All doors and windows were left open to get a current of air through". 9th October: "80 soldiers again billeted in the school overnight".

The entry on the 23rd and 24th October concerned a couple of boys each with a 'sweet tooth' who paid a price for their naughtiness: "Found a boy 'B' selling his hoop for a 1/- knife for 6d : 'A' was the purchaser and both were spending money on sweets. I sent the sweets on each and money to the parents. In 'Bs'case his father thrashed him. 'A' was punished by his mother (father at the War) who wrote me a note thanking me for sending 1s/5d, the sum remaining from 2s/6d, which he had taken from a box at home. Had a note from Mrs 'A' and visit Mrs 'B' who both thanked me for information given. They had inflicted punishment and asked me to do the same by keeping them from play and through the dinnertime".

Mrs Wormald was absent in the afternoon of the 27th October: "her husband, an Artificer in the Fleet, had just returned home after several months absence and she was anxious to welcome his arrival on a short holiday". On the 7th November: "Mrs Wormald absent this week .. her husband has got leave .. before going into the Mediterranean and she is spending it in Edinburgh with him". Mrs Lock had some sad news of the death of her husband's twin brother on the 22nd November but this had occurred at camp in Whitley Bay and the funeral took place on the 24th. Whether this was a death from illness or wounds HM did not say.

The 'Welfare State' of today means we no longer have the hardships of extreme poverty which were evident in HM's entry of the 4th December: "E.T. gone to stay with her grandmother in Leeds. She is one of 5 children who attend this school. The second child also comes and the next is absent owing to want of boots. The mother has applied for help: that is, food for the children, because they have been kept away owing to hunger. I sent for Nurse Taylor and asked if the "Care of Children's Committee (although in abeyance in this Parish at present) could help : or if the Act providing for the feeding of poor children could be put into force. I supplied her with full particulars and she has placed them before the Divsnl. Clerk".

The War's effects on peoples' lives continued – an entry on the 8th December recorded that Freda Hawkes, the emergency Teacher, was absent on leave as she was to be married the following day to a soldier home on leave. Her absence continued for a week on honeymoon and her married name became Mrs Bottomley.

The children worked their usual end of year papers to be taken home and Christmas holidays were from the 22nd December to the 8th January. During the holiday the school was cleaned as usual and coal delivered.

The War dragged on and 1917 started with cold wintry weather which we do not seem to get these days. Mrs Rhodes was absent on the 26th January "her husband on last leave again." It was often the case that soldiers would be sent home just before being sent overseas but they were not always sent abroad so this could happen more than once, with all the attendant heartache for loved ones.

Disruptions caused by the War occurred from time to time – on the 13th February: "received order for 2 tons of coal in advance. Owing to scarcity of delivery from pit to Aberford Depot and customers must take their turn in purchasing. I have sent the order to the agent to secure our turn in due course".

On the 8th March: "two rooms of school opened for R.T.C. Company stationed at Parlington Hall (ruins of) this evening. A Ladies Committee boiled hot water and made hot tea and coffee and provided meat sandwiches". On the 22nd March: "Mrs Bottomley isolated from school pending medical examination by a special Doctor. She visited the house of a youth suffering with, what has been determined as, Spotted Fever. Two deaths have taken place suddenly this week in R.T. Corps billeted here and the youth had been freely moving amongst them". Mrs Bottomley returned on the 26th March having been given the all clear.

The main road through Aberford has seen the passage of many soldiers as Aberfordians know and one such event took place on the 2nd May this year. "A very strong battery of R.T.A. fully equipped for Field Service halted in village during playtime. Children allowed to stand in street and witness the watering of the horses at the beck etc and continue their march. One lesson lost from Timetable but gained in object lesson". Mrs Wormald was allowed to be absent again from the 7th to the 14th May "her husband, a sailor, is home on short leave after six months absence".

In mid June of this year there were entries about what the procedure should be in the event of a raid by the enemy. On the 19th June: "Dr Abbot called in school to ask about how I should act in event of a Raid during school hours. I explained the method of Fire Drill and he promised to call unexpectedly and warn the school". On the 22nd: "Dr Abbott called 11.05a.m., rang a bell in passage. All teachers suspended work. Marched children in order into playground. The Doctor, by blackboard, showed children how to act in case of bombs dropping and they in the open and why windows should be partly open and doors. He recommended children at a distance should not be dismissed but retained in school along with teachers in their respective rooms".

In July Mrs Wormald received the welcome news that her husband was again back in the country having arrived at Liverpool and she was granted time off to join him.

The school holidays were for just three weeks this year, from 3rd to 27th August and the school received the usual thorough clean. However, 'cleanliness' of children from one family was to cause a problem in October. On the 1st: "Admitted a child 'I' to infants. The teachers of this family have notified to me on the filthiness of the children. I saw three very large fleas jump from the clothing of one and their skin under the clothes is literally covered with bites. Wrote for Mrs Taylor but find she has left. Brought the matter before Vicar when he called in school with a view to fetching the N.S.C.C. (think HM meant N.S.P.C.C.) officer but he promised to see the parents in the first instance". It may be that these same children are the ones referred to by HM on the 10th when he recorded sending the Nurse:

"to a case at Lotherton where the children (4) are verminous. She examined the three younger ones and saw their neglected condition bodily". The outcome was not recorded but hopefully the children were helped by the actions of HM.

A brief entry gave a glimpse of the horrors of the war raging beyond the school gates – on the 5th November: "Mrs Rhodes absent this week visiting her husband in hospital 'Gassed' at Rochester". Dr Abbott held an impromptu Air Raid practice on the 6th November which went very well and a curious entry revealed how the war was beginning to affect vital commodities: "Sent P.C. (postcard) to the Director of Propellant Supplies in response to circular stating we had collected about 3cwts of horse chestnuts".

A simple entry about the death of a pupil – on the 9th November: "Dorothy Heaton buried, aged 14, died of consumption". This was followed by a slightly longer entry on the 12th November: "Harry Chapman, an old scholar, killed by a stray shell and buried in France Tuesday 6th Nov. He was in Royal Engineers". Henry "Harry" Chapman was a Sapper, aged 26, with the 130th Field Company Royal Engineers. He was buried in Gorre British and Indian Cemetery, Pas de Calais. His parents were John and Sarah Alice Chapman.

HM did not write of his personal feelings at the growing losses amongst the young men he had known and taught but he recorded leaving school a little early on the 5th December to play at a concert for Soldiers Funds. Mrs Rhodes was able to welcome her husband home for a few days on the 18th December and she was recorded as being absent for the week. On the 21st a special holiday was granted. "The children's Christmas letter explains the causes and progress of the War. Master read 'the Proclamation' and after singing of National Anthem children dispersed 9.50a.m".

HM recorded at the beginning of the new year of 1918: "I have arrived at pension age but, by arrangement with the School Managers, and with the consent of the Board of Education and W.R.C.C. I am to continue for an indefinite period". Perhaps HM could have retired had he so wished but he obviously felt a deep obligation to remain in post whilst the war continued. The number on the books at the start of the year was 184.

There were many cases of mumps and whooping cough and, by the middle of January, the Medical Officer issued an order that the school should be closed for four weeks, to re-open on February 11th. The horse chestnuts collected the previous year were mentioned again on the 20th February: "Sent about 20 stones of dried chestnuts to Kings Lynn Harbour station by order of Minister of Propellant Stores London. These were gathered by the children in the summer and have been dried". What use these nuts were destined for is not known but we British are known for our ingenuity during times of crisis!

There was a measles outbreak in March. The severity of this illness in these times is often forgotten today but HM's entry highlighted its effects: "school again closed by M.O. Health on 11th March, owing to attack of measles of a bad type – one child died". School remained closed for a further three weeks after the Easter holidays this year, not re-opening until the 29th April.

Both Mrs Wormald and Mrs Rhodes had short periods of absence due to their respective husbands being home on leave. Miss Piercy had one or two short periods of absence due to her mother's illness and, in fact, her mother died in June. The 28th June saw Mr Cressey the Attendance Officer visiting the school to say goodbye "before joining up". Mr Dobson became the new A.O. visiting the school for the first time on the 29th August.

War-time shortages and more ingenuity were hinted at in these next entries. On the 12th and 18th September and the 4th October there were entries about the children being organised to pick blackberries; 12^{th:} "Stds IV,V and VI boys sent blackberry picking in the afternoon with Mrs Wormald (U.A.) They collected one stone". 18^{th:} "Std II, V, and VI boys and girls went blackberrying this afternoon. Former in charge of Miss Piercy to Ringhay Wood, latter with Mrs Lock to Hayton Wood. They returned with 36 and 27lbs respectively – sent to Brownhills Jam Factory, Leeds". 4th Oct:

"Standards V and Vi went blackberrying with Master. Collected 39lbs which were sent to jam factory, Leeds".

There was also an entry on the 27th September "Sent 5lbs weight of fruit stones and nut shells to Gas Works, Southend on Sea, on H.M.S. carriage forwards".

Astonishingly, HM made no mention in the Log of a personal tragedy which took place in October – the death of his wife Mary. The cause of her death was not known to the writer who thought she may have been a victim of the flu epidemic. However, information from her grandson was that she suffered from a goitre. This condition causes a swelling in the neck and is to do with the thyroid gland. In modern times it can be treated but perhaps not in this time. Mrs Freeborn (Polly) had been a great help both within the school and the community and her grave, which became a joint one with Mr Freeborn and a daughter, can be seen in Aberford churchyard.

By this time, after four long years, the War was drawing to a close. There was no entry in the Log about the ending of the War officially on the 11th November - perhaps because the school closed for the autumn holiday but, in fact, did not re-open for some six weeks. This was due to flu throughout the Country – indeed throughout the world. The HM recorded that it was "prevalent throughout nearly every home in the Parish". However, no child deaths were recorded.

1919 opened with 189 children on the books and deep snowy conditions. Mrs Rhodes was recorded – on 27th January – as being absent in the afternoon: "went to meet her soldier husband and say goodbye to her soldier brother sailing to Canada". We are not told why her brother was making this journey. There must have been a great many reunions going on – on the 3rd February Mrs Bottomley was absent for a week as her husband was on 12 days leave. Mrs Lock was absent 21st February: "her soldier husband arrived home from France just as she was coming to school". It's not difficult to picture how overjoyed she must have been! In fact she was given permission to be absent from school until the 10th March.

Mr Cressey returned safely from his relatively short service during the War and resumed as Attendance Officer – he visited the school on the 14th March. Both Mrs Wormald and Mrs Bottomley sent in their resignations to leave on the 31st March. However, Mr Standard the C.C. Inspector visited on the 31st March to discuss staffing and following his visit both Mrs Lock and Mrs Bottomley agreed to continue pro tem. In addition Miss Braham was engaged temporarily at the salary of 36/- per week of work.

The organisation of the school from the start of the new school year in April this year was recorded as follows:

Infants Class	On the Role	30	Miss Piercy (C.A.)	
Babies		14	Mrs Bottomley	(S)
Temporary				
Standard I		25	Mrs Rhodes (S)	
Standard II)		20		
Standard III)		22	Mrs Lock	(S)
Temporary				
Standard IV)		21		
Standard V)		20	Miss Braham	(S)
Temporary				
Standard VI)		18		
Standard VII)		16	Headmaster	

On the 30th June two events were entered in the Log in the same simple way in which many entries were made. One of them read: "Mrs Bottomley terminates her engagement after 3 years service. She came as an Emergency Teacher for Babies Class and last year became a Supply teacher". The second read:

"William Freeborn completes his engagement as Schoolmaster of this school. He took the school temporarily from the 4th Jan to 13th March 1875. Returned 28th March 1880 to above date".

The next entry – presumably in Miss Piercy's hand for she had been asked to take charge – read: "On Monday evening June 30th Mr Freeborn was presented with a Vol. of Music and a cheque for £57, from the Parishioners of Aberford, on his retirement after holding the position of Headmaster for 39 years. Dr Abbott made the presentation".

With these brief and unassuming entries the "Freeborn Years" were brought to a close. Mr Freeborn had steered the school through the Victorian into the Edwardian era. Momentous events had taken place in the world beyond the school – the Boer War and World War I to name but two. The community had suffered the terrible loss of many of its young men and they and their families would have been well known to Mr Freeborn. In addition to the two young men killed whom Mr Freeborn mentioned directly, research indicated that he must have taught at least 9 others – possibly several more, together with one who died from the effects of the War in 1920.

Mr Freeborn's grandson provided a copy of an article which appeared locally upon his retirement, reporting the gathering to honour him. In this it talked about his many important positions in serving the community outside of school including 38 years as Actuary of the Yorkshire Penny Bank held within school and, when Special Constables were appointed at the outbreak of war, HM was appointed Section Leader.

Mr Freeborn's family attended the gathering, including his son Edgar who had been hospitalised for over 12 months after being wounded by shrapnel in his leg. He had been brought specially from Beckett's Park Military Hospital in Leeds. HM had not expected such a 'send off' as he had been honoured for his service some 9 years previously and his closing words were:

"if he had succeeded in pointing out to them that the highest duty was to help one another, then his rest would be worthwhile. It would be satisfaction to know that his efforts had not been in vain, that they had appreciated what he had tried to do, and for that appreciation he could not thank them enough".

Appendix I contains some information about village people/children Mr Freeborn would have known/taught.

Finally it seems fitting that Mr Freeborn was buried in Aberford churchyard, close to the Church he had also served and his gravestone can be found on the left side of the path into the graveyard from Main Street. He lived for some 12 years after the death of his wife.

It is good to know that he had several years of retirement after all his years of service and he moved to Bridlington. His reputation in the family was of a scrupulously honest man who loved counting things! When he sold his house in Bridlington he insisted on accepting the same price he'd paid for it, being quite content with that arrangement. He played the organ in the Priory Church whilst in Bridlington and had also played music at Lotherton Hall on occasion for the Gascoigne family. He told his family a story that the Aberford children used to roll eggs down the steep field to the side of the school on Easter Sundays.

If you find Mr Freeborn's gravestone in Aberford churchyard perhaps you will stand there for a few quiet moments and reflect on this example of a life well lived.

Chapter Fifteen
THE INTERREGNUM
July 1919 to August 1920

Twelve months passed between Mr Freeborn's departure and Mr Rayson taking over. During this time Miss Piercy took charge and two male teachers held the post of Headmaster for a short time. On the 1st July 1919 Miss Piercy recorded that Mr Cook was to become Headmaster and Mr Chiltern was to assist temporarily.

A 'peace celebration' was held on the 19th July with children having tea in school and sports afterwards. A firework display was held on the 22nd July until 11.30 p.m. – as a consequence of which many children did not get up in time for school on the following morning! An extra week of holiday was added on to the summer break: "in accordance with the King's wishes in celebration of peace".

September saw Mr Chiltern still in charge of Stds V,VI and VII and a Miss Grace Dennis started in charge of Stds. I and II. Mr Powell visited on the 10th September: "to discuss organisation and stated that Mr Cooke … had accepted another appointment and would not be coming to Aberford on October 1st as arranged". Mr Chiltern left by the 22nd September. A brief entry on the 29th September mentioned a railway strike and the school was used on the 1st October for swearing-in of Emergency Constables as a precautionary measure in connection with the strike.

The shortage of manpower following the War and flu epidemic meant that the school was closed for two weeks in mid October to let boys help farmers in gathering potatoes. On the 30th October the Vicar called with the newly appointed Headmaster – a Mr Smith. Miss Piercy continued to keep the Log until Mr Smith commenced on the 12th January 1920.

On the 11th November, the first anniversary of the ending of the War, the day was referred to by Miss Piercy as: "League of Nations Day. All the children assembled in the big room to keep the King's silence for two minutes at 11.00 a.m. on the anniversary of the armistice. Short addresses were given by Mrs Gascoigne and the Vicar and the children gave appropriate songs and recitations". November the 17th saw Miss Dennis absent: "to Liverpool with her fiancé who is leaving for Canada". No reason for this was given and she returned on the 21st.

There was one of the regular medical inspections towards the end of November by Dr Allen and Nurse Ross; subsequently Dr Allen must have notified the N.S.P.C.C. of his concerns about some of the children for Miss Piercy recorded on the 2nd December: "N.S.P.C.C. Inspector to see children – T's, C's and G's. He had previously visited their homes and warned parents".

Eight children filled in forms to apply for the County Minor Scholarships this year.

There was an accident on the 16th December when Mary Abbott aged 7 slipped on the Infants' doorstep and hurt her arm. Dr Abbot called and found dislocation and fracture of the right elbow and she was taken to Leeds Infirmary.

Early in the New Year of 1920 Miss Piercy recorded on the 7th January: "I took boys in Stds V, VI and VII to the churchyard at 3.20 p.m. there being a military funeral. The deceased had died as the result of illness contracted in the Great War. The boys had not before seen a military funeral". Miss Piercy did not record the man's name or what the boys' reactions were to this event but it is thought to have been the funeral of James Cockrem who was 31 when he died. James was married to Agnes and the couple lived at Northern Cottages. He had served in the Yorks. Hussars Yeomanry where he had been a Corporal but was in the 509th (Agricultural) Company, Labour Corps when he died. James Cockrem's grave can be seen in Aberford churchyard fairly close to the Main Road. It was very likely that Mr Freeborn would have taught James in the early years of his time at Aberford. Cockrem is certainly an old Aberford family name and there were three children listed in the surviving Register who may have been from this direct family but almost certainly related.

On the 9th January the new Headmaster, Mr Smith, was met at the school by Mrs Gascoigne on behalf of the School Managers, together with the Vicar, and introductions were made to the children. Mr George H. Smith now took over the entries in the Log. There were illnesses in the early part of the year both to children and staff which disrupted the timetable. The usual entries were made about coal, cleaning of the school etc.

On the 10th May two Inspectors visited the school "with a view to introducing Domestic Training. The Vicar and Mrs Gascoigne also came in". Mrs Gascoigne also visited on the 17th May and "gave a descriptive account of life in Jamaica and Central America". The HM complained about the stench from "the offices" making physical training impossible and many children suffering from sore throats together with three members of staff. Mrs Rhodes left on the 31st May and on the 7th July "Gladys Hartley and Bessie Hawkett have been awarded Scholarships".

Further brief entries followed and, without any explanation, on the 22nd August "Mr Geo. H Smith terminated duties as Head Teacher of Aberford C..E. School".

This had been an unsettled period of twelve months for the children and staff after so many years of stability under Mr Freeborn but Mr W.D. Rayson was to bring a new style of leadership as the school moved into the 1920s.

Chapter Sixteen
THE RAYSON YEARS

Part One :1920 to 1939

Mr Rayson began as Headmaster on the 23rd August 1920 and gave the attendance as 154. His entries were less frequent than those of Miss Piercy and Mr Freeborn and within two years or so a whole month would pass with nothing recorded. After a short settling in period, he recorded the organisation of the school from the 1st October (Mrs Rayson joined the staff on this date).

Standards V,VI and VII	Headmaster	34
Standards III and IV	Mrs Rayson	41
Standards 1A and 2	Mrs Lock	40
Standards 1B and 1st Infants	Miss Braham	34
Babies and 2nd Infants	Miss Piercy	31

An Inspector visited on 6th October: "expressed his views on the organisation of the School. The possibility of establishing a cooking centre for the girls and gardening for the boys was considered". The first hint of some new initiatives appeared on the 20th October: "the first House matches were played today and aroused great enthusiasm. Their keenness has already had a marked effect upon the general work of the school. Boys: Football, Girls: Rounders". This was a reference to the children being divided into 'Houses' and these were named Parlington, Hazlewood, Lotherton and Becca.

On the 8th November Mrs Squires joined the school and Mary Squires was admitted to Infants Class – probably her daughter. There was a Mary Fearnside Squires in the Register, born 5.7.15 who started school 8th November 1920, with father "William" and address of Oriel Cottage so Mrs Squires and family must have been in one of the Oriel Cottages at this time.

On the 15th November HM sent off forms: "relating to May Selby and Sarah Kirby in Teacherships". Ivy May Selby was born 1.5.07 and started school 20.5.12; her father's name was James and her address was Parlington. She left school when she reached 14. (The school leaving age had been raised to 14 in 1918. and she was to start as a Rural Pupil Teacher on the 1st of June the following year.) Sarah Isabel Kirby was born 22.1.08 and started at school 1.4.13; her father's name was Edward with an address of Bunkers Hill and she left school 23.9.21: "Scholarship Tadcaster".

Mrs Gascoigne interviewed these girls and Bessie Gibson about this on the 1st December. Bessie was born 29.3.05 and started school 21.4.15, having previously attended school in Saxilby. "Ashlin" was given as a parent with an address of the Arabian Horse. There was no date of leaving or reason in the Register. On the 26th a Whist Drive and Dance was held in the evening to raise funds for the school Sports fund: "a most enjoyable function". The next day the School Eleven beat Bramham on the 30th October and they played a rousing game against the Selby Abbey School Team – resulting in a draw.

The move towards getting a Cookery Room was gaining momentum: "An Inspector (Lady) visited the school a.m. to discuss the question of converting the spare room into a Cookery Room. The Vicar came in and the question was thoroughly investigated. It was decided that the Managers wait until details of cost etc. were supplied by the W.R.C.C."

Mr Squires had an observation visit to the school in the middle of December – presumably this was Mrs Squires' husband who was undergoing teacher training. An entry in early January the following year recorded: "a communication from the Training College, Sarisbury Court, Hants. thanking the HM and staff .. for practice during the two weeks preceding the Xmas holidays". Mr Squires had a further two weeks practice in May the following year.

School broke up for Christmas on a happy note this year when HM recorded on the 23rd December: "The whole week has been a very happy one. The children and their parents co-operated keenly in making a fancy dress party on Tuesday – a big success. The Christmas Tree was greatly admired. The whole thing will do good throughout the village".

As the Vicar left in December, Mr Winterburn acted as Corresponding Manager and he called toward the end of January 1921 to discuss the appointment of a successor to Miss Braham, who left at the end of the month. A presentation was made to her on the 31st on behalf of the children and staff. Mrs Lock began a spell of temporary duty. After Easter Miss Moss began at the school.

Attendance remained consistently good – mostly over 90% - on the 1st July HM recorded that attendance had been 98% for the week with Stds IV and V making 100% for the third week in succession. The new Vicar visited the school on the 18th of April. In the outside world the Coal Strike continued as an entry on the 3rd May revealed "Mr Powell visited school re feeding of necessitous cases owing to the Coal Strike". There were probably quite a few families in the village suffering hardship at this time as many men were miners.

On the 25th June "the School played their first cricket match against Bramham away. They won easily 49 to 13". Another good win for the cricketers was recorded just before the holiday when Aberford beat Castleford – Castleford scored 33 but Aberford scored 37 for 8 wickets.

HM attended a two week course in July on 'Science for Rural Schools' at Cambridge and Miss Piercy as usual took charge. Several cases of whooping cough broke out and the Infants class was closed a few days before the summer holiday. The school was closed for a further two weeks at the end of the official summer break for the same reason, resuming mid September. Some extracts from the Inspector's Report of his visit on the 19th July show the changes and improvements which had occurred under the new HM:

"...the present Master has been in charge just a year and he has been eminently successful in enlisting the hearty co-operation of both teachers and scholars and the future is full of promise. The tone of the school is distinctly good and under the stimulating influence of the Master, a healthy spirit of rivalry between the different sections – into which the school is divided under the 'House System' – is evinced. There is a real atmosphere of work about the place and the interest exhibited by teachers and scholars both in day school affairs and in outdoor activities is a very commendable feature. ... many changes of staff .. much leeway to make up ... particularly noticeable with regard to Arithmetic and Spelling... every promise within a reasonable space of time. ..shortcomings ... will be amended. Increased attention .. to literature with good results, composition is good.... good practical work .. in history and geography ... house management lessons of older girls are much appreciated and some very good drawing is exhibited. The regularity with which scholars attend school is worthy of special mention".

The practice of taking children further afield began – on the 26th September – "Twenty-two children with Mr and Mrs Rayson paid a visit to Scarborough and had a splendid day".

The New Year of 1922 saw lots of bad weather in the first three months interfering with attendance but the percentage remained high and Mr Squires joined on the 3rd April.

Although not mentioned by HM, the War Memorial, sited close to the Almshouses, was unveiled in March of this year by Major General Sir Frederick Landon and it recorded Aberford men (or men who had close associations with the village) who were killed in WWI. Certainly many children would have attended this ceremony with their parents. The standard bearer was Arthur Banks, father of 'Dickie' Banks the author of 'Walk Through Aberford' (xiii)

In the wider world at this time things were changing. Young people had experienced the horrors of war and there was a feeling that life was short and should be enjoyed. Class barriers were being broken and change was on the way.

HM commented on the 19th May: "A system of awarding marks for good behaviour has been tried for three weeks and shows promise of being successful. Worked in conjunction with the 'House System' it is arousing a better idea of what is required in the way of behaviour".

Entries now began to have longer gaps with just brief notes about such things as receiving parcels/medical inspections/sewing requisitions/council meetings. On the 30th October the following brief entry appeared: "admitted the Masters' children from Barwick".

HM was very enthusiastic about sports; on the 9th December he wrote: "Saturday – we had a visit from Selby Abbey Boys Club with three members of their staff. A rousing game was played which ended in a draw of 3 each. The visitors were entertained to tea and the arrangements were made by our senior girls with complete success. After tea a short time was spent in musical items. Three of our old girls and one boy joined in this and the whole affair was voted a splendid success".

The good mood persisted as the Christmas break drew near – on the 20th December: "The children's party was held – the weather was atrocious but practically every child came and the evening was a happy one. During the interval between games and tea, Mrs Lund from Becca Hall presented a lovely picture with the title 'The Little Gypsy' to the School to serve as a trophy for competition between the different Houses in School. This gift was in answer to an appeal by the Headmaster". Unfortunately HM's house was ransacked during the holidays and the school keys stolen which meant a joiner having to remove the locks and fit new ones.

On the 12th and 13th January 1923 the school was used for a concert by the Raffle(s?) Concert Party and on the 27th the Football team reached the finals of the Barkston Ash Schools League. They played Garforth at Peckfield with Aberford being beaten 1 goal to Garforth's 3.

"Football – It used to be a thru'penny (old money) return to Garforth (on the bus). Me and Les Walton and Eric Bradley went to play East Garforth (school) but we didn't go on the bus. What we did – Les Walton had a little 2-wheeler bike and so Eric Bradley sat on't handlebars, Les Walton sat on't seat and I sat on't carrier at back and poor old Les peddled it right up the Fly Line to East Garforth. We played football there and then we come back the same way as we went. When we went to school on Monday morning the teacher said 'how many went to Garforth?' – so we said 'we three went' – we didn't tell him we went on't bicycle so he thought we went on't bus so he gave us thru'ppence a'piece. So what we did, we had a 'nosh up' – in other words we bought some sweets!" At that time I didn't have no football boots. Well, me father would have me play in me ordinary boots but I had a pair o' clogs so I played with a pair o' clogs on. Well, when the others saw I had a pair o' clogs on I could run through 'cause they wouldn't offer to tackle me 'cause in them days there wasn't all this whistling for fouls and that. If you couldn't get the ball you got the man in them days and that were how we played football". (xiii)

On the 14th February Mr Simpson presented a shield to School to be competed for by the Houses but the School had to close for a few days owing to no coal being delivered and the weather being very cold.

Brief entries appeared until the 9th July when: "Mrs Gascoigne sent word that she had approved our selection of a shield to be given by her for competition annually at the athletic sports[day]. To be inscribed each year in the space provided". Sports Day was held on the 25th July but there was no entry to say which House won. On the 19th September the Vicar presented the Gascoigne shield to the school for the first time and medals were given to the champions – Alec Walton and Nellie (aptly named) Swift.

There was a good Inspector's report which was copied into the Log on the 3rd Sept: "There has been a marked change in the outlook in this school since the present Headmaster took charge three years ago. The scholars are divided into Houses for games and for work in school and the Managers have presented shields for the competitions. This and the organised games have had an excellent influence on the behaviour and bearing of the children who now show self-reliance and self-control. A sports festival held recently out of school hours aroused much interest both among the children and their parents. Funds which have [been] raised by the teachers for games have also provided interesting and well illustrated reference books for Geography, History and Nature Study....".

In November HM hinted at the busy preparations going on for a concert to be held at Christmas – on the 20[th:] "In preparation for the School Concert, the proceeds of which are to be mainly devoted to the purchase of a piano and sports outfit, the Babies and Infants will spend from 11 to 12 in illustrating nursery rhymes and in learning action songs of educational value". An account of this concert was proudly given by HM and it was held in the Village Hall which was newly built in this year of 1923. Also at this time a daily bus service to Leeds began, using a Vulcan bus; this was later joined by a 16 seat Chevrolet. This was known to Aberfordians as 'the Red and White' service and soon another operator began; 'the Blue and White' – eventually the two were to combine.

December the 14th and 15[th:] "A highly successful Concert was given by the children in the New Village Hall. On Friday the audience filled two thirds of the Hall, on Saturday we were crowded out. The staff worked extremely hard and were enthusiastic to the last degree.

Programme: Sketch – The Old Woman Who Lived in a Shoe. The Doll's Wedding and Roses by Std I. Hail Smiling Morn. Ye Mariners of England. A Wet Sheet and a Flowing Sea. Viking Song. Minuet Keys of Heaven. Gay Little Girls from Japan. Six Egl ? The Village Blacksmith. ....songs. Rag Dolls. Jerusalem. Vesper Hymns. Highland fling. Irish Jig".

The HM's delight was again shown by a further entry in the March of 1924: "Another very successful Concert was given in the Village Hall. The programme was similar to that of the December concert with additions viz:

Comrades in Arms, Annie Laurie (McPherson?), The Ballad of S. Hilda (York Pageant), Caller Herris?   The dances included Scotch Reel, Sword dance, Highland fling.   There were two crowded audiences and the whole entertainment was a revelation to the village".

It was in this March of 1924 that the last passenger train was run on the Aberford Fly Line.   In part, the competition from two bus companies meant that there was no longer a future for the service.

On the 7th May HM recorded a visit by Mr Whitehead and an Inspector: "they saw the games and dances and heard some songs and were highly delighted. They expressed surprise and pleasure at the very smart appearance of the girls in their school costume".

In June Mrs Rayson ceased duty and Mrs Squires began supply duty. An outbreak of measles forced the school to close early on the 29th July for the summer break. By mid September Mrs Squires ceased and Miss Wormald started as a supply teacher.

The concert this year was performed on no less than five dates! - the 6th, 12th and 13th of December and again on the 29th and 30th of January in the new year. HM gave a full and proud description:

"The work given was the Operetta 'May Day in Well a Days' with several attractive additions. One, two, three and four part songs were sung with equal skill, the dancing and dialogue were equally good and the dresses, many of which were made by the parents, showed evidence of extraordinary care and enthusiasm. Our thanks are due to Mrs Miller for teaching the dance, Miss Townend and Mr Garbutt for supplying the music and Miss Heather Young for painting the beautiful scenery – 'Aberford' and 'The Enchanted Wood' The Saturday of the 13th was remarkable for a truly wonderful concert and an audience full of admiration. The takings were £46.8s.11d. £27 was handed to the Managers to add to the School Restoration Fund".

There was a favourable Scripture Exam in February. The usual medicals took place throughout the year and in July there seems to have been some centralising of dental services for HM recorded on 6th July: "Dr Scott the School Dentist visited the school .. the children from Barwick came in the afternoon" and on the 7th July "children from Scholes came to be attended by Dr Scott".

Miss J M Selby started as a Student Teacher on the 2nd September – "she was allocated for one month to the Babies Class where she will observe methods of teaching the youngest".

An outbreak of chicken pox caused a drop in attendance in November and the school had to be closed in the latter part of

November for four weeks in total which seemed to carry the closure over the Christmas period. No mention was made in December 1925 or January 1926 of any concert taking place – perhaps the chicken pox meant that it could not be done this year.

The first mention of punishment by this HM occurred on the 18th February: "Maurice W. punished for impudence". No further explanation was given but the offence and punishment were obviously of sufficient importance to be recorded in the Log!

February the 26th recorded the first instance of a short 'career break' or long holiday being granted to a member of staff. "Miss Piercy ceased duty for one month for the purpose of visiting the Holy Land". What an adventure this must have been at this time and what tales Miss Piercy must have brought back with her to tell the children! The tomb of Tutankhamun had been discovered by Howard Carter in 1922 in Egypt sparking worldwide interest in the ancient cultures of that part of the world. In addition Britain had a Mandate to administer a large area of Palestine at this time.

Whooping cough made one of its regular yearly visits to the village during July and there was very hot weather making conditions in school difficult – the thermometer registered 84 in Miss Piercy's room in the south of the building and 80 in the northern part of the school. Everyone must have been very glad when the holidays arrived.

An Inspector visited in early November and commented on weaknesses in Arithmetic: "Before any real progress can be made in Arithmetic, which is not a strong subject, particular care is necessary to ensure more facility in the fundamental principals". In addition there was the comment: "the work of the classes is periodically reviewed by the HM but he should give constructive guidance to his zealous staff".

HM was quick to act on this weakness and he called a staff meeting on the 17th December: "to discuss methods and means of improving Arithmetic. HM presented his suggestions which all were asked to read". He also made his feelings clear in his further comment: "Staff meetings are a regular feature of this school and it is the case that the 'constructive guidance' referred to in the HMI's report has usually been given".

The new year of 1927 saw HM begin to concentrate on arithmetic – on the 18th January: "... asked the Teachers to concentrate on the foundations in arithmetic and reading. Many of the children have had to be kept down owing to their not being fit to be promoted. These require special attention". HM began to take the different standards for periods of time to try to improve matters and Miss Selby concentrated on the older part of Standard I - the most backward part of the class - to try to get them ready for promotion in April.

July and August were very wet months this year and HM recorded on the 29th August: "A very wet August and a poor holiday for the children".

The 8th September had an entry about children being absent for pea pulling which was the first time this was mentioned by Mr Rayson.

The efforts to improve arithmetic appear to have begun to raise standards – on the 21st October: "I have given a short mechanical test to Std I and they are improving. 19 out of 30 got the division right. It seems as though the time I have spent with this class is doing some good". Mr Squires left on the 31st October to take up a Headship at Hipswell School, Richmond.

Early December saw Miss Piercy absent with ill health and she was advised to stay at home for at least two weeks. In fact she did not return until March the following year.

There was very wintry weather during the first months of 1928 and there were several staff absences through illness, culminating in the HM also becoming ill in mid-March. In fact, just after the Easter break, he was diagnosed with pneumonia and did not resume duties until July 9th. HM must have been quite ill for a note on the 7th May stated: "The Divisional Clerk called this afternoon and left instructions that, owing to the serious nature of Mr Rayson's illness, playtime each day should be for 5 minutes only and that the School should be closed 15 minutes earlier on Tuesday and Friday afternoons". Presumably this was so the noise of play would be less intrusive to Mr Rayson, whose house was close by the schoolyard. However, usual playtime was restored two weeks later.

HM must have been given a boost when, on the 11th July: "to mark the occasion in winning five Scholarships, school closed 15 minutes early by permission of the D.C. The Scholarship winners were Ronald Hudson, Clarence Brown, Philip Cockrem, Adah Stone and Dorothy Birdsall". On July 13[th:] "Standards VI, VII and VIII paid an educational visit this afternoon to the works of Messrs Rowntree and Co, cocoa manufacturers of York in charge of the HM". The good mood continued when the cricket team played Barwick on the 17th July and won for the first time for many years. The rest of the year continued much as previously with, again, no mention of any concerts.

It was a very cold start to the new year of 1929 – on the 17th January: "Temperature in Std IV and V room at 9.00a.m. 38, in Mr Rayson's room 40, in Std II and III room 38. The fires are not very effective in warming the rooms and the temperature is raised by keeping the windows closed". This problem continued throughout January and into February and may have contributed to HM becoming ill with flu in the middle of that month. He returned in the middle of March.

Children left and joined at times throughout the year and a General Election caused the school to be closed for a day on the 30th May. This election was the first in which women were allowed to vote on the same basis as men and resulted in a 'hung Parliament' with Ramsey MacDonald's Labour Party having the most seats but not an overall majority.

The state of the playground was a cause for concern as an entry on the 14th September revealed: "I wrote to the Vicar calling the attention of the Managers to the bad condition of the playground. It is nearly a cust heap and dangerously uneven". Again the yard was mentioned on the 30th October: "the schoolyard is again in a bad condition, the lower part being nothing but puddle and slime".

In February of 1930 HM recorded that there were now 181 on the roll and a period of illness for both Mr Rayson and Mr Salisbury meant that Miss Piercy was asked to take charge, although Mr Salisbury returned within the week. Several children contracted measles in February and school was eventually closed from 26th February to the 14th March by order of Dr Hill (the M.O.H). Miss Wormald ended her duties at the school during this period.

Mrs Rayson was pressed into service as a temporary Supply Teacher to take standards II and III. She continued to mid-July when a Miss Fawcett commenced as a C.A. on 21st July. Also in July the top class entertained 44 children from St. Andrews, Leeds with staff. Cricket, tea, games and a walk to Parlington. One proud pupil achieved a Scholarship (Harold Hudson aged 13) – the only one in the district – to Tadcaster Grammar School at the end of this month. Harold lived in Oliver Cottages.

The Inspector's Report of his inspection in September pointed to some weaknesses: "The good tone of the school is well maintained but absence owing to illness of the Headmaster and the staff has interfered with the work of the classes and the general attainments of the scholars are not as good as they have been. The HM .... now gives useful guidance to the Assistants .... the work of the Teacher of Class 2 being particularly thorough.... A definite attack on the defects of the composition exercises is securing some improvement in this subject but it is clear that the oldest scholars do not evince much interest in the reading of books, nor do they have their knowledge of Geography, History and Science thoroughly tested in writing. The foundations of arithmetic are still weak in all classes and the exercises worked during the inspection produced disappointing results. ....Children promoted to Standard I at the beginning of the present year were not well prepared especially in reading".

On the 31st October Mr Salisbury left to take up a position as Headmaster of Skelmersdale school near Southport. Mrs Rayson once again assumed temporary duties.

There was no mention in the Log of Mr Pickles joining the staff, he was appointed during this year. "Choice unanimous Mr Walter Pickles of Dewsbury who is now completing his training in Southampton. The decision was largely determined by a glowing account of Mr Pickles' character and work from Professor Cock the Principal of Southampton Training College". (xiv) This was to prove a very good choice indeed as Mr Pickles went on to be a long-serving and well-liked teacher!

An unusual event was recorded on the 8th June: "newspapers report earthquake – felt in Aberford". No damage was reported in Aberford but this earthquake was the strongest ever felt in the British Isles and measured 6.1 on the Richter scale. Its epicentre was some 60 miles off the Yorkshire coast on the Dogger Bank and the coastal communities of Filey, Hull and others all had a little damage to chimneys, roofs etc.

In July the older children went on an interesting educational visit, in charge of HM and Miss Fawcett, to York and visited Rowntrees in the morning and the museum and grounds of York Minster in the afternoon. In the early evening they also visited the Bar walls and Merchants Hall in Fossgate returning from York at 7.00p.m.

1932 began with 174 children on the books. There were two cases of scarlet fever but no general outbreak. However the seriousness of this disease was underlined when, in October, HM recorded: "Beryl Foster dead – scarlet fever – two others serious cases". Beryl was the daughter of Christopher of Chapel Yard and she had only just started school, aged 4.

In February this year, Oriel College sold off its final holdings in the village with the sale of the Rose & Crown cottages and property nearby which included the two cottages up School Lane. This block of property was sold to John Smith's Tadcaster Brewery Ltd. It was around this time that the Rayson family moved into a property at the north end of the village and the Walton family began to rent their old house. Subsequently Mr Walton's son bought the house in which he lives to the current time.

In March there was the usual delivery of boots to the school for Miners' children and in June the welcome news that Tom Freeman had won a Scholarship. In August Albert Dickenson had news that he had won a scholarship to Tadcaster Grammar School – one of five offered.

In September Miss Piercy became ill and it is not clear just how long she was absent but a Mr Reed started as a Supply Teacher. In fact it was not recorded that Miss Piercy returned but HM did record on the 22nd December this year: "It was announced during the holidays that Miss Piercy had resigned her post as Certificated Teacher on the staff owing to ill health".

In the minutes of the Managers meeting Miss Piercy's resignation was: "accepted with deepest regret and with many expressions of appreciation of her wonderful work and influence in the school during her 33 years of service". (xiv) Astonishingly there was no mention in the Log Book of Miss Piercy's long service. She had started as a Pupil Teacher in 1894, progressing after 4 years to Assistant in 1898 – some 34 years of qualified service. No 'leaving' or 'presentation' ceremony was recorded in the Log.

She was to live for just a few years longer – for HM recorded on 12th February 1937: "The HM attended the funeral of Miss Piercy, for over thirty years a teacher on the staff of this school. The funeral was at 2.30p.m. and was attended by the children of the top class". Miss Piercy's grave is in the part of the graveyard which is now a conservation area and may become obscured by vegetation as it does not have a vertical stone. Though not marked, this grave also contained the remains of a Sara Stead and Miss Piercy's mother. Two graves further on is the grave of her father and siblings. The wooden gates at the bottom of the steps fronting Main Street were donated in Miss Piercy's memory and are by the 'Mouseman', Robert Thompson of Kilburn.

A modern innovation on the 28th November: "work commenced on the provision of water lavatories". This work was completed on the 17th December. The School Caretaker became ill in early December and he died in Leeds Infirmary just two weeks later but HM did not record the cause of death.

In January 1933 there were difficulties with staff illness and there was a great snowstorm at the end of February: "the worst within living memory" which caused attendance to drop drastically.

At the end of March Mr Reed ceased as a temporary Teacher and Miss Margaret Irving started as an Assistant. A Miss Robshaw came on an observation visit on the 25th April prior to her entering Hull Training college in September.

In June, though no acknowledgement of Miss Piercy's long service had been noted in the Log, it was recorded: "The Managers reported that a piano had been given by Miss Piercy for the use of the Infants Division".(xiv)

On the 31st August Miss Fawcett left to become Head Teacher of Killinghall Church of England School and Miss Mary Ellis replaced her after the summer holidays. Miss Fawcett returned for a visit on the 23rd October and was presented with a flower vase from the staff and children.

On the 10th October: "Miss Heaton, an old scholar of this school, who commenced her singing career by singing solo contralto at one of our School Concerts in 1925, left today for Vienna to be trained for opera. She has successively passed through training at Leeds and the Royal Academy and now on to Vienna". From this entry it appeared that the school concerts continued to be a regular feature although the HM did not mention them. In the following year HM recorded on the 12th June: "Miss Heaton ... took one of the solo contralto parts at Covent Garden in this year's season".

The Register recorded that three Heaton siblings attended Aberford school. A little has been researched about Maud Heaton. She seems to have had a good career for she was mentioned in a book (xvii) about a Concert Agency which represented many famous artists including Dames Janet Baker/Clara Butt/Kathleen Ferrier and Rachmaninov, so Miss Heaton was in illustrious company! Artists would audition for the Agency and Miss Heaton was recorded as being a Contralto, experienced in German opera houses, who had "an exceptionally good voice, even throughout the register, sings with intelligence, think highly of her". She very quickly went into the top third of the Agency's names listed in the 1938/1939 brochure. These brochures were available to promoters putting together concerts who would then book the artists via the Agency. Further, there was a Maud Heaton singing in an opera 'Elektra' by Strauss conducted by Sir Thomas Beecham in October 1947 – the part of a maid sung by an Alto. Surely "our Maud"? If the war years had not intervened, who knows what heights Maud's career may have reached!

A death was recorded on the 14th November: "Eric Perkins 1st class Inf. was knocked down on his way home by a car. He has been taken to the Infirmary. The news has just come through to say that poor Eric is dead". Eric was not quite 5, his father was "Nathan" and the family lived in Grove Terrace.

There were outbreaks of colds, tonsillitis and diphtheria in December and cases of scarlet fever with, on the 11th: "Elsie Bellerby died on the 10th a victim of diphtheria". Elsie was 8 and had previously attended Trinity school in Ripon. Her father was Roland and the family lived in Galton Cottages, Lotherton Lane. A rather sad end to this year of 1933.

Attendance during 1934 was affected by sporadic cases of diphtheria, whooping cough and chicken pox. During the early part of the year it was reduced to 70 - 75% but by April attendance picked up and hit 90%: "the first time since November". The number on the books was 140 in May – considerably reduced from the numbers in the Freeborn years.

In June the girls of the school won the Shield at the sports meeting at Garforth with Freda Brownridge winning the cup for the best individual score. Freda was nearly leaving age at this time, her father's name was Joseph and the family lived in Chapel Yard. She seems to have had several family members at the school.

On July 31st Miss Moss left: "she was presented this afternoon with a writing case as a token of appreciation from the children, staff and

Managers". Here is an incident recounted by a former pupil: "Then you moved up into Standard One and the teacher there were Miss Moss. Now then, when you first went in there Miss Moss were asking people when they were born and what date and my mother always used to call Good Friday 'hot cross bun day'. So, being a bit of a comic like I always were, she said to me 'when is your birthday?' – I said 'hot cross bun day' – so she give me a good hiding and told me not to talk like that! Well, all the kids in the class laughed and that made her more vexed so she give me another hiding!". (xiii)

The entry at the start of the September term this year contained a record of the arrangement of Classes: " Std VA, VI and VII Mr Rayson, Std VB IV and III Mr Pickles, Std I and II Miss Ellis and Infants Miss Hindley".

Extracts from the HMI's report on visits on the 12th June and 26th October read: ".. Number of children has been falling for some time ..school organised in four classes in place of five. Instruction is planned on generally sound lines .. lessons are well prepared by the teachers and the terminal examinations are carried on systematically and thoroughly by the HM who gives useful guidance to his young staff as the result of them. With the exception of one class where control and effort are decidedly weak, the scholars are in good order .... arithmetic and English still show much weakness throughout.....The scholars .. difficulty in expressing themselves adequately both in speech and writing .. composition exercises .... older scholars.... too many elementary errors .... should have been eradicated at an earlier stage .... indistinct speech.. spoils... reading and recitation. Geography, history and nature lessons ... two top classes ... well illustrated ... singing particularly well taught and is worthy of special praise. Infants Class promising .... as the teacher gains in experience she will no doubt be better able to keep all the children more actively employed".

School was closed for the day on November 29th for a Royal Wedding – in fact it was the first live radio broadcast in Britain of a Royal Wedding - the marriage of the Duke of Kent to Princess Marina at Westminster Abbey in London.

In December HM brought Stds I and II back to Classroom 3 as he was not satisfied with the order and this was to continue to be a problem with this class under Miss Ellis for some time to come. In an effort to improve spelling, Miss Ellis was asked: "to make a list of the weakest spellers and to use an exercise book for each of these; to enter a list of each child's errors and to test these periodically". The usual parties were held in late December and the school had various repairs done over the holidays.

In January 1935 a couple of boys had a difference of opinion. On the 15th: "Alfred Oldfield Std III was sent to my desk from drill lesson for fighting. Willie Banks was sent by Miss Ellis to Miss Hindley for attention to his bleeding nose. I have asked Miss Ellis to tighten her discipline up". Young Willie seems to have come off the worst from the scrap! Willie (William) was a few months older than Alfred – both c12 years old – and both lived in the Bunkers Hill area. Hopefully the warring neighbours patched up their quarrel!

A very important entry on the 1st February: "all children who so desired were immunised this morning – after adults were also treated – 117 in all". This was the first reference to the programme of immunisation against the scourge of diphtheria which was being rolled out in schools across the country. Further sessions were held on the 8th, 15th and 22nd February.

A reference to the continuing practice of corporal punishment appeared on March 5th: "There was disturbance in Class III – Eric B. shouting at his teacher – I have punished him – two strokes on each hand". HM was still having trouble with lack of discipline in Stds I and II as he recorded on the 1st April and a longer entry on the 2nd July stated: "I have had to go into Miss Ellis's room half a dozen times this morning. .. Groups of boys in reading lesson discussing out of school affairs – pigeons – and writing names on desks. I have told Miss Ellis that good order is essential before progress can be made. The objectionable feature is that I am having to employ methods of discipline which would be quite unnecessary under normal conditions".

This year was the Silver Jubilee of King George V and Queen Mary and, to commemorate this, there were two extra days of holiday on the 6th and 7th May and each child received a Jubilee pen and pencil presented by Mrs Gascoigne.

There was trouble in Miss Ellis's class again on 23rd July: "I have had Mrs Capper and Mrs Garbutt to see me today. They complain that their two girls went home at 12 bruised. I have investigated the matter and find that the troubles started in the Phy. Trng. Lesson this morning. Miss Ellis seemed to know very little of what was going on although at least half a dozen children were involved". The outcome of the complaints was not recorded.

During the summer break the boys' yard was improved, being levelled and tarred. It may have been this work to which the National Society contributed £22 at this time. HM made no mention of his daughter Elizabeth, who had joined the school in September of 1929, having won a Scholarship. This was her recorded reason for leaving August of this year.

The teaching in Stds. I and II was still causing concern in the autumn term with: "the [teacher's] ability to secure attention through interest is the great weakness". There were disappointing results in the HM's test of times tables and he made a suggestion about using a game : "Buzz – which has proved very popular in former years". However Miss Ellis felt this was useless! November saw the HM giving a demonstration lesson: "as to how tables can be taught in an interesting manner".

Despite the immunisation programme there were three cases of diphtheria in December but the programme continued in the new year of 1936. Colds, flu and heavy rain affected attendances in January and school was closed on the 28th January for the funeral of King George V.

Miss Ellis was absent attending an interview in mid-January – she had obviously had a difficult time at Aberford and perhaps she felt she would do better somewhere else. During the rest of the year Miss Ellis would attend interviews for posts at Wombwell in

February, unspecified in March, Rothwell in July, Shrewsbury in October and Mirfield in December.

Miss Hindley was away for about a month from 7th April for an operation and Mrs Rayson helped out during this time. Miss Hindley actually left Aberford on the 30th September as she was to be married and Miss Simpson started as a temporary Assistant – she had been trained at Sunderland Training College – and was to stay until February 1st the following year when she left to go to Garforth.

HM was having to constantly visit Stds I and II in October and on 1st December: "In the reading lesson three boys of one group took it in turn to blow the teacher's whistle. I observed this through the window but the teacher failed to notice anything unusual".

During December HM made no mention of the events taking place concerning the monarchy. The future King had decided to abdicate on the 1st December in order to marry an American divorcee, Wallis Simpson. The marriage took place in France on 3rd June 1937.

For those who believe in such things, perhaps 1937 began with a bad omen. HM recorded on the 11th January that the school clock had fallen down during the Sunday School – just a few weeks later Miss Piercy died as recorded earlier. The clock must have broken when it fell for a new one arrived on 13th April.

Misses Staley, Jennings and Sunderland all came and went for short periods of time during this year to help out for the absence of staff and in March Miss Ellis left but there is a one line entry with no mention of where she was going and HM did not record his feelings (having made them amply clear in several entries!). However one former pupil recorded: "Now then, when you finished in the class [Miss Moss] you moved to another class which was Standard Two and it was a lovely young lady teacher called Miss Ellis". (xiii) Mr Jack Reed took the place of Miss Ellis as temporary assistant and stayed until August the following year.

School closed for an extra four days, tacked on to the Whitsuntide holiday, in celebration of the Coronation of King George VI and Queen Elizabeth.

School had to be closed for two weeks in March 1938 owing to a measles outbreak and only one out of six eligible children was able to sit for the Minor Scholarship examination. In fact school was closed for an additional three weeks and four days as well as the six days for Easter.

In June of 1938 there was a very large sale of sections of the Lotherton and Parlington Estates of Col F.R.T.T. Gascoigne who had died in 1937. This must have been a much-talked-about sale within the village and the children would have heard it being discussed without doubt. The sale included some thirteen farms, amongst them Church Farm at Saxton, Scholes Park Farm, three farms at Sherburn and Sturton Grange Farm. There were also eleven lots of cottages, some of the lots being themselves of several cottages. The farmland involved was over 2400 acres.

The gathering war clouds were hinted at by an entry on the 29th September: "At the request of the A.R.P. authorities, HM – Chief Warden – was on duty fitting gasmasks from 3.15p.m". HM did not say who was being fitted – perhaps the children?

On the 7th November a Mrs Hall commenced as a C.A. Arithmetic was still weak throughout the school, according to the HMI's report this year.

At the beginning of the significant year of 1939 there were approximately 116 children on the roll. Towards the end of March the school was used on three occasions for a lecture to A.R.P. Wardens. In June HM recorded that four children, including his son John Rayson, had won County Minor Scholarships. John Christopher Metcalfe Rayson had begun at Aberford in April of 1933.

Part Two : The WWII Years and Retirement in 1948

In early September the school remained closed, having opened briefly after the summer break and there were visits from Inspectors to discuss future plans. School eventually re-opened on the 11th September with 211 on the register made up of 117 from the previous Aberford total, 86 from Crossgates and 8 others. The staff consisted of four Aberford staff, three from Crossgates (Miss M. Steel, Mr Critchley and Mr Burton) and "helping in the reorganisation" were Miss Young and Mr G ? also of Crossgates. These numbers of children had not been seen for a number of years. The reason for this influx was that children were being moved outwards from the city centre in case of it being bombed.

HM continued to record brief details only, so the disruption and difficulties can only be glimpsed. The classes were recorded as: Class 1 Mr Critchley with 36, Class 2 Mr Burton with 34, Class 3 Mr Pickles with 37, Class 4 Miss Steel with 33, Class 5 Miss Staley with 35 and Class 6 Mrs Hall with 34 – there is also a note of "7 Mr G ?". Extra chairs and tables were received by the 9th September.

From October, gardening assumed great importance for the older boys. On the 20th: "20 boys with borrowed tools did gardening on plot by the windmill". On the 24th: "gardening Tuesday p.m. windmill plot Group B – Vicarage plot Group A". On the following day: "Wednesday – 11 – 12a.m. Group A".

The Ministry of Agriculture had very quickly launched 'Dig for Victory' within a month of the outbreak of war and began a campaign to encourage people to transform their private gardens and other spaces into mini-allotments. It was believed, quite rightly, that this would not only provide essential crops for families and neighbourhoods alike, but help the war effort by freeing up valuable space for war materials on the merchant shipping convoys. Over just a few months Britain was transformed with gardens, flower beds and parkland dug up for the planting of vegetables. By 1943, over a million tons of vegetables were being grown in gardens and allotments.

The very low temperatures within school in January 1940 caused it to be closed for several days and Mr Burton ceased duty on the 2nd February. Whether he and Mr Critchley had been called for War service was not stated.

There was disruption of travel arrangements for teachers and some illness – in early April HM became ill and Miss Steele ceased duty and a Miss Jackson took her place for a short while. HM did not return for a month.

Frequent entries now appeared concerning gardening efforts: 26th April gardening instead of nature, 7th May – two rows of potatoes planted p.m. 8th May – Std VII prepared nursery bed for greens, two rows of potatoes planted p.m. Std IV 1.15 – 2.15 dug a long row for potatoes.

Despite German measles breaking out: 14th May – 4 boys planted onions in windmill plot p.m. 15th May – p.m. made pea trench in school plot, planted lettuce and Fr beans in windmill plot. 21st May – 5 seniors prepared windmill plot for planting greens in afternoon.
Further gardening entries appeared throughout May, June and July.

On the 27th August there was a morning visit from A.R.P. Wardens and an air raid alarm during the night – the all clear was sounded at 3.00a.m.

How heartbreaking it must have been for the boys who had put in so much hard work gardening when, on the 5th September, HM recorded: "Reported that all greens on windmill plot have been eaten by sheep. I went to the plot at 1.30 and found that no greens were fit to be used. The parsnips (17 rows) had their tops eaten away and the beet had been uprooted and eaten". However, gardening still continued despite the setback – potatoes were lifted in October and a plot was dug and cleared.

On the 19th December a Christmas party was held for the London evacuees which the other children also attended. Who these children were and how many of them is not known.

In early January 1941 HM received a War Emergency Plan for the distribution of supplies and Nurse Clough began to give lessons on First Aid to the children. Immunisation continued as did gardening. Indeed entries about the gardening efforts became a major topic in the Log. In March there was digging and sowing of onions, leeks, lettuce, radishes, parsnips and beans. In May 500 onion plants were received and history lesson was cancelled for the boys as it was essential to plant immediately.

Although there had been no specific entries by HM about fund-raising going on in the village for a Spitfire plane, it was around this time of June 1941 that a plane bearing the name 'Aberford' went into service. The story of the plane which bore our village's name is told in Appendix III. Whether the children followed her adventures is doubtful but, if they did, there would have been plenty to fire their imaginations!

In August Mr Pickles was 'called up' and a Mrs King took his place – the staff, with Mrs King, were now Mr Rayson, Miss Staley and Mrs Hall.

On the 3rd October the school: "received 120 yards of protective material for windows".

There was illness amongst the teaching staff which caused difficulties in December and January of 1942. For one period of time at the end of January only HM and Mrs Hall were teaching. Mrs Hall left at the end of March: "appointed to a school in Southport". HM had some personal sadness when his sister became ill and he went to York to visit her on the 14th January; she must have died shortly after for he attended her funeral on the 21st.

It was not until the 23rd of March that: "the weather has been suitable and the soil friable enough so that I am taking gardening".

In April of this year Walter Lock Jnr. was killed in action. He was aged 26 and in the Royal Air Force. Although not traced in the School Register he was one of an extended family by the name of Lock in the village and would almost certainly have been known to HM. He was the son of William and Margaret and husband of Barbara, all of Aberford. He was commemorated on the Aberford Memorial and on Runnymede Memorial.

Nurse Clough gave the seniors lectures on first aid with practical work on the 19th May and throughout June. Staffing difficulties continued and Mrs Rayson helped from time to time. In addition,

HM's daughter Elizabeth helped out in September and October. Mrs Rayson attended a meeting of the Tadcaster Food Committee in May and further sporadic entries over the next few years of the war showed that she was involved on other Committees and meetings such as one for Rest Centre Supervisors.

It was in June of this year that the son of one of the prominent families in the village was killed in the war. Francis Fawcett was a Captain in the Royal Army Service Corp. HM made no mention of this sad event but all in the village would have been talking about it at the time no doubt. He died on the 26th and was aged 35. He was the son of Thomas Percy and Margaret Joan of Byram, Brotherton. He was commemorated on Brotherton War Memorial in addition to the one in Aberford and in El Alamein War Cemetery.

Toward the end of September: "a meeting was held to discuss the question of a school canteen". During the autumn the seniors were often absent in the afternoons potato picking which interfered with singing lessons.

There was early good weather in 1943 for on the 24th February HM reported: "it is lovely gardening weather so I am taking gardening instead of composition with the boys in Stds IV and VII – we are sowing broad beans and parsnips". On the 17th March: "the weather shows signs of breaking and as the soil is in splendid order I am altering the Timetable ....to get the gardening in now".

The hard work of gardening was not without a bit of fun on at least one occasion. Mr Terry Parkinson recounted that there were lots of 'cow pats' in the field adjoining school garden and one day some of the boys removed a strip of grass and made a channel beneath it into which they carefully put plenty of the cow pats. They replaced the grass to make an inviting path and Mr Rayson began to walk down it, only to sink up to his knees in the nice juicy cow pats beneath. The consequences for the culprits can only be imagined!

There were major National Savings campaigns from time to time to raise money for military equipment and one of these during 1943 was entitled 'Wings for Victory'. In connection with this HM recorded on the 12th April: "The children have prepared for sale a very interesting collection of toys. They have had extra time allotted for this. The sale is to be held on Saturday April 17th in the Village Hall". Again on the 17th "Sale .. realised £55 approx".

On the 21st June HM recorded a sad entry: "Admitted two children, one under 5 – Barbara Hudson – whose father has been killed and whose mother is working". In fact Leonard Hudson was commemorated on Aberford War Memorial. He was a Gunner in the 5th Battalion of the Lincolnshire Regiment, Royal Artillery and was aged 26. He was the son of Albert and Mary and husband of Gladys all of Aberford. He was buried in Aberford churchyard.

There was another National Campaign to salvage books and on the 20th August the children were told about this; HM recorded on the 17th September that the huge number of 5080 books had been collected and this was in addition to raising the sum of £66 by means of 'handwork' and a sale of work in April. Perhaps due to the long history of education in the village, there were plenty of books in circulation locally!

Yet another campaign followed shortly – this time an appeal was made for the collection of rose hips and the seniors went, on a lovely sunny day in late September, to Woodhouse Farm and gathered over 5lbs. There was a further collection on the 27th September. Great efforts continued in the production of food with eighteen children over 12 years of age out potato picking on the 26th October and seven boys picking at Walkers Farm on the 7th November.

HM made no mention of it, but another ex-pupil was killed in the War raging beyond the world of school. HM would have taught the young man; Leslie Richard Kemp who was just 21. He had left school in 1936 and had lived in Markham Cottages. This man was a Trooper in the Reconnaissance Corps of the 56th Regiment. He died on the 25th October and was the son of Ernest William and Mary Kemp of Aberford. He was commemorated on Aberford Memorial and in Tripoli War Cemetery. Leslie was recorded in the school records born 25.6.22.

HM made an entry about school dinners, which started on the 8th November and on the 16th a longer entry appeared: "The school dinners are popular – 80 having ordered them this week". However HM went on to express his dissatisfaction with all the additional 'extra-curricular' activities taking place: "the children finish their meal at about 12.30/12.35 p.m. We cannot arrange for milk in the morning as it does not arrive until 11 a.m. at the earliest and lately there has been too much interference with the lessons in the morning. Potatoes, meals, measuring for boots etc., dentist, medical inspection, immunisation, have all made systematic work difficult in the two senior classes".

There were again staffing difficulties at the end of the year with Mrs Butler and Mrs Rayson absent ill which meant the school had to be divided into two sections only, under Miss Staley and the HM. Miss Staley left the following February.

Seed potatoes were received in early February – 16 stones of Arran Banner and 8 stones of Arran Pilot. However on turning them out it was discovered that they seemed wet and a scuttle-full had to be discarded with dry rot.

Mrs Gledhill started temporary duty in place of Miss Staley on the 2nd March and she continued until the end of April when Miss Schofield started as replacement for Miss Staley. However, by June, Miss Schofield informed HM: "she may have to stay at home for an indefinite period owing to the illness of her mother. She has sent a medical cert stating that she herself is unfit for duty – influenza is feared". Although she returned for a few days she went on indefinite leave by the middle of June, sadly HM recorded: "she has proved herself to be one for whom the school has been waiting, very good in the very subjects for which I want her, Phy. Trng. Art Handwork and Needlework. Her departure is a blow".

Throughout March, gardening replaced drawing for the boys and a great deal of digging went on with Stds V,VI and VII going to a Horticultural Show in the afternoon of the 9th March.

There were further staffing difficulties with Mrs Butler having an operation – and a further one later in July. Mrs Rhodes helped temporarily from mid June but by early July she told HM she could not teach any longer and Mrs Gledhill had further periods of helping out. When school reopened in August there were only three teachers – Mrs Butler taking Std 1 and Infants, Mrs Rayson taking Stds II and III and HM taking the upper Stds. By the end of August Mrs Butler left to take up a Headship at a school near Cheltenham. Yet again, Miss Gledhill helped out temporarily.

In August there was the first of two war deaths in this year of Aberford men. The loss for each family would have been equally great but the loss of Douglas Wilder Gascoigne would have reverberated around the village due to the history of that family being so bound up with that of Aberford down the years. Captain Gascoigne of the Coldstream Guards had been the only surviving son of Sir Alvary and Lady Sylvia of Lotherton Hall.

He was commemorated in Aberford churchyard and also in St Charles de Percy War Cemetery in Calavados, France. The Allied offensive in north-western Europe began with the Normandy landings of the 6th of June 1944. St Charles de Percy War Cemetery is the southernmost of the Normandy cemeteries. The majority of those buried here died in late July and early August 1944 in the major thrust made from Caumont l'Evente towards Vire, to try to drive a wedge between the German 7th Army and Panzer Group West. The cemetery contains 809 WWII burials.

Entries throughout this time were brief, in October HM recorded that eighteen children were potato picking, there were several cases of mumps and he was trying to take foundation work in arithmetic with each class. Mrs Rayson attended a meeting in mid-November as Aberford's representative on the Tadcaster Food Control Committee. She was also to be found helping at the regular Medical Inspection at the end of the month: "The nurse is away so that I have had to arrange for Mrs Rayson to help the Doctor".

Although HM made no mention in the Log of his death, it was in November 1944 that Jack Bulmer was killed whilst serving with the Yorkshire and Lancashire Regiment. He was one of several siblings who went to Aberford School, having left in 1936 so would certainly have been taught by HM. He was not found under the name of "Jack" – but there was a John Bulmer in the records, born 22.9.22. Jack is a common alternative name for John so it is presumed this was the same man. He was the son of Albert and Priscilla Bulmer and an address of Green Hill was given. He left school 16.10.36 aged 14. He was a Private was commemorated on Aberford Memorial and in Cessena War Cemetery.

There were some joyful times for Mrs Gledhill during mid-November for she was recorded as being absent for an hour in the afternoon to attend to her son home on leave. She was also able to have the pleasure of her son being home on leave unexpectedly in mid December. Mrs Gledhill was absent once or twice in December and January but her daughter was also home on leave in mid-January. Sadly this lady became ill again in March of 1945 and, on the 19th March HM recorded: "Mrs Gledhill did not arrive this morning and at 1 o'clock I heard the sad news that she died very suddenly".

There began an extremely difficult period of staff shortages at the end of 1944/early 1945 with the HM's daughter Miss E M Rayson helping out at the end of December, together with Mrs Rayson taking Std I and Infants. From the 15th to 22nd January HM was the sole teacher at school – he recorded on the 15th: "had no alternative but to place seniors in charge of groups" – on the 16th: "two old scholars have come in this morning and have given valuable help" – on the 18th: "no new arrival to help – a wet day – children managing group work". Heavy snow hindered matters.

The war which had been raging for so long continued to touch the lives of all classes of society, reaching now the son of Leeds Solicitor E.O. Simpson up at Hazlewood Castle. Although Mr Simpson had died in 1927, his widow lived there at this time. Philip was 45 and a Petty Officer in the Royal Navy; he died in January of this year and his joint grave, with that of his parents, can be found in Aberford churchyard. His name appears on Aberford Memorial and he is also commemorated at Portsmouth Naval Memorial. This news must have been received with great sympathy and sadness in the village for Mr Simpson had been a friend to the school (donating to the Extension Fund of July 1912 for example).

Finally Miss Braham came from Garforth Parochial School as a temporary help on the 8th February – she stayed a week. A Mrs Coleman began to take needlework for a while and a Miss Marshall also helped temporarily during March, April and May.

During March of 1945 the war very nearly directly touched the village for a bomber came down in Hayton Wood. The Halifax bomber of the 420 "Snowy Owl" Canadian Squadron crashed owing to bad weather. The plane had taken off from Tholthorpe airfield and it caught fire on crashing.(xviii) There was only one survivor with the other crew members being subsequently buried in Harrogate. Whether the brave pilot wrestled to bring the plane down away from any habitation we cannot know, but half a mile away the villagers nestled in their beds unaware of the tragedy unfolding. The Squadron's motto was "We Fight to the Finish" – and we can be sure that they did! No doubt the school would be buzzing with talk about this incident which so nearly could have caused many deaths and injuries to Aberfordians.

A Mrs Skillington started temporary duty in May with the Infants but Mr and Mrs Rayson were the stalwarts of the teaching staff. Mrs Rayson was still involved in outside community work – she attended another meeting of the Tadcaster Food Committee on the 28th May.

There was a joyful personal occasion on the 10th July: "Mrs Rayson absent attending Degree ceremony at Durham University. Accompanied her daughter Miss E M Rayson who has passed the B.A. exam. She is an old scholar of this school". Miss Braham covered the absence of Mrs Rayson. It seems a great shame that HM could not also attend though he does not record requesting leave.

After the summer break Mr Rayson had a period of illness in October and a Mr Pratt of Micklefield school took over his duties. He recorded that a Miss Spence, Music Organiser, visited on the 18th to prepare the children for a visit to a forthcoming concert. On the 23rd of October a party of forty-one children attended the concert at Scholes school. Mrs Rayson had a bout of illness in November when a Miss Todd covered temporarily but she was well enough by the 6th December to attend another Food Committee meeting. Both the HM and Mrs Rayson seem to have suffered short bouts of illness throughout this year which was a very difficult one for them struggling to teach so many children. HM did not record the ending of the war in this year but he continued for a short while longer.

It must have been a great relief when Mr Pickles (who had taught at the school for ten years between 1931/1941) returned to the school in January 1946. For a while, Mrs Skillington continued to help. She eventually left at the end of May and HM recorded: "she had done valuable work for over a year but is now leaving the district".

In February HM described the poor state of parts of the school: "the girls lobby is dripping wet and for months I have allowed the girls to hang their clothes in the spare room. The girls' yard is a quagmire and the boys not much better. The school approach is awful". Again in March: "the gas radiators are apparently in a poor condition. The smell is objectionable and there must be leakages of gas. Every room, except the canteen room, is under suspicion. I have reported them to Mr Page and also have asked for a plumber to turn the metre off".

Mr Pickles attended an art course on two occasions early in the year and HM recorded on the 10th May: "Mr Pickles to conduct a survey of Aberford district – this to be done on Tuesdays p.m. and will take the place of drawing".

When school re-opened after the summer break, Miss Freda Thorpe helped out for a month. Freda was an 'old girl' of Aberford School and had gained a Scholarship to Tadcaster Grammar in 1938. She was the daughter of Herbert and the family lived in the Little London area (now St Johns Garth); she was 19 at this time. However, by October, 125 children were being taught by three teachers – HM and Mrs Rayson and Mr Pickles.

Dinners often arrived late, due to a variety of reasons such as vehicle breakdown; which meant that afternoon lessons were disrupted by having to start later than they should have done. Several children still continued the tradition of potato picking in the autumn and Mr Pickles took a group of children to Lotherton on the 29th October in connection with the local survey course.

On the 20th November HM recorded with obvious relief: "Mrs Hilda Beevers (Telford) commenced duty – I for once have a full staff".

Attendance was down as seemed to be usual in winter due to colds, chicken pox and snow and dinners continued to arrive late. HM and Mrs Beevers both had periods of illness. Amusingly, HM did not record if there were any ill effects when, on the 13th May: "Derek Howson was sent home 9.45 a.m. as he had swallowed a wireless terminal"! Presumably the terminal successfully passed through young Master Howson.

The school yard continued to give concern – on 30th September a girl fell and scraped her knees and face and, on the 3rd October, Mrs Beevers badly bruised her hand when demonstrating a physical exercise in the yard. She slipped on the loose surface. At the end of October Mrs Rayson complained about smoke and soot belching out into her room and Mr Garbutt had to repair and alter the chimney.

1948 was to prove a landmark year once more in the history of Aberford School so far as the HM and Mrs Rayson were concerned. Throughout the short entries in the first half of the year there was no hint of a forthcoming change of Headmaster.

In January a pane of glass in Mr Pickles class was blown out by a gale but luckily caused no injuries. Mr Pickles took seven children aged 14 to York visiting The Atomic Train, Railway Museum and the Kirk Museum. In January HM made a return on pupil numbers to the Education Authority and a copy was within the Log Book, dated the 16th January 1948. There was a breakdown of Males and Females and ages which showed there were 39 boys and 51 girls between the ages of just under four to just over twelve years. There were 23 boys and 11 girls between the ages of just over twelve to fifteen years. This totalled 127.

In February HM was absent for most of the day on the 11th: "attending interview at Wakefield re son's future career". No details are recorded of the post the young man was interested in. Both HM and Mrs Rayson had bouts of illness in February, March and April. Also during April twelve seniors went with Mr Pickles on an educational visit to a woollen mill in Dewsbury and HM once again emphasised the dangerous condition of the playground when two boys badly bruised their palms on the loose grit. On the 16th April Mrs Rayson was taken ill at school and had to go home – she was never recorded as returning.

School was closed for a day on the 26th April to celebrate the Silver Wedding Anniversary of King George VI and Queen Elizabeth.

On the 5th May 19 children went by bus in the morning to York Road baths for swimming instruction. "Edward B using very foul language was told to apologise before having dinner. He showed no sign of regret and was sent home unless he did apologise". Edward was quite lucky the HM did not inflict stronger punishment on him!

The final entry in Mr Rayson's hand was the commonplace one on the 14th May "school closed for 2 weeks". There was no written record in the Log of him ceasing as Headmaster of Aberford School, nor any record of his departure being marked in any way, after almost 28 years guiding the life of the school.

During his Headship Mr Rayson had introduced the 'House' system and the children had put on sports festivals and concerts in the new Village Hall to which parents had been invited. He had seen much progress made against the scourge of some childhood illnesses but had lost a valued teacher in Miss Piercy. In the world outside the school there had been many significant events –the poverty of people in the 1930s, the rise of the Labour Party, universal suffrage, 'flappers', the increase in motor traffic, a twenty year interlude of peace and then the rise of the madman in Germany to mention just a few.

As with Mr Freeborn, Mr Rayson had experienced the great sadness of the deaths in WWII of young men he had taught and witnessed the grief of their families. He had had to cope with the disruptions and difficulties within school of the war years whilst, at the same time, giving extra service to the community. He did have the personal pleasure, however, of the graduation of his daughter from Durham University. After his retirement Mr and Mrs Rayson moved to Harrogate.

Chapter Seventeen
THE COWELL YEARS

Mr J. Cowell took over as Headmaster from the 1st of June 1948 which was two months before the end of the school year. The staff consisted of Mrs Beevers in charge of Infants and Standard 1 with 46 pupils, Mr Pickles in charge of Standards II, III and IV with 44 pupils and HM in charge of Standards V, VI and VII with 38 pupils. In addition two senior girls, Margaret Bye and Jean Knowles, helped Mrs Beevers with the Standard I and Infants.

Margaret started school in November 1938 and her father was Walter; the family lived at Bunkers Hill. She left school at the end of the year aged 15. Jean and her sister Audrey both attended Aberford School. Their father's name was William and they lived at Mill Farm; both had previously gone to school in Selby. According to the Register both girls returned to Selby in July of 1940 but Jean would have been 17 at this time in 1948 so perhaps she had gone on to further education and returned to help at Aberford.

During June the usual life of the school continued with children being taken to York Road Baths and HM asked children to notify him of any they knew who were due to start school in the September. When Mrs Beevers had a short absence from school for two weeks, the two senior girls helped with her classes and Messrs Page and Hood (School Managers) asked if Mrs Cowell might help out temporarily; it's not clear that she did. By the middle of June a Mrs Humphreys came to take temporary charge of Stds I and II.

There were short entries about the late arrival of dinners; the village Policeman gave a talk on Safety First and two children were hurt in the rough playground. The nurse distributed and collected immunisation forms. The 'handicraft organiser' took the age and numbers of senior boys. There was a hiccup in the late arrival of a pay cheque when HM recorded: "Post Office has been asked by someone to hold the morning mail (Mr Rayson)". No doubt this was quickly sorted out but HM did not comment further.

There is a sense of a proper 'new beginning' when HM wrote in large capitals "NEW SCHOOL YEAR" on the 31st August 1948. He recorded that Miss Ramsden had joined on permanent staff teaching Form 1. The school was now divided into "Forms" with Mr Cowell taking Form 3(Stds VII and VIII) with 30 pupils, Mr Pickles taking Form 2 (Stds IV, V and VI) with 34 pupils, Miss Ramsden taking Form 1 (Stds I, II and III) with 31 pupils and Mrs Beevers taking Infants Class 1 and II with 33 pupils.

The nearby 'camp' was referred to for the first time in the Log on the 2nd September when HM arranged for a room there to be used to show a film by the recently-established National Coal Board. This film was shown by a Mr Dowding to children of Forms 1 and 2 on the 8th September. The camp was in the area where Parlington Villas now stands and little has been discovered about it, but it had been used to house personnel engaged in the repair and maintenance of military vehicles during WWII. There were several Nissen type huts which had been left empty and presumably transferred to the Education Authority.

During the rest of September the dentist came to treat those children who required attention, there was a Band of Hope lecture, coal was delivered ready for winter and old books were gathered (for return).

The P.T. Organiser visited and there was another minor accident in the rough playground.

Early in October several boys were absent with permission to go potato picking and HM made enquiries about using the P.T. facilities at the adjoining camp. Attendance continued to be affected by potato picking throughout the month. Mrs Beevers left at the end of October and Mrs Cowell began as a Supply Teacher for the infants – she was to continue for some time.

HM had to warn boys about using catapults in and about the school in mid-December and they were also told not to bring chewing gum to school. There was a rearrangement of classrooms – Form 3 was moved into what was the kitchen, Form 2 was moved to the dining room and their former classrooms made into a hall. In December each class gave a short play in the hall and the afternoon of the 22nd was given over to Christmas parties – 8 senior children left this year end.

1949 began with 121 pupils on the roll but attendance was badly affected by an outbreak of measles towards the end of January. Miss Pollard called to check up on the number of girls who would be doing domestic science and this resulted in three girls going to Tadcaster Domestic Science Centre during the morning of the 22nd February. This was to continue.

On the 16th March: "all classes left school at 11.40a.m. under Teacher supervision to see the meeting of the hounds at the Almshouses". Also during March an N.C.B. representative called to make arrangements for a film show to be held in May – this was shown in the camp cinema on the 5th. Mr Stone and a Building Inspector called to look at the buildings and decide upon repairs and alterations. Miss Schooling, the 'gardening organiser', called to look at the garden area and "considered the boys had made considerable improvements in the garden".

In April a Mr Hebden called (organiser for 'bees' for W.R.C.C.) He discussed the keeping of bees which was to start in the summer. On the 21st May: "all members of staff visited Kippax Junior School for course in Beekeeping". On the 24th May: "a hive of bees loaned to school by Mr S. Brownridge – also indoor observation hive complete with bees". This became part of the school curriculum.

There was an accident on the 21st June: "Derek Senior, Form 1, was hit by a lorry on his way home from school at lunchtime. He was taken to Leeds Infirmary with bad head cut. Children warned about playing on the pavement when near the main road". Derek lived in the Bunkers Hill area and was aged 6 at this time. (He transferred in 1954 to Aberford Modern School).

There was an exciting journey for some of the children at the end of June when, on the 30th: "a visit to London by the 4 members of staff and 25 children between the ages of 10 and 15". On the 4th July: ".... all children were very tired but had a good day – saw King and Queen, went round Houses of Parliament with Colin Ropner". Research showed that the M.P. for Barkston Ash at this time was actually a Leonard Ropner (Conservative) which it is assumed HM meant.

The new school year began with a good intake of ten children with five having left and children began to be issued with halibut oil capsules. Nine girls began to go to Tadcaster for domestic science each Tuesday afternoon but visits to the swimming baths were suspended owing to repairs to the building. All of Class I and half of Class II went to Scholes on the morning of the 30th September to hear the West Riding String Quartet play.

There were two cases of scarlet fever in early October and attendance was affected by the usual absence of children for potato picking. Needlework lessons had been presenting difficulties to Miss Ramsden because of the large age range of the girls so it was decided on the 21st October: "needlework to be changed from Mon. to Tues. so that Juniors will have needlework while Seniors are at Dom. Science".

There was a peculiar accident on the 8th November: "Diana Jackson's forehead was cut and needed one stitch at the Doctors. Terence Capper went out to ring the bell and Diana (who is short-sighted) ran towards him and the edge of the bell caught her forehead". Little Diana was only 6 – she went in 1954 to Aberford

Modern School. Terence was a big boy of 13 at this time who also lived in the Bunkers Hill area. If he was ringing the bell vigorously as might be imagined then poor Diana must have got a real wallop!

In December there were the usual school parties; children went to Church and sang carols on the 21st and a 9-lesson carol service was held in the afternoon of the 22nd with children of each age group from 7 to 15 reading lessons.

The new decade began with 134 children on the roll and on the 10th January: "Children to be given chance of attending Elton Park Camp near Beverley". Eleven children went to this camp from the 16th February to the 15th March. Also in January HM recorded that the school was to come under the control of the W.R.C.C. from the 16th; the usual N.C.B. film was shown in the camp cinema. On the 9th a Mr H. Smith gave a talk with lantern slides to Forms III and IV on Cock Beck.

At the beginning of May the school took delivery of four boxes of apples – a gift from British Columbia – these were distributed to the children over the next few days. At the end of May, 29 children, teachers and parents went on a day trip to Windermere, Mrs Cowell completed her 'temporary' appointment and Mrs Stephens joined the school at the beginning of June as the Infants teacher. All 37 children in Mr Pickles' Form 2 started to go to the Union Street Baths on Monday afternoons.

In July a 'canteen organiser' called to measure up for a new kitchen and safety films were shown on two occasions during the remainder of the year. Three children qualified to go to Tadcaster Grammar School. The 1944 Education Act meant that children passing the 11+ examination would now go to 'Grammar' school. A Youth Employment Officer came to talk to the children who would be leaving this year.

Many children were absent in early 1951 due to an influenza outbreak and the dentist came to carry out treatment – at this time treatment was still carried out in school including those children 'needing gas'. School was closed for a day in mid-February for children to take the County Selection examination and on the 27th

June four children learned they had secured places at Grammar school. There was an Easter service to which parents were invited and in May a Miss Pollard, the W.R. domestic science organiser, called and asked HM to show her the huts on the camp which were to be used for domestic science. Parents were again invited to attend a Whitsuntide event when readings and songs were performed by the children and HM recorded: "I was pleased to see so many".

Miss Pollard seems to have been free with her opinion on appearance, for on the 5th June HM recorded: "Miss Pollard visited school to see Mrs Stephens about further studies. She said Mrs Stephens dressed in a very dull manner for infants to look at – I said I would pass the information on". On 11th June: "Mrs Stephens much smarter". During this month many afternoons were given over to rehearsing Robin Hood with dancing and music which was to be performed in July. A child was knocked down again when crossing the busy main road and children were once more reminded of the dangers – particularly when crossing between the Swan and the Village Hall. The end of year ceremony on the 27th July was attended by seventy-five parents when four boys who had reached 15 left.

School re-opened with 132 on the roll and in October builders started to repair the roof. HM made entries about the harvest celebrations on the 2^{nd:} "children bringing harvest offerings all week for harvest service". On the 5th Oct: "harvest service held in the Hall at 3.p.m. there were 4 tables of produce and flowers".

Photograph No: 2 shows the wonderful Harvest Festival displays which used to be a feature in school life at this time. The produce is shown in the Hall. What a contrast with the Festival of 2008 which took place in the packed Church when children had been asked to bring only tins of food. No fruit and vegetables, no flowers, no autumnal boughs from trees, no sheaves of corn, no specially baked bread and cakes. For each hymn the children turned to face the balcony where words were displayed and the large congregation did not join in (no hymn sheets having been supplied). The up-to-date way no doubt, but the children of this earlier time surely recall the joyful and colourful occasions they attended.

An interesting entry appeared on the 6th October which opened a small window into the past: "heard that an old sword, which was found by Alan Perkins in the old defence works of Aberford up Field Lane, was a Saxon or Medieval sword and is to be kept at Kirkstall Abbey museum". Alan was 13 at this time and lived in the St Johns Estate area – he left school in 1953 aged 15. There was an outbreak of mumps which affected attendance in late October and several children were also absent with permission to go potato picking. The mumps continued to affect some 50 children this year.

The sad death of a child occurred in mid December – HM recorded on the 12[th:] "Jean Wharton (8yrs) who has been absent for over 18 months due to illness, died in Leeds Infirmary. She had rheumatic fever for a second time". On the 13[th:] "children contributed to a wreath for Jean". Jean's father was John Kenneth and the family lived at 'The Bungalow' but which one was not recorded. There were many Whartons in the Registers – perhaps a large related Aberford family. Jean's death must have been particularly hard for her family so close to Christmas. The year ended with the usual Christmas party and a carol service to which parents were invited and was "very successful".

When school opened in 1952 HM recorded: "much work has been done on the school during the holidays. Spouting and outside walls have nearly been completed. All floors were covered with linoleum. 2 porch floors had been concreted. Kitchen equipment had been removed to lower porch. Radiators removed from Hall".

On the 6th February the death of King George VI was announced to the children before they went home and on the 14[th:] "Forms 3, 2 and 1 assembled at 1.40p.m. to listen to the broadcast of the King's funeral at Windsor until 2.45p.m".

In March HM stated that teachers were to take dinner duty from then on and younger boys had to be warned about coming to school with dirty hands. The children were again allowed, on the 26th March, "to go out immediately after dinner to see the meeting of the hounds at Parlington". However there was an unfortunate incident when "Gerald Wilson had his leg badly bitten when coming to school via the field, by Dennis's dog". (This was the farmer's dog – not a hound). The unfortunate Gerald was 9 at this time and lived at Hook Moor Lodge – he went to Aberford Modern School in 1954.

The Easter service was held on the 9th April and attended by many parents; three children left at this time. During the break new light fittings were put in all rooms and stoves were fitted in the hall in place of open fireplaces.

In late May the W.R. 'horticultural organiser' called – HM recorded he checked on the size of the garden hut required but "suggested that if the seniors were to be taken away the whole plan of the garden would have to be changed". This referred to the plan to move older children to a new secondary school the following year.

The school dentist made the regular visit and gave treatment as necessary – there was, as usual, a session for those whose treatment required 'gas' on the 23rd July. Four children left at the end of the term with one going to the grammar school and another to Whitwood Technical School but another child was later told that she had gained a scholarship to Tadcaster Grammar.

Several repairs were carried out over the holiday, including the school yard being "newly laid except for rough patch under tree". Three fire extinguishers had been supplied and the children were told about the fire drill which was to be practiced. This fire drill was tested and refined on the 15th and 16th September when HM recorded: "Bell rung for fire drill at 2.45p.m. Children were quickly out of the building but arrangements still not satisfactory. 1. Difficult to disperse children from the front of the school. 2. Some doors still do not swing outwards. Children to move to back of school into the garden. Infants and Form I straight into garden for roll call. Form II and Form III boys into boys' playground. Form III girls remain in girls' playground until Infants and Form I are in garden, then join boys for roll call and proceed into garden. Children were shown positions and then told drill and they were out in ¾ minute".

This year eight children went to school camp at Bewerley Park. There were several children absent having contracted impetigo-

some of them were to be away for several weeks - and in early October there were two cases of scarlet fever and one of german measles.

Although not specifically mentioned by HM, Mrs Stephens must have left over the Christmas holidays for he recorded in January of 1953: "Infants without teacher so Miss Ramsden moved down to Infants and classes were split with Mr Pickles in the Hall". There were 144 on the roll. A supply teacher helped for a short time and, on the 2nd February, Mrs Beanland commenced as an Infants teacher. After Easter: "a further request was made to the Divisional Education Officer that another Infants teacher should be supplied for, in addition to 41 in Infants class, up to 10 children in Form I are only of infants age".

Preparations for the forthcoming Coronation were mentioned in May this year. On the 4th May: "started a collection of objects having connection with previous Coronations or with the life of the time – parents to be asked to visit after school to look at the collection". On May the 8$^{th:}$ "afternoon tea was made and children were given the Coronation Souvenir Beaker, presented by the West Riding. Children all had tea on the school lawn".

When school re-opened after Whitsuntide, there were thirty children absent due to an outbreak of whooping cough and twelve with german measles so that, although there were 149 on the roll, attendance was down to 57%. Nearly all returned by the middle of July but one child had a nasty accident just before the summer break. On the 21st July: "John Hunter, at 2.25p.m. fell on the school lawn, walked into school and I carried him home because he was in pain and I thought he had twisted his knee. In fact he had broken his thigh just above the knee". John was 9 at this time and lived in Main Street - it was unfortunate occurring just before the summer holidays!

When school re-opened there was a shortage of seating for the 41 infants and a wall had been broken by a coal wagon. A Mrs Brookes came from Barwick to help with Form II when Mr Pickles was absent sick. By the end of September the numbers on the roll had increased to 158.

The scourge of polio was touched on in an entry on the 12th when HM recorded: "J Jackson returned to school after more than a years absence – still wearing calliper – to be allowed to leave school a few minutes early for this reason".

On the 6th November there was a reference to the forthcoming opening of the Parlington Secondary Modern School: "... called re staffing of Modern School when seniors are transferred. Mr Pickles will be surplus to staff and will either be transferred or apply for another appointment in the meantime. Not much hope of an additional teacher in the juniors". Also in November the preliminary intelligence test was taken by the children of selection age.

The forthcoming changes began to affect decisions in the school, as per an entry on the 2nd December: "Mr Day, horticultural adviser, agreed to the sowing of half the garden with grass now that seniors are definitely to go to the Senior Modern School. Also noted that gardening tools are not locked up since no space is available in school. I again suggested that the spaces between the lavatories should be enclosed for this purpose". With some sadness HM recorded on the 22nd December: "This was the 6th Carol Service held – commencing in 1948 – and the last of its kind in this school for the senior children leave before the end of 1954".

Early in the new year of 1954 Mrs Beanland left and she was presented with a travelling bag from the children and staff. A Mrs Brookes, followed by a Mrs Armitage, came on supply until a new teacher – Mrs Joyce Molesworth – started in early May.

The school garden was referred to on the 16th and 17th March: "Mr Page informed me that we have been given notice to quit the school garden for it may be sold as building land. Play Field team ploughing up half of garden to make into small field for juniors – operation suspended. Informed by Divsnl. E. Office that nothing can be done to retain garden". HM was also told that three teachers plus himself would be retained after the re-organisation. In July HM recorded that all the children who would be over 11 years on the 31st

August were told to attend the Secondary Modern School after the summer break.

When the school re-opened it was as a Junior and Infants School and there were now 117 pupils on the roll. HM recorded that the garden was no longer for school use and all outside activities would be confined to the playground which he stated was not adequate. A large detached house was subsequently built on the old garden area – many old Aberfordians felt it was a great mistake that children no longer had this area to learn about horticulture. Indeed, at this time of 50+ years later, how short-sighted the policy seems when society is trying to reintroduce healthy eating and knowledge about how our food is produced.

Dinners began to be supplied from the Modern School, being delivered in containers just before noon. The rest of the year continued much the same as previous years with visits by the dentist, doctor and nurse; several children started swimming lessons at York Road Baths and children of 10+ years took selection tests in November. An outbreak of flu in late November and early December reduced attendance to below 70%, which was the lowest for some years.

The start of 1955 saw the same number of pupils on the rolls. HM recorded that he was not satisfied with the results of his testing of the children in Forms 3, 2 and 1 in standard spelling tests. He decided that a special effort should be made throughout the school to improve English.

The hall floor was found to be suffering from dry rot when Garbutts started to make air vents and took up the lino. Additionally, on the 13th May, HM recorded: "I reported the condition of the floor at the entrance to classroom occupied by Form 1. The boarding underneath lino is very weak. Children told not to use the corridor door but the one into the Hall". During the summer break the rotten floors were taken up and replaced with "red wood" and air vents for floors were formed. Gutters for water were also made in the boys' playground.

Selection examinations were held in February but it would seem no children were successful in achieving a place at grammar school.

Miss Ramsden went on a course for a week at the end of June entitled "Round and about the Junior School" and some twenty children left at the end of July to continue their education at the modern school. This left 113 children on the rolls in September.

There were one or two housekeeping tasks during September with surplus desks and chairs being removed, lino taken from floors removed, a reclining chair/lawn mower/1cwt roller all being transferred to the modern school together with a half hundredweight of grass seed which had been intended for the garden. Surplus and worn-out books were readied for collection. On the 9th September HM recorded: "visit by National Savings Rep. with view to starting savings group".

Twelve children sat selection tests during late November and thirteen children went swimming on 29th November. HM recorded: "baths much too crowded". This must have been brought to the attention of Miss Dawson for "she arranged for children to go to baths Wednesdays at 11a.m. to ease numbers on Tuesdays". HM was asked, by the County Library representative, why books were not being renewed and he replied that he had decided the school library could manage quite well enough with the current stock of books due to the older children being transferred.

The Carol Service was not very well attended due to a heavy fall of snow in late December.

Mr Pickles was delayed in getting to school when the new year of 1956 started – he had been detained in Lincolnshire due to heavy snow. Lots of children had colds and attendance was low in early February but the preliminary selection test was taken by twelve out of fourteen children and a Mrs Douthwaite began to supervise them at lunch time and in the playground from early March.

There was a two-day inspection in late February and some of the Inspector's findings were: "... children now arranged in four classes of 27, 30, 30 and 34 ....cramped site set back a short distance from the Grt North Road ... premises disadvantage .. old building puts many difficulties in the way of a full and satisfactory education as the term is nowadays understood. Fortunately there is a Hall of reasonable size ... Artificial lighting is by gas and heating is by open fires and gas radiators. The wash basins are of an antiquated pattern and there is no supply of hot water." The Inspector stated that the Infants were progressing satisfactorily but the learning situations available could be enriched considerably and ways of doing this were discussed.

".. too low a quality of written English... reconsider its handwriting policy. Too many untidy books, careless mistakes and poor handwriting. .. reading satisfactory ... beginnings of a school library....Arithmetic tends to be concerned chiefly with mechanical processes, there is a need for closer connection with everyday situations and the environment of the school .... Several lively physical education lessons taken by the HM and thoroughly enjoyed by the children, were seen. ... History, Geography and Nature Study have their places on the timetable but it is suggested that the children should be given a more active and positive role then they enjoy at present...."

The Inspector was interested to find a group of boys doing needlework – probably due to a disparity in numbers between boys and girls – and he noted that the older boys were introduced to simple weaving and bookbinding skills. Finally the Inspector stated that the school was a happy one and: "the children are friendly and independent but, in various ways, greater demands could be made upon their individual powers and interests. Many of them are capable of better work then is being accepted from them, especially in written language".

Several children were vaccinated against polio on two occasions in May and June and Miss Ramsden gave notice of her intention to leave the West Riding Authority for she was to commence duty under the jurisdiction of the Leeds Authority in September. When she left at the end of the summer term she was presented with a reading lamp and two children – Elizabeth Robson and Marian Raffel – were presented with prizes for a full years attendance.

Elizabeth lived at Ashfield House and left school in 1958 to go to Tadcaster Grammar. Marian lived in Lotherton Park Cottages. Miss Ramsden went to teach at Brownhill School in Leeds.

When school reopened HM again called on the services of Mrs Armitage from Barwick as there was no certificated teacher available; he spent a morning with her in mid September on the preparation of lessons and grading of reading books.

Perhaps in response to some of the comments by the Inspector, an engineer from the Heating Dept came to school and said he would suggest central heating be installed, failing which a slow combustion stove in each room. In October Mr Minett and Mr Porter visited: "to consider improvements which have been suggested in the past – electric light, stoves in classrooms, playground completion, wash basins". Improvements to floors in some areas were made in October/November.

In late November twenty-three children took the 'intelligence test' and Mrs Armitage was still in charge of Class 1. The frosty and foggy weather caused attendance to drop due to colds and the Christmas party had to start early because of fog and difficulty in travelling.

At the beginning of 1957 there were 116 children enrolled. A boy received a nasty cut across the back of his hand, from a knife he had brought to school, when another boy bumped into him. HM later warned all boys about knives and they were told not to bring them to school.

Mrs Molesworth was absent for around four weeks in February and March due to tonsillitis. She was absent again for a few days in early April and on the 8th HM received a letter from her stating that she would not be returning to school as she was expecting a baby. By the middle of April HM had attended an interview session at the Vicarage and two young teachers were appointed to start from September but earlier if they were able. Difficulties were experienced due to lack of staff throughout May and June but there was some improvement to facilities with some wash basins being installed.

On the 1st July a Miss Peet "arrived without warning to take up a temporary appointment teaching Form I. She will take up permanent post in September" and Miss Warrington started on the 3rd July to take the Infants Class, again temporarily until September when she would join the permanent staff. On the 4th July HM recorded a visit from the photographer. During the rest of the month three girls heard they had passed the 11+ to go to Tadcaster Grammar, several children caught german measles and eight children were recorded as having attended throughout the year – Elizabeth Robson, Anthony Cockrem, Dennis Mallorie, Wilfred Robinson, Martin Cockrem, Alfred Horan, Peter Hayton and Susan Armitage.

School re-opened in September with 98 children on the roll and HM recorded: "Open fires are being replaced by Searchlight stoves. ... 3 new wash basins installed in infants' porch and white tiles round walls. 7 new wash basins in W. Porch in preparation for transfer of kitchen equipment to E. Porch".

A nasty accident occurred on the 9th September when a boy collided with another and his nose was broken. These days there would have been a lengthy investigation and reams of accident report forms to fill in but, at this time, the incident was treated in a very matter-of-fact manner. An outbreak of flu badly affected attendance in late September and there was a brief visit by an HMI who stated: "Miss Warrington and Miss Peet to be given more guidance – said there should have been more evidence of fresh ideas straight from College".

On the 8th November: "Beech in school yard is to be felled due to unsafe branches and branches overhanging school". A few days later a playhouse was delivered to the Infants class.

In the hope of getting an electricity supply, HM recorded on the 10th December: "accepted delivery of a record player and loud speaker (in preparation for A.C. mains)". The usual Christmas party, plays and carol service were held.

The numbers had increased at the start of 1958 to 106 and, curiously for the time of year, children from Form III were taken to see the Triumphal Arch. That must have been a bracing walk! Polio injections were given to children – including those below school age – during January and February. Heavy falls of snow during late February caused disruption to transport for teachers and children from outlying areas could not get into school.

On the 6th March Miss Peet took a party of 28 children to The Grand Theatre in Leeds to see a matinee performance of Peter Pan. The visit went well and the children returned to Aberford on the bus from Leeds at teatime. Also in March HM made several entries about repairs and renewals and mention was made about there being no store-place in the school. It was suggested that the coal-place should be emptied and fitted with shelves and made into a store room but the Div Officer "held out little hope of new cupboards. He offered old cupboards but the offer was not accepted. The question of making the coal place into a store would have to be given further consideration". Just the sort of comment given these days sometimes!

Miss Warrington married during the Easter holidays and changed her name to Mrs Poulter. Workmen were busy about the school. Miss Spence the W.R. 'music adviser' visited on the 23rd April: "She heard all classes sing and was pleased with what she heard. Shocked to find no electricity for record players and wireless!"

The transfer of items to the Parlington modern school took place from time to time: "transferred 24 gardening books and coil of galvanized wire to Mr Backhouse at Parlington School".

On the 16th HM complained about the staffing situation: "A reply to my letter to Mr Clegg states that, for the time being, staff at the school is to remain at Head + 3 Assistants. We now have a situation of having two vacancies which need not have existed. Miss Warrington's vacancy (due to resignation on marriage) was not filled due to proposed reduction in staff and Miss Peet did not want to teach infants so, due to the uncertainty of the position has found another post". HM was asked to see if Miss Peet would reconsider but, due to the long delay, she did not feel she could do so.

Work done to the school during the May break pleased HM: "... completely redecorated. Everything looks fresh and clean, playground has been completely renewed, gives us for the first time a good stretch of playground... old coal store underdrawn but not decorated". Unfortunately HM was informed by Mr Stone in mid July "electric light still cannot be fitted". He did, however, get a new Headteacher's desk on the 18th. At the end of the school year, Miss Peet left to take up an appointment at Manston and Mrs Poulter agreed to return on a temporary basis in September.

On the 17th October an extra day holiday was granted "for visit of the Queen to Leeds".

In November children were warned about bonfires, there was a talk by an R.S.P.C.A. lecturer and children were warned about scattering paper in the schoolyard and the streets. Later in the month children were told "they must not go out of school after school meal unless written request is made by the parent and all children to be outside school during break unless instructed to do something by member of staff".

During December the usual Christmas preparations took up extra time and Nurse Brigham said she would be paying a final visit before she left at the end of the year. There was the usual nativity play, school party and visit of Santa Clause.

The new year of 1959 saw a teacher shortage when Mrs Moulesworth was unable to continue on supply and classes were split between Mrs Poulter, Mr Pickles and HM. Frozen toilets caused problems and there were bursts when a thaw came. The new vicar Rev Burton called and made arrangements as to when he would attend to give religious instruction and to arrange for a service after school during Lent.

Toward the end of February HM went on a two-day course on "backwardness in schools" and, in early March, a Miss McGuiness was interviewed and subsequently appointed to teach the infants. This was to be the start of a very troublesome period when there were many incidents concerning Miss McGuinness which seemed to indicate she was not well.

During June garden troughs were put out in the playground and the base of the tree cultivated. Only one child was informed of selection for transfer to grammar school in September. There was a Road Safety Quiz which saw Aberford losing by four marks to Scholes. A Lecturer from the Band of Hope spoke to junior children on the 17th and a photographer came to take both individual and group photographs. At the end of the school year Mrs Poulter had completed her year as a temporary teacher and she left with Mrs Lawrence taking over Form 1 in September.

An insight into the school Managers at this time can be glimpsed from two sheets within the Log Book. The first sheet was a record of minutes of a meeting held on the 21st October 1959. The Managers at this time were Rev. P. Burton, Lt. Col. F.W. Lane Fox, Mr H. Brook, Mr J.R. Heaton and Mr S. Hood. Rev. Burton was elected Chairman for the forthcoming year. Mr Brook had been appointed in succession to a Mr Birkbeck as a County Council representative.

There was a discussion about reinstatement of a boundary wall between the school and the house opposite and about the wall between Vicarage Drive and School Lane – whether it was to be reduced and repaired and, if reduced, to what height etc. In his report, HM said there were 92 children on the roll and attendance had been fairly good. There was a full complement of teachers and Mrs Lawrence had settled down very well. Electricity was to be installed in the porch. No mention was made of any difficulties with Miss McGuiness. The second sheet informed HM of a meeting of Managers to be held in March 1960 so it seems these meeting were probably held twice a year.

On the 14th September HM recorded: "Miss McGuiness made a strange remark at morning break – would I as HM inform her of any scandal about her if I heard any!!" There were many entries from this point with Miss McGuiness becoming increasingly alienated from the other members of staff. One instance on the 30th October gave a flavour: "Saw no change in Miss McGuinness attitude. She now considers that she is the one who is being treated 'abominably'. Again on the 6th November: "Mr Pickles reported Miss

McGuinness odd behaviour. After afternoon break she went into his classroom and took away his tea without any reasonable explanation – then to Mr Pickles or to me later".

The normal small entries about school life continued such as the piano being polished and retuned, two old looms transferred to the modern school and fog preventing children going swimming in mid-November. There were increasing difficulties with Miss McGuinness during late November and December with a Miss Mayo (Asst C.C.I.) coming to school to see her and the other teachers. On the 4th December HM recorded: "Miss McG stated that each time I entered her classroom I upset the class – they became emotionally upset!"

On the 8th December Miss McGuinness was unable to open the door when she arrived at school and accused HM and the caretaker of fastening this on purpose to annoy her. HM recorded: "I could not convince her that the door was only tight because of the rain" and "in the discussion she said that she was being 'got at' in exactly the same way as at other places in the past. She said she had at this school been given 'phenol barbitone' in some way and I knew about it". HM tried to phone Mr Minett but was unable to reach him so he wrote to Mr Minett and Mr Stone asking that some action should be taken about the situation.

It must have been a welcome relief when the usual Christmas preparations made life busy in school and Mr Stone informed HM that some action would be taken (re Miss McGuinness). Children enjoyed their party, carol service and the ceremony of the opening of the 'post box' and distribution of Christmas cards.

1960 did not start well for there had been a break-in at school; some boys had opened HM's desk and taken keys and a small sum of money earmarked for paying the bill at the village shop for the school Christmas party. At first HM recorded on the 5th January: "Miss McG much more normal – asked about planting of trees and shrubs in garden". However the next day a complaint was received from a parent that her daughter had been slapped by Miss McG. when the child went into the porch to watch her attend to another who had fallen. When HM questioned the teacher he recorded: "in her way she honestly believed that her action was right in correcting the actions of the child". Later in January when Mr Pickles was in charge whilst HM was with the children at the swimming baths, he reported that Miss McG. had interfered with an order he had given at playtime – she stated she had not been informed that Mr Pickles was in charge.

In early February there was a woollen collection for the World Refugee Fund' a policeman came to speak about road safety and children were warned about going into Mr Lumb's garden and not to stand on the gate into Vicarage Drive which was spiked. Mr Pickles took his class to Lead Church on the 16th February and HM went on a course from the 26th to the 1st of March at Woolley Hall on religious education when Mr Pickles was left in charge.

In early March a group of children were allowed to go and see the hounds gathered at the Almshouses. There had been a "quieter" period with regard to Miss McGuinness but, unfortunately, difficulties began again in mid March. HM recorded on the 9th: "Miss McG again rather 'odd' – She said I was untruthful. She said she would not be attending the Friday afternoon service for 'conscientious reason' which she would not reveal to me but only to 'the Authority' I reported this to Mr Minett Div.Ed Off and Mr Stone C.C.I."

On the 18th: "Miss McG said she would not attend assembly. Asked if her class could be excused – I said no since this was the only time we met as a school. Later decided she would attend with her class". However, on the 21st, HM recorded: "Miss McG much more normal to me". Just a few days later, however, Miss McGuinness seemed to focus her feelings of alienation and resentment on Mrs Lawrence and relations between the two broke down badly. HM asked Mr Minett and a Mr Armstrong the W.R. psychologist to call which they did but the situation was not resolved. There was also a visit from a Mr Smith' the N.U.T representative, to see Mr Pickles and Mrs Lawrence about the difficulties they were experiencing with Miss McGuinness.

The Easter break brought an interruption to the situation – HM had been informed just prior to the break that electricity was at last to be installed later in the year. In fact, in June the Managers accepted a tender for the work and it was started in mid-July. (All did not go smoothly – how often do such jobs cause problems in our homes! When school opened after the summer break, the gas had been removed but the electricity was not working so there was no power for heating meals. HM got over this by taking the children across to the modern school. The YEB arrived after lunch but in the afternoon they cut through the water supply! There were many more niggles during September and October before everything was sorted out.)

School was closed for an extra day on the 6th May for Princess Margaret's wedding. There continued to be problems with Miss McGuiness – she had wanted a tap to be installed at the front of the school but this was refused by HM and the Chief Education Officer called to discuss the situation. Finally matters came to head when a further incident occurred during which Miss McGuinness tore up the meals receipt book. HM had to contact the Div Officer who wrote a letter of suspension to Miss McGuinness and she left school without comment on the 27th May.

School was temporarily reorganised into three classes and children again warned about traffic and road safety following an accident to a girl on her way home. After the Spring holiday, a temporary teacher – Mrs Greavy - came to help and some children went to a Road Safety Quiz in a police car which must have exciting for them. They were just beaten by one mark in the quiz.

HM was informed by letter that Miss McGuinness had resigned but she came to school on the 1st July stating that her suspension was for only a month and intending to work until the end of term. Mr Minett was telephoned to clarify the situation and she was informed her services at Aberford were terminated – apparently supply work was offered to her in the interim. Bizarrely the W.R. psychologist called to see her on the 6th July – not knowing of her suspension. A case, then as now, of the left hand not knowing what the right was doing!

When school re-opened after the summer break, Mrs Greavy continued on a temporary basis in charge of the infants class. The School 'meals organiser' visited several times to help get the kitchen running correctly and eight children were seated at each table. After the autumn half term the kitchen was much more complete but little had been done about the old stoves despite the fact they were inspected during half term. Many children and Mrs Greavy were away with colds and there were instances of mumps.

During late November some repairs were made to the stoves but the hall stove was found to be beyond repair. Stacking chairs were delivered and preparations began for a carol service and Christmas party. The service was recorded and the children listened to the recording instead of R.I. on the 22nd December.

Mrs Greavy was still helping when school opened in January 1961 and children had to be warned about an accident which had happened – "found later that a woman was killed at the Swan Hotel". This was presumably a traffic accident.

The children must have been disappointed on the 23rd January: "Infants classes 1 and 2 went at 10.45a.m. up to Almshouses to hounds. They returned by 11a.m. for the meet has been delayed for 2 weeks".

On the 15th March: "Found writing on wall of the Boys Toilet. Boys of Class 2 and 3 to be kept in at playtimes until culprit found". This punishment did not produce an immediate result – the boys stuck it out for a couple of days until the 17th: "Kenneth Birch and Kevin Loveday, after some delay, at last own up to above". Kenneth lived at Wellhouse Farm and was 11 and Kevin lived at the north end of the village and was also 11. HM did not record what his punishment of the culprits was but, on the 20th, he wrote: "Children reminded after morning assembly to be truthful and listen to the advice which is given to them".

A further modern improvement to school for, also on the 20th March: "Post Office engineer called to check on position in which the telephone would be put when eventually installed. I decided that just inside the hall outside my door would be best". On the 27th

March there was a Managers' meeting to interview Miss Tyler who was appointed to take the infants class starting from the 1st July. There was an Easter service to which parents were invited and school closed for two weeks.

The rest of the year continued much as previously with small improvements to the fabric being carried out and there was an extra day of holiday on the 8th of June for the wedding of the Duke of Kent and Miss Worsley. Also during June the vicar brought a lady from an overseas Mission to talk to the children and she showed slides of Tanganika.

As the school year drew to a close there was a collection from the children and staff towards a leaving present for Mrs Greavy and on the 29th June: "Mrs Greavy in afternoon had picnic with infants in field prior to leaving". However she carried on until the 6th July until Miss Tyler started.

Sports days were held on the 24th and 26th July and HM took thirteen children on an educational visit to Kirkstall Abbey. Only one boy made a full attendance during this year and school closed for 5 weeks of summer holiday.

When school re-opened there was just 89 children on the roll – the hall stoves had been replaced and the HM had some personal sadness when he received news, on the 7th September, that his mother was seriously ill. She had died before he reached home but he was only away for a day.

The school nurse visited to weigh and measure children and the school doctor also inspected them. On the 13th September children of Forms 2 and 3 were allowed to listen to the BBC broadcast of the enthronement of the new Archbishop of York – hopefully it was not a dry and boring event!

Surprisingly to us these days, only four out of twelve children eligible for the old 11+ examination indicated they wished to continue further than the secondary modern school. This meant that they would not go forward to sit the old G.C.E. examination at 16 but would leave school at 15.

Some hyacinth bulbs were delivered and planted up towards the end of October and children were warned about the dangers of fireworks and bonfires in advance of the half term break. There was thick fog on the 10th November which meant that Miss Tyler did not get home until 8.00p.m. Colds took their toll on both teachers and children during November and attendance was down to 55% on the 1st December. Severe frost after snow made the playgrounds very slippery with ashes being put down on the paths and lamps placed in the outside toilets in an effort to keep them from freezing up which is evidence of the more severe winters at this time. A telephone was installed on the 13th December and rehearsals were held for the Christmas carol service – the money collected was donated to the Save the Children fund.

School re-opened with HM pleased that there was only one burst pipe in the toilets despite the severe frost! The school meals helpers had to be reminded that they were using too much detergent – the 4 gallons supplied in the previous September were to last for a whole year!

In February there was a visit from a Miss Benshead checking on children's speech to see if any needed therapy. Attendance was down due to several children contracting German measles. On the 12th February HM recorded: "the worst gale for many years was experienced in the north of England – particularly in the vicinity of Leeds. Trees were down in great numbers. This prevented children reaching school from Parlington, Lotherton and Becca who had to travel through woods. Many children were absent because they and parents had been up for long periods during the night". HM also recorded that no damage was done to the fabric of the school and comparatively little within the village itself.

There was a heavy snow on the 26th February and contractors began to install hot water heaters in both porches. The weather and German measles continued to disrupt attendance into March. Also during March and April HM selected colours for painting the school and some preparatory work was carried out. A fire bell was also fixed when school opened after the Easter break. HM recorded that there was more trouble than usual with new arrivals crying in the infants class but does not record how Miss Tyler dealt with them! Overall attendance gradually improved but the cold weather meant that fires had to be lit in the two classes on the north side of the school with Miss Tyler and HM managing with electric heaters.

In May a policeman called to make arrangements for instruction for cycling proficiency tests to be held in July or September and a cycling film was shown in June in preparation for the test at Thorpe Arch in July which five children subsequently took.

Miss Tyler's progress in her probationary year was checked by someone from the Administration Dept/Wakefield and presumably found to be satisfactory.

HM recorded an incident in May which serves as a reminder that teachers were allowed to physically punish pupils at this time. On the 24th: "Mrs B at 9.00a.m. to complain of Mr Pickles slapping Y's leg. It was bruised but, on investigation, found that she had not been more than 'tapped' on the back of her leg. She bruises very easily". It seems that HM felt Mr Pickles' action was appropriate.

It was at this time that the bypass for the village was being built and HM referred to it: "Carried out a traffic survey all day from 9.30 to 3.30, two children at a time checking on vehicles travelling in both directions. To compare with numbers after August when the bypass will be open". HM made a further reference a few days later: "1.00p.m. I set off with my class to see the old Roman Road at Hook Moor to take measurements and compare with the new bypass which is almost completed. We walked back along the bypass to Lotherton Lane and were back by 2.30p.m".

In late June the photographer took individual and group shots plus 'activity photographs'. HM also recorded that potato picking suddenly started – which was surely early this year – and as a consequence of many parents taking part in this activity there was an increase in the uptake of school dinners from 48 to 62. Mechanisation had not yet replaced this hard labour.

The infants had a treat on the 2nd July: "17 infants who normally stay for dinner were collected by senior girls from Parlington Sec.

Mod. who had prepared and set a meal for young children. They were returned before 1.00p.m.and all seemed to have thoroughly enjoyed it".

On July 5th a road safety team, consisting of Kenneth Oaten, Andrew Watson, Dorothy and Martin Cockrem, met a team from Micklefield in the first round of the Blackburn Shield and won to go forward to the next round. During rounds held later in the month Aberford's team won through to the semi-final for the first time but were beaten by Rothwell C.P. who went on to win.

School re-opened in September with 90 on the roll and HM was very pleased with the repainting which had been carried out over the summer. In November HM wrote on the 16[th:] "this week being the 40th anniversary of the opening of the BBC we decided to see 'wireless through the years'. We were fortunate enough to find an old crystal set and an old set with a horn speaker".

There was a meeting of Tadcaster District teachers to discuss the adoption of the Thornes Scheme of Selection with Mr Minett from the Authority. It was decided to use the scheme as a 'shadow' to the normal selection tests of November and February and make the complete changeover the following year.

There were the usual Christmas festivities which included a party and nativity play which HM recorded. The older children acted as a choir in church at a service for the older people in the Tadcaster area.

January of 1963 saw hard firm snow and frozen toilets caused problems with bursts - lamps had little effect this time. By the end of the month the water was only being turned on at lunchtimes for the kitchen. The heavy snow had its upside when a snowman and igloo were built in the school yard. Much fun must have been had in the igloo which could hold 7 children and Photograph Nos: 3 and 4 show Mrs Lawrence and Mr Pickles joining in!

Photograph No: 5 shows the snowman. Would 'political correctness' prevent a teacher getting inside an igloo with children in 2008? Sadly, the answer is probably 'yes'.

1: Oriel Cottage

2: School Harvest Festival 1953

3: Mrs Lawrence 1963 *4: Mr Pickles 1963*

5: Snowman 1963

6: School Uniform 1990

7: Sports Day 1992

8 : Library Room 2009

9: Computer Room 2009

10 : New Mobile Classroom 2009

HM had to cope with his father's death in early February and having to go into hospital with appendicitis. He was away from school for a few weeks and returned on the 18th March.

A few days later some children were taken on an interesting visit to Tadcaster by HM, Mr Pickles and Mr & Mrs Burton: "We visited the exhibition for the end of the Christian Family Year. In the Parish Church were vestments, silver, documents from all the Churches. In the schoolroom were layouts on various subjects connected with Christian Family Year. Winning entries from schools which had entered the painting competition were there. Leslie Arnell was the only winner at our school". Leslie lived at Wellhouse Cottage and was 7 at this time. Later the children wrote a composition on what they had seen and the prize-winner was Andrew Watson. Andrew lived at Swan Farm and was 12 at this time – he went on to Tadcaster Grammar.

The school dental inspection was commented on in April "Whether the teeth of the children are so much better [think HM meant 'worse'] or whether it is the new dentist who has this time included every dental defect, but defects are nearly 90%. Children must be reminded much more frequently to take care of their teeth". In fact at the end of July HM recorded: "16 children went to have dental treatment in a.m. Several not fit to stay for lunch and went home". How this brings back memories of a dreaded school dentist in the late 1950s – a woman who had no patience with children and rarely offered pain relief. Why she chose to work with school children was a mystery as 'sadism' seemed to be her middle name!

April saw the usual Easter choral service, carols and readings and the collection was for "Freedom from Hunger" campaign which raised £5.

The old drainage system was a constant difficulty – there were two systems, one of which was in operation before the toilets were water closets and was a 'soak-away'. In May a buildings inspector with a contractor had a look after school to work out a contract for improving the drains.

Two children learned they had been selected for grammar school – Andrew Watson and Peter Whitehead. There must have been a 'Brooke Bond Tea Painting Competition' for six children received prizes on the 19th June in connection with this and the school photographer called to take individual and group photographs.

At the end of the year HM recorded his arrangements of classes for the coming year: "Infants 4+5+, Form 1: 6+7+, Form 2: 8+ 9+, Form 3: 10+. Exception will be brighter ones in each of the 5+ 7+ 9+ age groups which will be passed to upper class. Infants will start as a small class to allow for build up at Christmas and Easter". At this time there were multiple starting dates for infants unlike these days when some little ones are only just over 4 when they start in September.

There were 94 children on the roll; the wall between school and vicarage drives was lowered; coke was delivered ready for winter and fires were being lit by the start of October. HM recorded that only five parents out of a total of seventeen in the 11+ age group requested that their children should be considered for grammar school places.

Interestingly for the author HM recorded on the 14th October: "I am making an effort to find out the early details of the history of our school (in addition other schools in the village)". However, no further mention was made by HM about this. On the 16th he recorded: "my class went to look at Field House which, in the late 18th century, used to be a Dame School for boys and girls (boarders)". (This school is mentioned in Volume I of the story of Aberford School). On the 18th HM again: "Miss England (80yrs) an old pupil came up to school to tell us of the changes since she was in school". It is likely Miss England was at school when Mr Freeborn was HM so it would have been interesting indeed to have heard her reminiscences. The Registers did not show a definitive candidate for her.

During November children were warned as usual about the dangers of fires and fireworks. An Inspector called and was pleased with what he found, suggesting that encyclopaedias be ordered. There was also an unfortunate incident this month when HM had to deal with a mother complaining about Mr Pickles slapping her son as he had allegedly been insolent. Her son had said he'd bumped himself at school but the following morning other children had given a different story. HM wrote of the boy: "... 8yrs old and has already been in 7 schools at least and has had no opportunity to settle down and get any grounding in any subject. His reading is still at infant stage, written work of a connected nature is not possible and arithmetic is simple addition and subtraction – counting on fingers and with counters...". (Later in the Log Book it is revealed that the boy was probably from a travelling family who were temporarily on land at Black Horse Farm to the north of the village.)

The next day Mr Pickles was confronted by both parents and there was an altercation in front of children and parents with the father being very aggressive – HM wrote that the father volunteered: "he hides [beats] the child at home and gives permission for the same thing at school but objected to him being slapped on the cheek!! .."

HM also wrote: "the child had last night asked me for work to take home which seemed encouraging. The father this morning made fun and laughed at his feeble efforts and said the child was only a 'creeper' ...". Eventually the father shook hands with Mr Pickles and it was agreed to forget the matter.

(There were no further incidents but a year later HM was first informed the family were going back to Hampshire, then that they would be staying until after their son had had an operation. Finally a few days later the mother informed HM she would not be sending her child or his brother to school again and asked for the dinner money she'd paid to be returned but HM could not do this as it had been banked. A few days later the father telephoned to say the family were indeed moving back to Hampshire. Whether the young boy had enjoyed his time at the school and/or his progress over this year of settled time was not recorded).

The usual Christmas festivities took place and early in the new year a Junior Encylopaedia and Children's Britannica were delivered. In late February HM recorded that there was a selection test for sixteen children and four from modern school: "this will probably be the last test of its kind set by the Authority for the Selection of children for grammar school".

In March the School Meals Organiser told HM that one helper was not fit enough to continue – this lady was a Mrs Oldfield who was actually 76 years old and still helping! Mrs Oldfield was reluctant to resign – the suggestion being gently put to her. However, she did eventually agree but continued until the Spring break, having worked since the School Meals Service started in 1945. She had probably really enjoyed spending some time with the children each day but it was not recorded if any presentation was made to her. A Mrs Burlingham took her place and a Mrs Bradley started as a Dining Room Assistant in the summer.

Later in March the Art Organiser visited and pointed out that some of the pictures were fading and suggested HM apply for a grant from the Divisional Office. A "Banda" [duplicating] machine was delivered. HM was not very happy with the swimming progress of the children who had been going to the baths from the beginning of the school year. Of the twenty children, four of whom could swim a little to begin with, only five others could swim a little: "11 can still be considered to be non-swimmers".

On the 25^{th:} "Brian Rawlings had an accident last night. He ran out into the road without looking and was hit by the Post Van". Another child had an accident later in the year – in June Arthur Tiffany ran out of his garden gate onto the road in 'the housing estate' and was knocked down by a small van. Although his head was badly cut he recovered well.

In June HM's daughter, Miss S. Cowell, came to help on a couple of occasions at the end of July. (She became "Mrs Cox" and was to go on to teach at the school for a number of years). Two swimming certificates and a book prize were awarded to children at the end of the year and school closed for five weeks and a day.

When school re-opened in September HM told his staff something of the new thinking he had learned on a vacation course at Ilkley and which was to be introduced into the teaching of children. He recorded: "The aim now with Junior children being to produce conditions in which the child can learn from firsthand experience – where he can experience and discover. I told them that the Set Test Geography Nature schemes as they stand could be ignored and introduce more and more a discovery of the environment, a process of finding out that starts with each individual child. The aim would be that this would operate in the whole syllabus so that starting from one subject or one visit in the locality children should work in different ways and in different directions. As wide a range of books and apparatus as possible should be made available".

In October of this year the children would no doubt hear their parents and others discussing the sale of most of the core properties of the Gascoigne estate. This sale was perhaps in an effort to reduce death duties as Sir Alvary Gascoigne was 71 at this time. Several well-known farms were sold: Park House Farm, South Lodge in the very heart of the village, Leyfield Farm along the Aberford/Barwick road, Home Farm within the Parlington Estate, Manor Farm,

Throstle Nest Farm, Swan (Mill) Farm. In all this amounted to over 1500 acres.

In mid and late November HM recorded admitting two children to the school from the Black Horse caravan campsite. The children were from two families who seemed to move around together. The attainment of both children was much lower than the average for their age and such admissions must have caused a little difficulty for the class teachers from time to time.

In January 1965 the children were told about it being the 700th anniversary of the beginning of Parliament under Simon de Montfort and in June they would be remembering it was the 750th anniversary of the signing of the Magna Carta.

HM recorded in February: "a number of children from the Infants to read for me who have now started on I.T.A (Initial Teaching Alphabet). The children appear to be reading very well and read particularly fluently and without hesitation". The Initial Teaching Alphabet was introduced into schools at this time as it was felt that it was much easier for children to learn to read and write by this method. Spain for instance had long had a phonetic writing system – this was an attempt to simplify English and quickly establish confidence in children. By October Mrs Lawrence told HM: "the children she has now from the Infants class can read better than any others she has had – this would seem to be a result of the I.T.A. reading in the Infants class".

During a visit from two HMI's the HM said that the school needed some staff facilities and better urinals for boys. In May a buildings inspector called and said there was a possibility the urinals might be brought up to standard!

There was an outbreak of "tummy upsets" in mid-May which persisted and children were reminded about washing hands, keeping fingers out of mouths etc. The sinks and toilets were not being as thoroughly washed as HM would have liked and the area M.O. called to explain to HM that the outbreak was a form of dysentry which could be easily spread; toilets should be cleaned each day and disinfected with Dettol. There was a second wave of mumps and tummy bugs in June.

Also in June the photographer called and in July just three children were told they had gained places at the grammar school. On the 14th there was an 'occasional day holiday' which allowed for attendance at the popular Yorkshire Show. The school dentist brought a mobile clinic and sited it at the front of the school so that children requiring treatment did not have to travel to Tadcaster.

When school opened after the summer the West Riding Architect called to show HM plans in rough for proposals for installing toilets. 15 children joined making 92 on the roll. HM pushed for staff toilet facilities.

During late September/early October HM recorded a disagreement about a boy whose mother requested he be allowed to wear 'plimsolls' for P.E. (This seemed one of those small but intensely irritating matters which headmasters must deal with from time to time!) HM pointed out that the general rule for schools in the West Riding, where conditions permitted it, was for bare feet. The parents (the father was a County Councillor) approached the W.R. senior P.E. Advisor who informed HM that if the parents insisted then the child should be allowed to wear plimsolls. HM recorded that the child in question seemed to want to have bare feet like the other children – having been told to wear plimsolls. His teacher found them too small so he went barefoot! HM recorded: "a ridiculous situation".

There was a pleasurable occasion for HM on the 15th October when he attended his daughter's graduation (later Mrs Cox) in Aberdeen.

In November HM made reference to three children being admitted "from caravan site" at Black Horse Farm. Poppies were sold in school and the architect visited. Three days of dull rainy weather kept the children confined and there was a heavy fall of soft snow just before school and into mid-morning on the 29th making both Mr Pickles and Miss Tyler late.

HM made reference to the old records kept in school – a Mr Perraudin telephoned to say he would call to collect the old log book. Presumably this man was from the W.R. Authority. In fact he called on the 6th December "He looked at the old documents belonging to the Church with all the school accounts and found them most interesting". He did not return the borrowed log book until October 1967.

In December there was trouble with fumes coming from the stoves due to wet coke being put on them. Alarmingly HM recorded: "sulphurous fumes and sometimes flames have gushed out from the doors of the stoves and classrooms have had to be vacated until the air has cleared". HM pressed for cover for the storage of coke but it was April of the following year before a proper bunker was installed. The usual Christmas festivities took place with the tree supplied, as usual, by 'the estate'.

Ten new children started after Christmas as there were multiple starting dates at this time, giving 99 on the roll. With the usual brilliant timing, it being winter, joiners began fitting windows in Class 3 and that class had to be moved into the hall.

In late January 1966 a parent complained about a teacher nipping her child's bottom! (a light-hearted act at the time, according to the teacher – which no teacher in these politically-correct times would ever think of doing.) HM informed the teacher this sort of thing must not be done in the future.

Snow and sleet affected attendance and school was used on a Sunday by the Church due to the boiler having burst. School meals take-up increased to around 70 per day due chiefly to increased numbers of children from outside the village or children living on a new estate who are too far away to travel home each day.

All but two children were found to require dental treatment in Class II and HM must not have been pleased that he had to ask one of the dinner ladies to stop giving presents to children as they had started to expect and ask for them!

Alterations began in April and HM made two small sketches of the them in the log book. HM was not very pleased with Messrs Hood and Burton saying they could not change plans "Plans are worked out in detail by the Architects Department and those directly concerned have little say in the matter".

HM recorded his criticism: "The boys porch with a floor space of approx 3sq.yds. is to accommodate 46 boys (34 pegs to be put in) adjacent to a similar space for 35 girls (34 pegs). This is going to cause delay on wet days when all children have coats and waste of time while children go in and come out. Changing for P.E. is likely to be another complication with 15 boys and 15 girls changing in such small space adjacent to each other. There is a sense of weary resignation. It is hoped that the confusion and delay caused will not be so bad as we imagine. Girls and infants porch is to become a toilet for the girls opening onto the central corridor and toilet and cloak for infants (a small part has now been allocated as toilet for teachers). This makes the Infants classroom self-contained for the entrance door now feeds only the Infants classroom. Other teachers, than the infant teacher, can only reach the staff toilet by going through the classroom or by going outside and via the infant porch entrance. One toilet for the infants also is very restricted. On plan these alterations look well but in practice they are producing confined small spaces which look, at this stage, as though they will not cope with the rush of children which takes place at beginning of school, playtime and dinnertime".

In May there was a complaint from the mother of the child involved in the 'plimsoll incident' of some months previously, that her child had arrived home 'with a flea!' She asked HM to investigate "or she will have to report to the Health authorities". The health visitors were called in but cleared all the children except for bite marks on the child affected so HM wrote to the mother saying that the flea must have been picked up out of school. Nothing further was recorded but in the September the child was removed from school and sent to a boarding school in Rishworth – hopefully without the flea!

Work caused disruption during the summer and this at a time when there were 118 on the roll - the highest number since 1957. There was a shortage of desks and dining tables and limited porch space meant cupboards and boxes in corridors, tables in the hall and painting easels in classrooms. At lunchtimes the hall was nearly up to capacity.

Late in July two men visited the school and asked to look around for they had both attended in Mr Freeborn's time. One of them – Charles J Pratt, was on a visit from Sydney, Australia to where he had presumably emigrated. The other man was his brother S.L. Pratt. The elder man would have been 66 and Charles 61 at this time. Their time at little Aberford School must have been strongly impressed in their memories – hopefully in a good way.

(The Pratt family were in the village in 1901. Father Henry Frederick was 30 and a drayman, originally from Bath in Somerset. On census date he was living in Main Street with his wife Frances Beatrice and sons George Henry age 3 born Scarcroft, Edward Arthur age 4 born Aberford and Sydney Langstone age just 1 also born Aberford. The existing school records do not cover the older children but Charles, who was born 9.10.05 was shown as being admitted 12.10.08. There was also a younger child, Henry Frederick, born 29.3.11 and admitted 12.4.15. Both of them, presumably together with the whole family, were recorded as leaving the school and village 6.12.15.)

When school re-opened in September HM's misgivings about space for changing proved right – on the 13th he recorded "Decided that we will try changing in classrooms instead of in porches, especially with a view to the state of porches when wet and cold of winter arrive".

At the end of September, HM recorded giving information to a Skyrack reporter about the approach of the 250th anniversary of the school. On the 7th October he recorded that pictures of pupils and staff and a story of the anniversary of the school appeared in the local paper. HM "issued an invitation to parents and others who are interested to attend school any evening from 3.30 to 4.15p.m. during the week commencing October 17th (the real date of 250 years ago) and for others from 7 to 8p.m. on Tuesday and Thursday. I passed an invitation to Mr Minett and Miss Milne C.C.I." HM did not record how many Aberford folk saw the exhibition he mounted but perhaps many in the village from that time remember it.

After half term there was much painting in school – windows inside and out and classrooms, which meant each class in turn had to use the hall. The job was not completed until mid December and the usual Christmas festivities took place but without the carol service due to the upheavals of building and painting work.

During the early part of 1967 the stock of library books were changed and HM decided to make a more careful inspection of books returned as some were in a poor state. The piano tuner said that the instrument could do with replacing. Following a medical inspection the doctor recommended that children with poor sight and/or hearing be placed at the front of their classes. During May the photographer called and in the early part of the month there was a heavy fall of snow, a keen frost and thick fog.

HM recorded on 20th May: "Spring Bank Holiday (the first time) was on Monday May 19th whilst Whit Monday, which in the past has always been Bank Holiday, was May 15th. Most work people in addition to May 19th as holiday are also taking today so only 60% of children are in school".

On the 3rd of June HM recorded: ".... these are the last children to undergo any form of selection for, from September 1968, children at 11+ will go to Sherburn Comprehensive School".

In July the Warden at Woolley Hall called to arrange for a German teacher to visit school for several weeks in September. Frau Hampel was collected from Leeds on the 18th September and introduced to staff and children and she stayed initially with Miss Tyler.

After the October break, Mr Minett the local Education Officer informed HM he was to retire in the new year.

In early January of 1968 it was decided that Mrs F.J. Cowell (HM's wife) would be employed three half days a week. This was to be all day Wednesday and Thursday mornings. There were 105 children on the roll at this time. She was: "... To spend this week chiefly in groups of readers from Form I which is the stage at which children have changed over, or are changing over, from I.T.A. This will also help her to become familiar with I.T.A. before she begins to help in the same way with the infant class. In addition she will take hymn singing and songs with the younger children".

After Easter two student teachers started their practice - Mrs Browne and Mr Bradshaw. HM found that Mrs Browne had her nervousness to overcome whilst Mr Bradshaw had not quite adjusted his teaching to the level of the children of seven but was "interested in children and has a pleasant way of dealing with them".

In May there was a committee meeting to appoint a new teacher to replace the long-serving Mr Pickles who had reached retirement age. In the event only two out of three applicants arrived for interview, one being a Mr Jacobson from Birmingham who had a BSc Degree gained in Natal, South Africa.

Mr Pickles had been at Aberford since 1938, around 30 years, which had been interrupted by war service. He had served under two headmasters. Although not mentioned in the Log Book, there was a retirement presentation evening held for Mr Pickles in the school. Mr Pickles' son recalled people attending from all over the village and some families were represented by three generations his father had taught. Many years later, in Mr Hewitt's time in1985, Mr Pickles was to visit the school again to show children the Maundy Money he had received from the Queen at Ripon Cathedral. Many older Aberfordians will remember Mr Pickles with fondness. He was a very kind and caring teacher with a great interest in the natural world, taking children on many nature trips and collecting flowers etc. to be dried in the classroom.

Sparse entries for the rest of the year concern winning the group road safety quiz, the visit from the photographer and a Mr

Backhouse speaking to the children who were to go to Sherburn comprehensive school in September.

It was during this year that Sir Alvary Gascoigne presented Lotherton Hall to the city of Leeds, together with the surrounding park, gardens and art collection and it was opened as a museum the following year.

Mrs Cowell began work on a temporary basis in September, all day Tuesday and Thursday mornings. HM asked Mr Jacobson: "to as far as possible aim for an integrated timetable with group work". Initially he seemed very conscious of discipline with HM pointing out that if he kept the children busy they would have little time for misbehaving. By the end of September two parents complained about their children being slapped by Mr Jacobson and HM had to point out to him that all forms of corporal punishment were banned. This was in marked contrast to earlier times when headmasters frequently used corporal punishment.

In early October the West Riding Woodwind Quartet came to play to all the children. In mid November Mr Jacobson's absence saw a supply teacher taking HM's class for 4 days whilst he had Mr Jacobson's class. He commented "it is potentially a good class – good written English and activity Mathematics – changed children onto divider-lined English books for written work".

Classes began work on Christmas preparations by December and, on the 17th, there was an opportunity for parents to visit and see children at work, talk to teachers and enjoy a programme of music in the afternoon. Mr and Mrs Pickles helped at the party.

In January 1969 HM decided to spend much of Tuesday and Thursday in the morning with Mr Jacobson – particularly to help with 'movement' on a Tuesday which Mr Jacobson would follow on Thursdays "until he feels more confident".

HM complained to the School Meals Organiser in early February that the meals were cold but the situation improved after her visit. There was heavy snow on the 7th and school was closed for three extra days at half term "to cut W.R.C.C. expenses".

The James Graham Training College asked HM if a student could come for practice and two students called to collect timetables – a Mrs Steele and a Mrs Lennon who were both on their practice from April 28th to May 23rd. In the middle of May HM recorded both students were doing well and their Tutor was pleased with this work.

There was a heavy fall of snow in mid March causing great difficulty for all staff to get to school. Miss Tyler had tried several ways and even by lunchtime was not able to make any progress. There were no playtimes and children were sent home by 3pm.

A Miss Spence called to arrange a guitar class for teachers and suggested introducing an instrument class for children. On the 30th April HM recorded: "first lesson in playing brass instruments by 4 pupils. Taken for 1 hour each Wednesday morning by Mr Walker. Some difficulty in collecting instruments. First lesson only one cornet which I borrowed, by the following week a cornet which Mr Walker brought and a trumpet which one girl had loaned to her + trombone which I borrowed. Pupils chosen were those who would have one more year in school – Peter Hey, Pamela Knowles, Anne Bradley, Janet (?) They will be given a trial period up to half term".

Towards the end of the school year preparations were made for a parents open evening. "Older children put on musical play 'Gypsy Gay' and sang 'Jonah Ja(ck?)'. Tea was provided and parents enjoyed the evening. Those who could not come were invited to come to school to see me on Tuesday or Thursday".

After the summer holidays an H.M.I called to see Mr Jacobson and she was not entirely satisfied with the way he was teaching "class must be worked more in groups – each days work to be seen by HM before 9am. each day".

There was a reference to the village 'flower show' on the 18th when pictures and work were prepared for exhibition in the village hall at the show. Mrs Cox began to help out from time to time in school. In October HM went to Germany on an exchange trip for three weeks, being two weeks in a school and a week of personal holiday with Mrs Lawrence left in charge and Mrs Cox taking his class.

On the 3rd of December: "all staff on strike for half a day (a.m.) along with the rest of the Barkston Ash N.U.T. on salary claim". This strike was a stoppage in protest at the refusal to give teachers an interim pay award before annual pay talks were concluded. HM did not record his personal feelings on the matter.

It was decided to split the Christmas parties for the first time and they were much more successful in this form. School was open to parents in the afternoon of the 22nd and there was singing in the hall for all classes.

At the beginning of the new decade of 1970 there was snow and school was very cold after the break. Snow in the playground made things very slippery and a crate of milk was dropped with sixteen bottles broken. There was news that the outdoor toilets were to be demolished as a hut was to replace them for a store. Mrs Cox helped out whilst Mrs Lawrence and Mr Jacobson were ill.

In February a new tape recorder was delivered and demonstrated and an H.M.I. spent an afternoon in Class III "discussing the linkage which exists and is to be developed between Junior Schools and the High School at Sherburn".

Also this month the school managers discussed the demolition of the toilets, all outside stores were cleared and the Vicarage stable used to store items. Demolition was carried out over the half term break.

In March the West Riding String Quartet gave a concert and HM went with some children "to see new lambs at the farm". At the end of the month Mr Jacobson left to take up an appointment in Welwyn, Hertfordshire and a Mr Lang – the County Supply Teacher – helped after Easter. In May a Miss Cromack was appointed to start in September in place of Mr Jacobson but it would appear she did not start and a Mrs Ness was shown in the log book from September in charge of Class II.

On the 5th May HM recorded that he attended a memorial service for Sir Alvary Gascoigne but he did not say where this was held – presumably in Aberford Church. 'Master Alvary' was first mentioned as visiting school back in March 1903 when he accompanied his mother and sister – on that occasion his mother had been judging the sewing and knitting for a prize-giving. Sir Alvary inherited Lotherton Hall in 1937 and had a distinguished career in the Diplomatic Service which included serving as Ambassador to Japan and later in Moscow. After his retirement he lived at the Hall until his death. His only son Douglas Wilder had been killed during WWII and the Hall and contents were presented to the City of Leeds in 1968 together with an endowment fund for buying works of art for the collection housed there.

In June there was a General Election causing school to be closed for the day and contractors began to check on replacing the coke fired radiators with gas fired. The work was completed during the following months.

Mrs Ness "proved to be interested in livestock" and a hut and four guinea pigs were bought which were to be kept outside. Early in 1971 Mrs Ness started to teach oral French to her class from tapes and apparatus provided via the Nuffield Foundation. She was to continue with the children the following year with French. Mrs Greavey, who had worked previously at the school several years earlier, started as a temporary teacher for Class III on Monday/Tuesday and Wednesday mornings. She also covered for staff who went on occasional courses. The remainder of the year proceeded as usual.

Two students from the James Graham College did teaching practice during February and March and HM attended a Junior Art course. A postal strike saw HM having to collect letters for a short time. The children were entertained to a concert of brass instruments which was very much appreciated. There were no entries from the end of March to September when, on the 7[th:] "the vicar Mr Burton decided to recommend the appointment of Mrs Glenville as combined Clerical Assistant and Non-teaching Assistant". A Speech Therapist made the first visit of this kind and saw three children.

A student teacher, Mrs Thom, took top class for six weeks in mid-October. At the end of November new chairs and desks were delivered for the infants class with the old furniture being sold off locally to children, staff and parents. The usual Christmas entertainment was put on with singing and plays together with cornet and recorder players. Everything had to be packed away in preparation for painters over the break.

There were power cuts in February of 1972 which caused the heat to be off – this happened again on the 1st March causing school to be closed at 2.15pm. Mrs Greavey's husband became ill in February and she ceased work at the school in early March. Mrs Picken took Mrs Greavey's place from the middle of April. Mrs Ness and HM were to attend six sessions of a Guitar class at South Milford during the course of a week and slides of France were shown in the Hall to all three classes.

There was some bad news in June: "Sherburn High School almost completely burnt down"!

The last weeks of term were busy ones. Practices were held of singing and recorder playing for an open evening. A concert was given "much appreciated by parents". Tea and biscuits were served and parents were given a tour of the classrooms. Some poems were sent to Lady Gascoigne and she replied thanking the children. A visit was made to the Triumphal Arch and sports day was held. Unfortunately two children fell (in different races) – Carol Ward and Philip Fisher – and they were later found to have both broken a wrist! (What a panic this would cause these days when a full enquiry would doubtless have to be held. There is probably a requirement in 2008 for a full Risk Assessment and report in writing to be made prior to sports days. Are the 'sack race' and 'three legged race' still permitted?) Finally the older children went up to Lotherton for a leaving party, games and a good look around the garden.

In September Mrs Trayford joined as a helper for lunches and she was to stay for many years becoming well known to very many children. School meals changed to a 'cafeteria system' and 4 School Meals Organisers helped. HM met the new Education Chief and also attended a meeting at Bramley Grange with other HMs concerning Boston Spa School. It was around this time that this school was being constructed and it was planned for Aberford children to be able to continue their education there.

At the end of the year the long-serving caretaker, Mr Robert King, retired and HM recorded: "presented .... with a wristwatch and travelling clock ... after nearly 23 years service at the school". There was a short article and photograph in the local newspaper. When he started the school was lit by gas and heated by open fires. Mr King was to carry on his other part-time work as Verger at the Parish Church and he and his wife lived in Main Street towards the north end of the village. Mr King will be remembered by older Aberfordians as a kind chap to all the pupils – after he retired he would often give sweets to the children passing by his house.

There were further meetings to liaise with Boston Spa School throughout 1974 and in March: "the 'Maths Master' explained the approach to maths which children face when they start at high school. Subject matter covered by Junior schools now but there should still be certain basic concepts and standards which should be expected as a minimum". Later in March a P.E. teacher from Boston Spa came to observe the methods used in junior schools. In April a teacher of juniors from Boston Spa talked to those children due to transfer and in June the Deputy Head gave a talk to them.

In February the children were taken, in two groups on different days, to the Leeds Playhouse to see a pantomime: 'Beauty and the Beast'.

In March a leaking hall roof caused problems with the building inspector deciding it would be a fairly large job and would have to wait until April: "when we are in the Leeds Metropolitan area". This change took place as from the 1st of April.

Mrs Lawrence had been accepted on a three month French course at Leeds Polytechnic and was given leave to attend so Mrs Picken increased her hours to full time to cover the class. A Mrs Campbell came to replace Mrs Picken from May: "working chiefly with remedial reading".

A group of children from Ninelands Lane school, Garforth had a sandwich lunch at the school as they were having a days visit to the area. Later in May the older children attended a Deanery Service in Church: "to see the Bishop of Selby and to observe the new Communion Service". Infants and Class 1 children had an educational visit to Flamingo Land in mid-month.

Miss Tyler's mother died in early June and she was absent for just a few days. In early July HM took the children due to transfer to Boston Spa to that school: "to be given classes and to learn the layout".

There was a musical evening in the Village Hall in mid-July, the usual sports afternoon and an open evening for parents to look around and talk to teachers. Mrs Lawrence returned to duty, Mrs Picken reverted to part-time and Mrs Campbell finished helping.

In September Mrs Lawrence and Mrs Ness continued French lessons and Mr Burton attended regularly on Friday mornings from 9am. to approximately 9.35am. Mrs Robinson taught clarinet and flute on Wednesdays. HM pressed for a Staff Room as the hall was being used by too many people at the same time, such as the clerical assistant, doctor, part-time teacher etc.

The windows giving onto the flat roof were sealed to prevent the mischief of children using them to get access. The state of the school drive was brought to the attention of inspectors but, in common with the previous West Riding Authority, it was felt the allocation of cost would be very difficult.

HM was absent due to a bout of bronchitis during late February and early March of 1975 and school meals increased to the princely sum of 15p! In April some children visited Harewood Bird Garden. This year HM recorded there was the longest summer break ever of six weeks and a day and that the weather had been sunny except for a few days. Mrs Picken increased her hours to almost half time and there were the highest number on the roll for some time – 111.

There was a visit by the Leeds Primary Organiser for the east area who was pleased with the rural setting and running of the school and was to check: "on the new school and possibility of portable staff room". A subsequent visit by the Administrator for the area was disappointing in that he knew nothing about a new school or future developments.

In late September Mrs Picken was away for a day or two looking after family members who had been involved in a car accident. Mrs Ness had an interview for a post at Green Lane School, Garforth but she was not successful. It fact Mrs Ness left in April of 1976, to have a baby, after six years at the school and was presented with a food mixer and a reclining chair. Mrs Picken increased her hours to full time to the end of the school year with Mrs Campbell teaching half time – every morning. In March HM had been informed the staffing levels were to be himself plus four.

There were a huge number of applicants for the vacancy for a Class 2 teacher – 67 in all and a Miss S.E. Blake was successful. However, it seemed that she probably married in the interim for a Mrs S.E. Maddison was recorded in September. The other vacancy drew over 250 applicants from which a list of 15 was made resulting in a shortlist of 5 to be interviewed. Eventually a Miss Massey was appointed.

From September 1976 the classes were arranged as follows:

Class III	Mr J. Cowell
Class II	Mrs S.E. Maddison
Class I	Miss J.M. Massey
Infants 2	Mrs P. Lawrence
Infants 1	Miss B. Tyler
Part-time teacher	Mrs Picken

There were now 127 children on the roll and school meals were averaging between 95 and 98 per day plus adults. By the middle of September HM reported that the two new teachers had settled in well but Miss Massey was arriving at school rather early – just after 8am. each day – due to the timings of the service bus to the village. The caretaker gave notice to leave and a Mrs Ingle was appointed by the end of October. Two children were admitted to top class: "they are much below standard due to the wandering life they live – over 20 schools since they started schools".

When school opened in January 1977 there were 137 on the roll with some 120 for dinners and there was a shortage of plates, cutlery, glasses and desk coverings with children dining both in the hall and two classrooms. It was at this time that the first temporary classroom was mentioned. A site in the boys' playground was decided on as planning rules meant the structure could not be sited in the bordering field. There began the delays so often experienced in getting matters sorted – the owner of the school had to be formally found to be entered on the planning form – HM was able to tell Leeds Council that the owner was the Archdeacon of York.

The classroom actually arrived in four parts on the 20th May; it was painted in June and the Y.E.B. connected it up in July and presumably brought into use either immediately or after the summer holidays. HM recorded in July that "no further classroom could possibly be supplied – I did not consider one would be needed in the near future".

It was the Queen's Silver Jubilee during the summer with five children joining in the planting of a tree on Pump Hill and 'festivities' on the 6th and 7th June involving sports for children and parents. There was a visit to Hornsea and the older children went, on the 12th July, to Elland Road: "to see the Queen on her visit to Leeds".

Mrs Lawrence went into hospital on the 29th June and did not return to school until the last day of term with Mrs Picken covering. Sports day was rained off this year on the 18th July but a play, "The Golden Fleece", was performed by the children on the 19th and 20th with: "a crowded hall".

In September the children were divided into five classes with Mr Cowell having 26, Mrs Maddison 29, Miss Massey 22, Mrs Lawrence 28 and Miss Tyler 16.There were brief entries for the rest of the year indicating the very busy time.

In mid January 1978 tree trimming took place, particularly those over the temporary classroom and HM recorded the bank branch in the village finally closing.

Indications of HM's approaching retirement were recorded in March when he talked about attending a two day course for people considering retiring. Mrs Lawrence was away with a cold for a week in mid March with Mrs Picken again covering and there was a meeting of managers in the school on the 16th. In early April, Mr Hood and his wife, visited school. Mr Hood was a school manager and at this time he was Deputy Lord Mayor of Leeds. The couple went round the school, spending a short time with each class. They told children of their duties during the year and answered their questions.

Later that month HM was involved in discussions about admitting a disabled child to the school from September. Teachers from the child's existing school visited and HM visited them – in the event the layout of the old building was considered too difficult for the child to cope with.

Mrs Lawrence was again absent ill during May with Mrs Picken covering. A supply teacher, Mrs Brown, came to help out and it appears Mrs Lawrence did not return until towards the end of June. In mid July there was a pleasant trip by Classes 1 and 2 by coach to Pickering and then by train to Grosmont. When school opened after the summer break HM recorded the staff and numbers and it seemed Miss Massey must have left for a Miss Brockbank was recorded as being the teacher for Class 1 in her place

TV aerials were fitted for each classroom and a TV trolley delivered so that it could be wheeled around school. Teachers continued to go on various courses, including Miss Tyler in December to the Language Centre taking a German examination. There were the usual Christmas plays which were well attended: "school was pleasantly decorated and children made cards, calendars, small gifts etc for Christmas. We had a lovely Christmas tree which was given by Fawcetts of Becca".

1979 was to be a significant year in the history of Aberford School for it was at the end of this school year that Mr Cowell retired. Firstly, to record the small 'happenings' of the year.

Many children were absent in January with chicken pox and there was a one day strike by N.U.P.E. members which closed the school on the 22nd. The Adviser Mr Lamond called on his last visit as he was being transferred to N.W. Leeds and a Mr Elliot was appointed by early March.

Snow continued through early February with many roads blocked and Radio Leeds advising children to stay at home. No doubt they made the most of the enforced holiday and enjoyed lots of playtime in the snow. There was a visit from the newly-appointed vicar, Rev. Harris, in March who began to visit regularly on Friday mornings as Rev Burton had done.

Unusually, HM gave a fairly full account of the managers' meeting of the end of March. Rev Harris was attending his first meeting. HM wrote that the school caretaker would be leaving, informed them of his resignation and that the post was advertised. The clerk told HM a staff room could not be provided as permission would not be given for a further extension. Replacement lighting might be carried out during the current year.

At the beginning of April Mrs Brockbank contracted chicken pox which caused HM to miss a meeting and a two-day course on preparing for retirement. When Mrs Ingle, the caretaker, left on the 27th April she was presented with a picture. There was an unusual heavy fall of snow on the 1st May.

The Managers met to draw up a shortlist of applicants for Headmaster and HM recorded he was concerned about the late interviewing but was assured that "the person appointed would be released to take up appointment in September". On the 28th June Mr Hewitt came to look around the school as did Mr Hirst from Oulton – both candidates.

On the 5th July HM was invited, with other teachers leaving in the year, to the Civic Hall when the Mayor and Chairman of the

Education Committee thanked them for their service. There were now several longer entries by HM in the log.

On the 12th July: "7.30p.m. I was presented with a bureau as a leaving present at a gathering in school of many people connected with the 31 years I have spent here as Head Teacher – Mr Johnson (Director of Education L.C.C.) Mr Platts (Junior Schools and W.R.C.C. Divisional Off) Mr Mauchan (Prof. Assistant) Managers – past and present, Staff – ditto, Parents of past and present pupils, old pupils and friends. The meeting was chaired by Mr Pickles, an old member of staff, and the presentation was made by Mr Peter Walton. The choice was appropriate for he was one of my first pupils and his youngest child is in my 11+ class now – added to which he is now a School Manager".

On the 19th July: "Leavers party arranged for my class during the afternoon ...at about 2pm. I was asked to go into the Hall where the rest of the school and staff were assembled for their presentation of a beautiful armchair to go with my desk. Each class had made its own giant-sized retirement card for me. Mr Hewitt, the newly appointed Headmaster, came just after the above proceedings and spent a little time with each member of staff and worked out a few points with me after school".

On the 20th July: "My last teaching day. My children collected their books and artwork. Reports were issued. Closed the day with a final assembly and a prayer for all leavers – a rather emotional ending.

I would like to record my thanks for 31 years here as Headmaster. I have had great pleasure in that time for the many children I have taught and very co-operative members of staff. I would also like to record my thanks to my present staff of Mrs Lawrence, Miss Tyler, Mrs Picken, Mrs Brockbank, Mrs Maddison and Mrs Glenville for all the effort they have made contacting old pupils, parents and friends and providing food for two presentation parties".

Thank you all . John Cowell ...July 20th 1979.

Mr Cowell and his family moved into one of the houses to the rear of the Church which, until quite recently in 2008, could be reached on foot via a gate in the rear wall of the churchyard.

Postscript:

On July 3rd 1987 Mr Keith Hewitt recorded in the Log Book "The school heard today of the death of Mr J. Cowell, who was my predecessor as Headmaster of Aberford C.E.School from 1948 to 1979, a staggering total of 31 years. He had been ill for only a few days. His daughter, Mrs Cox, my present Deputy Headteacher, was absent today. Mr Cowell, naturally over such a great many years, made a great contribution to the life of this school and he will be very much missed within the community". A commemorative plaque, bearing the names of John and Florence Joyce Cowell, together with a tree, can be seen on the right hand side of Aberford church graveyard, going up the steps from the main road.

Chapter Eighteen
THE HEWITT YEARS

The new school year opened in September 1979, with Mr Keith Hewitt as Headmaster. The classes were divided between Mr Hewitt with 15, Mrs Maddison with 32, Mrs Brockbank with 32, Mrs Lawrence with one Infants class of 28 and Miss Tyler with the other Infants class of 28, making a total of 135 on the roll.

Increasingly throughout Mr Hewitt's tenure there were all sorts of initiatives and controls brought into school life. Children began to be examined more and more – as did teachers' performance. This 'state' involvement will be seen as the Hewitt years unfold.

Mr Hewitt wrote: "this was my first real opportunity to get to know the staff and children of the school. Having been the Deputy Head Teacher of Langdale J & I school in Woodlesford, a new school in suburban Leeds, then working in a very old school in a rural environment is a considerable change but one which I shall indeed relish. Both staff and children made me feel very much at home straightaway and I appreciated the visits of the Vicar, Mr Harris and the Head Churchwarden, Mr Hood who offered me their best wishes. I am looking forward to what I hope will be a happy and successful stay at Aberford C. E. School".

In these early days HM held discussions with staff, made small changes to the lunchtime running of dinners, got permission from the local farmer to use his nearby field after school for football, saw netball start as an after-school activity and discussed some urgent repairs to the school fabric. There were many visitors to see the new HM: Miss Pearsall the General Adviser for East Leeds, Mr Thompson who was responsible for repairs and maintenance, another Mr Thompson the Authority P.E. Adviser, Mr Machen the Admin Assistant for East Leeds, Mr Elliott the Pastoral Adviser, Mr Newsome from the Development Section, Mrs Reamer the Health Officer and, finally, P.C. Cooper. A photocopier was obtained and surplus furniture removed from the Hall allowing much more room for P.E.

Following a complaint about the reading progress of a pupil by his parents, HM informed Miss Tyler: "I wanted her class to be able to take their reading books home so parents could help their children". A little later, in October, Miss Tyler felt her class would not have anything ready for Harvest Festival but HM recorded: "I had to insist that her class would be a contributing part of the occasion".

A Mr Levon from Radio Leeds visited to ask about using some of the children's work and this was recorded on the 24th October: "their work on tape sounded very impressive".

In early October a parents meeting was held to discuss the formation of a social group to raise funds and organise social occasions after school for children and parents. At their first meeting later in October it was decided to hold a 'disco' for children at the end of November. This proved to be extremely successful with almost all the children attending and £50 was raised for school funds. Later a parent held a coffee morning and a further £38 was raised.

The boys' football team had a match against Barwick: "something that hasn't happened for many years" and though they lost 2 – 0 "it was a most enjoyable occasion". In November another match against Thorner brought another defeat (1 – 0) but an honourable score!

HM held discussions with staff about Christmas activities: "in addition to the parties and Carol Concert it was decided to hold an Infant Nativity Play and a Junior Pantomime". Two members of staff indicated their unwillingness to attend evening performances but, despite this, it was felt that the junior concert might be held in the evening so that working parents would be able to attend.

Preparations forged ahead for the coming Christmas production with the Christmas Tree being delivered in early December and decorations put up; the final dress rehearsal was held with the juniors watching the infants and the infants watching the pantomime. HM recorded: "the Nativity Play was rather under-rehearsed and therefore rather more humorous than should have been the case at certain of its more dramatic moments". The concert proved a resounding success. The first afternoon performance was attended by some 130 parents and raised £14.50 for funds; the evening concert was attended by 160 enthusiastic parents. As two members of staff declined to attend: "we had to replace the Nativity Play with a programme of recorder, guitar and flute pieces with some singing added for variety. Nevertheless the evening was most enjoyable and a plate collection raised £24.36 for school funds".

The year ended with the usual parties and HM was told the school was to get a portable classroom: "so that Head and staff accommodation can be made from another inside classroom". There was a carol service in Church: "it was something of an anti-climax, it was cold in Church and there was no decoration .. nevertheless about 80 parents came along and joined us". That evening thirty-five children and four staff went around the village singing carols and raised £41 for the Blue Peter appeal for Cambodian refugees and Dr Barnardos. HM recorded he was ready for a rest "having spent a most hectic but enjoyable first term".

At the start of 1980 there were 135 children enrolled – HM looked at a possible new maths scheme – netball practice resumed with new posts – workmen replaced the dangerous chimney stack above

HM's room (whether he had previously been ready to leap up and make a run for it he does not say!). A wall mounted screen was installed for the projector and arrangements were started to seek a replacement for Mrs Brockbank. Two people were shortlisted with Mrs Knowles being chosen "as she can offer some music as an extra-curricular activity". She started after Easter.

Various fund-raising events were held which resulted in uniforms being purchased for the football and netball teams and one boy, Stuart Robson, designed an Aberford badge.

Mrs Maddison left in March with Mrs Cowell replacing her and Mrs Lawrence had a period of absence when Mrs Picken took over the class. Mrs Lawrence did not return for 8 weeks.

Chicken pox caused lots of children to be absent through most of March – most had returned in time to listen to the broadcast of a radio programme that some children had made in November on the theme of 'fire'. HM recorded the children who took part: Louise Campion, Susanne Tait, Paul Robinson, Stuart Robson, Robert Whitaker, Mark Hunter, Jeremy Elphick, Carlene Dalton, Iain Graham and Nicholas Cox.

An Easter Parade was held in school with more than 60 parents present. The children showed off Easter bonnets, painted eggs, cards, Easter gardens and baking .

There were new faces in the staff: Mrs Knowles; Mrs Fowler, an 'extra' due to high numbers, who was to teach in each class each day; Mrs J. Wright temporarily in place of Mrs Lawrence and a temporary caretaker.

Playground markings were painted to stimulate play and HM expressed a wish to introduce "a traditional orthographic programme in place of the I.T.A. scheme (for reading) currently in operation. Miss Tyler is reluctant to change but I hope she can be persuaded to do so".

Discussions were held about the positioning of a further temporary classroom and Mrs Glenville the N.T.A. accepted the position of

First Aid representative at the school. A visit by three of the staff to a local school gave them much inspiration for P.E. lessons and Mr Hood, one of the Managers, gave a talk on the history of the village to two classes.

HM mentioned the 'crossing lady' – there must have been one before for he spoke of a replacement starting duties under the training of P.C. Cooper the Road Safety Officer. Many children had always had to cross the very busy main street which continued to have bursts of heavy traffic, particularly when the nearby A1 suffered any hold-ups. The crossing lady had a very important job and often developed quite a rapport with her charges.

There was a heatwave in May with several classes being held outside and planning continued to form a secretary's room/HM's room/staffroom and store room but the work could not begin until the temporary classroom was in place. HM recorded that most children stayed at school for lunch with 85 having school dinners, 41 bringing a packed lunch and 10 actually going home for lunch.

Later in the year the Leeds String Quartet visited, the two infant classes made a visit to Harewood Bird Garden with five staff and the usual photographer's visit was held. Mrs Maddison resigned and HM offered the post to Mrs Fowler and was told he could have a further fulltime member of staff for one year due to the high numbers on the roll. A Gala Queen was chosen by 'lots' together with four attendants.

The 'nanny state' was growing in the outside world; a Fire Prevention Officer visited to check on arrangements for a social night! In previous times the occasion would just have gone ahead. However it was still possible for HM and Mrs Cowell to take 18 children to Horton in Ribblesdale for a weekend in June without the necessity of a prior risk assessment. The social evening was a great success and raised £100 for school funds, going towards Hall curtains.

Towards the end of the school year a special effort was made to put up displays of children's work ready for an open night and parents were allowed to bring along their children. Attendance was excellent, with only 13 children not represented by their parents.

HM held discussions with Mr Elliott, the Pastoral Adviser, about the long absence of Mrs Lawrence due to illness and the Staffing Officer brought out the application forms for the recently advertised position for HM to look at. A shortlist was drawn up from 48 applicants and Mrs Adams (with 10 years experience) was appointed.

Sports Day went well, a leavers' party was held and the new children who would be starting school in September had a visit to Reception Class with their parents. HM had a long chat with Mrs Lawrence during which the possibility of her considering early retirement was raised. HM recorded "if there are any further and protracted absences next year I shall consider using our new teacher as class teacher in J2 thus making Mrs Lawrence the floater".

The base was laid for the new temporary classroom and HM hoped it would be ready for the start of the new school year; he recorded: "It is the end of my first year ... has been an extremely hard year but most stimulating and rewarding. Many changes have been made and there have been staff changes too. The support I have received from the pupils, staff, parents and Managers has made this a most enjoyable and satisfying year, I hope the first of many such years".

1980 began with 126 children on roll and the staff consisted of HM (assisted with his class by Mrs Picken) plus Mrs Knowles, Mrs Fowler, Mrs Lawrence and Miss Tyler. Mrs Fowler was now permanent and Mrs Adams was appointed for one year teaching across all classes.

At this time there were two peripatetic music teachers coming to school – one to teach classical guitar and one a woodwind teacher taking a group of flute and clarinet players. A parent offered to play the piano at Harvest Festival which was gratefully received as both Miss Tyler and Mrs Fowler were beginners. There was a change of two Managers, from Messrs Hood and Watson, to Messrs Thompson and Councillor Mrs K M Smith.

Some boys had to be admonished about playing around the gravestones after leaving school and 17 children over age 9 passed their cycling proficiency course during the summer holiday, receiving their certificates during assembly. The large lime tree in the playground was examined and found to be quite safe but some lower branches were scheduled to be removed. A Parents Social Group film night raised £90 for school funds.

The temporary classroom site was prepared but a strike of crane drivers delayed matters. There were to be many hitches before this was finally delivered in early December and occupied on the 12th: "Mrs Knowles and her class was able to occupy it this afternoon much to everyone's relief as the Hall is now released for next weeks festivities – parties, carol concert etc".

Harvest Festival was held on early October on a sunny day with approximately 100 parents attending and the produce was later taken by HM and a small group of children to the Vietnamese refugee centre near Wetherby. There was an evening meeting concerning the new mathematics scheme which all staff and around 40 parents attended and new books and equipment were on display. Mrs Knowles, Mrs Fowler and Mrs Adams began a course on 'art in primary schools'. An October football match saw Aberford triumphing 7 goals to 0 against Thorner with Stuart Jackson scoring 4 goals: "the spadework done in football last year is beginning to bring results and good ones too!".

In mid-November work was carried out to create a Head's/secretary's/staff and storeroom and a disco later in the month was attended by 131 children raising £35 for school funds. Rehearsals began for the Christmas production – this year "Joseph and the Amazing Technicolour Dreamcoat". There was also a preparatory meeting between HM and the parents of children who would be going to Ingleborough Hall.

In late November HM had to ensure that the crossing lady was operating correctly and: "in discussion with staff (today) I reiterated my policy on corporal punishment, i.e. that there is to be no corporal punishment in the school and that any child presenting any behavioural difficulties must be sent to me to be dealt with". What a change from the first couple of hundred years or so of the school's history when corporal punishment was an every day occurrence and thought to be a useful tool to maintain discipline!

On November 25th: "in the afternoon my Class J3, listened in to a Radio Leeds programme about the history of Aberford in which both the previous Headmaster Mr Cowell and myself referred to and quoted from the school's old Log Books. References were to events in the late 19th century when Mr Freeborn was Headmaster".

There was a bit of excitement in early December when "during afternoon playtime the workmen allowed 2 horses to escape from Mr Dennis's field into school lane... ... we were able to prevent them from reaching Main Street. Eventually they were persuaded, reluctantly, to return to their enclosure". School "is looking very Christmassy now .....classrooms decorated with festive murals and pictures .. almost a half of the windows on the giant Advent Calendar opened ... Christmas Tree lights switched on". The usual festivities took place at Christmas. HM wrote " .. we managed to stage a Nativity Play and Carol concert in school .... I doubt if so many bodies have ever been squeezed into Aberford C of E School Hall. In addition to 8 staff and 120 children there were more than 100 parents seated...". All went very well.

Class J3 spent the weekend before Christmas at Ingleborough Hall Outdoor Education Centre at Clapham near Settle. "The group of 22 children was accompanied by myself, Mrs Hewitt, Mrs Picken and her daughter and Mrs Knowles". The activities included climbing, caving, local walks and evening activities included carol singing, a disco and a Victorian evening. Late in January the children gave a display of their work in school, together with a slide and tape show and entertainment which was attended by 80 parents.

During early 1981 the staff and administration areas were fitted out and heating was sorted out in the new mobile classroom. The Parents Group arranged a dance at the Village Hall in March to raise funds in support of a new reading scheme and Mr Bennett, a resident, gave a slide show on Aberford 'old and new'. The Vicar donated £25 towards the new reading scheme. The dance raised £217.

There were increasing meetings outside of school that HM had to attend such as one in February on "The Advisory Committee on Falling Rolls" – in March Head Teachers met education officers of the Authority: ".. gave mostly bad news on matters such as staffing, maintenance and capitation allowances". HM's membership of the Advisory Committee involved him in visiting one or two local schools later in the year.

A sponsored 'spell' took place to raise more funds for the new reading scheme and HM recorded: "90 out of 131 children took part ..... if all the sponsored money is collected some £450 will be raised – a quite staggering amount by any standards and one which will enable us to buy all the material needed. I think that this shows how supportive and interested in their village school the local people are". Sentiments which hold true to this present time and are sure to continue given the quality of teaching Aberford children have most often enjoyed! The new reading material arrived in mid-May with plenty of time to prepare it for September.

Pancake Day was enjoyed – display boards in the corridor were covered in hessian to improve the general effect – a road safety quizz competition first round brought victory to Aberford – the area around the mobile classroom was landscaped – victory in a second round of the quizz – defeat in the semi-final! Football and netball teams had mixed fortunes throughout the year.

In April the children enjoyed a visit from a natural history expert who brought some animals to show: "a Surinam Toad, an Indian Eagle Owl, a Honey Bear, and a Boa Constrictor .. the children and staff were fascinated to be able to see these exotic animals at such close range".

In late April, Mrs Lawrence told HM she would be taking early retirement – she had been with the school since 1959. HM set in motion the arrangements to appoint a replacement so that the new teacher could start at the beginning of the new school year. In May three candidates visited for discussions and there was also a visit by two disabled people: "they talked to the children and answered their questions – a most worthwhile visit in the International Year of the Disabled...". In June four candidates were short-listed for the position of Deputy Head and, on the 26th, Mrs Mason from Barwick C of E School was appointed.

School photographs were taken and a final dress rehearsal of 'Joseph' was performed for the infants, the children of the local play group and some senior citizens. There were two performances on the 16th/17th June and HM wrote: " splendid performance .. to a full house of 110 parents. The children were magnificent and the production colourful and vibrant. The children received tremendous applause and the whole evening was a most enjoyable and rewarding occasion which those who were involved in it will remember for a long time".

The usual choosing of a Queen for the local Gala took place – Dawn Evans was Queen this year with attendants Ruth Holt, Karen Cooper, Denise Davies and Polly Plaskitt. Class J1 visited Aldborough Roman museum and on to Lightwater Valley. Classes J2 and J3 went to Castleton in Derbyshire going down two caves and then up Mam Tor – quite a contrast!

A cycling proficiency course was arranged during the summer holidays – a head inspection found a few cases of lice – Mrs Mason had a look around school.

School open evening was well attended: ".... a colourful red/white/blue display to commemorate the wedding of Prince Charles and Lady Diana". It was attended by almost all parents and the following day Classes J1 and J2 visited Lotherton Bird Garden. There was a visit by four families with children starting school in September - a very low intake this year.

Sports Day was warm and pleasant: " ... usual round of flat, hoop, sack, potato and skipping races and the teachers and parents sack races provided some humour especially when two of the mums were unable to get into the sacks because of their large size!".

At the end of the year 22 pupils left – all of them go to go to Boston Spa school. Mrs Adams left after her one year and Mrs Lawrence after 22 years. A presentation was made to Mrs

Adams of a piece of Wedgewood and to Mrs Lawrence of a watch on behalf of the whole school and parents.

There were 108 children on the roll from September – HM had to speak to someone in authority about a fair which had camped on the school field from 28th August to 1st Sept. Bailiffs had tried to move it on but without success but it was hoped that it would not try to do this again in the future.   There were discussions about resurfacing school lane.

Lice reared their heads again! HM had to send a note and leaflet to all parents with advice about identification and treatment. A minor invasion of mice had to be dealt with and money for new heaters was allocated by the Development Section.

Three former pupils, all attending Boston Spa, came into school as part of a community education course and HM attended a course on 'the preparation of English schemes in primary schools'. He also attended another course on 'craft design and technology'. A fire drill showed that an internal bell system was needed to alert the outside classrooms and Harvest Festival produced the usual splendid response with recorder and guitar players adding variety.

On 30th November: "Mr Peter Russell, a local artist and expert on heraldry, came into school to talk to the children in J3 and to show them some of his work which has been commissioned by the Prince of Wales and Lady Diana for the birth of their first child. A great honour for Mr Russell and the village of Aberford".

An arranged visit from a fire engine must have excited the children in early December and a family film night organised by the Parents Social Group raised £50 for funds. Preparations hotted up for the Christmas production.

On December 14^{th:} "morning school was in a state of confusion as very heavy overnight snow coupled with drifting made it very difficult for both pupils and staff to get to school. More than 20 of our 100 pupils were unable to get into school.... it was Infant Party Day but some of our mums came to the rescue by preparing and helping with the party and eventually everything went ahead as planned. The deep snow made an ideal setting for Santa Claus who came along and distributed presents to the children".

The concert this year had three elements: "a play based on WW1 from J3, musical items on flute, clarinet, guitar and recorder and the Nativity Play".   There were two afternoon performances which were well attended and when school closed for the break there was still deep snow laying.

During the new year of 1982 a new meals system was introduced – the 'cook/freeze' method. HM recorded expecting much disruption whilst the work was done and that dirty plates etc would have to be sent away for washing up.   One of the dinner ladies had a bad accident when she tripped over the heel of another lady and fell breaking her pelvis.   Later the lady made a claim for damages.   In March a long-serving dinner lady – Mrs Douthwaite – retired after 22 years service.

There was a visit from an HMI in February; HM wrote a full report in the Log which contained the following extracts: " He thought great progress had been made in school over the last two years.... impressed with the competence, enthusiasm and industry of staff....children happy and responsive to the staff. ....reception class .... unlike the rest of the school in that it had an air of sterility about it. .... room lacked activity and needed a book corner, constant sand and water and large apparatus....he made an interesting suggestion to merge the two infant classes J1 and J2 so as to dilute the lack of stimulus ... on reception children at a central stage of their school life...." HM felt it was a most rewarding day for the school.

A new innovation in March was the arrival of some pets.   Two guinea pigs were named by infants class 'Prince' and 'Princess' and two rabbits 'Bomba' and 'Victoria'.   The pets were housed in their cages just outside school and proved very popular at playtimes.

Miss Mason, who had only joined the school the previous September, had been away on sick leave and in March informed HM she was considering leaving the teaching profession – toward the end of the month HM wrote: "she intends to resign with effect from the end of the school year... hopes to return after Easter to complete the summer term.. she seemed much fitter physically and hopes to find a job outside teaching which will give her the self-satisfaction she has been unable to find in teaching generally". In fact she did leave at the end of the summer term. Mrs Susan Cox, daughter of the previous Headmaster Mr J. Cowell, was appointed to replace Miss Mason – she had previously attended Aberford school and taught at Ledston Lady Betty Hastings School.

June saw HM being informed that the lighting throughout school was to be updated, including the external brick sheds. External lighting on the main building would be revised to make things easier and safer in the winter months.

On the 21st June HM reported on a burglary at school – complete window panes had been removed and internal doors and desks forced. Some £82 was taken which had been collected for photographs of the children. "The only consolation was that the thieves did little damage and did not make a mess so that clearing up was done quickly".

There was a nice treat at the end of June for two classes who visited Scarborough – rides were enjoyed on donkeys and the miniature railway. There was paddling and digging on the beach and the weather was reasonably kind.

The village summer Gala was still a reasonably sized event at this time with the school well represented. HM wrote: "We also entered a float on the theme: 'The Video Road Show' with 20 children in the costumes of pop stars, T.V. and film personalities. There were 5 floats altogether and the school entry won first prize in the competition".

In the last week of term HM and Mrs Knowles, together with four student helpers, took classes J2 and J3 to Ingleborough Hall.The weather was very good: "we had an exciting week fell walking, caving and visiting local places of interest and in the evening there was folk dancing, barbecue, camping and bivouacing. A memorable week for all concerned".

In September 1982, thirteen children joined reception class with another 4 joining in various year groups together with Mrs Cox commencing as Deputy Head and class J1 teacher. Twenty of the boys from Mrs Cox's class turned up to the first after-school football practice of the new school year and HM commented: "as the 'seed corn' of future teams they were most enthusiastic if, at this stage, lacking the finer arts and skills of the game".

The long-running problem of the surface of school lane crept closer to a solution when HM was informed by a school Governor that he had heard it was to be re-surfaced but HM remained sceptical! In November a deputation of 2 Governors, a Parish Councillor and 2 parents presented a petition to the full meeting of Leeds City Council to lobby for money to be granted to resurface school lane. It was to be April before the work was carried out: "the whole job was completed in about 8 hours ....makes the building look more attractive and cared for ... campaign waged over many years... is now at an end".

A dental inspection found only three children out of 100 were in need of any sort of treatment – a remarkable difference to the children of earlier times.

French was being taught in school at this time: "Mr Donaldson, Head of French at Boston Spa, came to speak to myself and Mrs Picken who teaches French here, about the desirability of continuing teaching French in the Primary School. Despite 'rumours' to the contrary he emphasised that he thought the two years our pupils spend on their French was well worthwhile and so we shall continue to teach it as before".

A Mrs Gledhill covered for Miss Tyler for two weeks whilst Miss Tyler did jury service and HM recorded his pleasure at Mrs Gledhill's performance: "all of us in school will be most sorry to lose Mrs Gledhill who has worked splendidly with reception class and who has been a most popular member of staff".

The Christmas production went well and, like a previous Headmaster, HM recorded the details of the programme for this year which are given below:

1. The Bell That Cried – a modern interpretation of the traditional Nativity story.
2. The News at Ten – comedy news from J3.
3. The Rehearsal Sketch – comedy playlet from J3.
4. Dashetty Dash – a copy of the popular T.V. game "Blanketty Blank" from J2.
5. Thoroughly Modern Millie (a musical) and Close Encounters of the Third Kind (a film)
   - Singing and dancing from one of our most talented pupils Caroline Pickering.

During January 1983 the whole school was painted internally and some new anti-glare curtains fitted in J3 classroom. The playground was also resurfaced. HM had the offer of lower suspended ceilings but "I said I would think about his offer as I think that such an alteration might rather spoil the charm and character of our lovely old building". He also wondered whether it would be another 13 years before the school was re-painted!

At a Governors' meeting, Mrs Cox – standing in for HM who was absent having a minor operation on his foot – reported in the Log that there was a heated discussion concerning the discontinuation of corporal punishment in the school. "The Governors pledged their support to the Head on matters of internal discipline and were aware that corporal punishment was not approved of by the Headmaster and staff".

A new cine projector was purchased and the Parents Social Group began to organise a social evening with an American theme celebrating the bi-centenary of the Triumphal Arch at Parlington.

There were a growing number of educational visitors to school combined with children themselves going on various visits: a party went to Tadcaster Riley Smith Hall to see a ballet "the performance was polished and those children who went enjoyed themselves greatly". Abbey House Museum at Kirkstall was visited. The folk guitar group visited Parlington House. There were conducted tours of Hazlewood Castle and Lotherton Hall for class J3. This same class went to Armley Mills in Victorian costume "to experience an authentic Victorian school morning" – they went on to Abbey House museum to see Victorian streets.

Visits were also made to Whitby Abbey and Lifeboat Station and Flamingo Park zoo. BBC Radio Leeds recorded the comments of some children for a programme they were making.

In June HM had a surprise on his 40th birthday: "Mrs Fowler somehow found out that it was my birthday, indeed my 40th ... unknown to me gathered all the children in the Hall and set out a cake with 40 candles on it. .... children sang ... each also received a bun..... a lovely morning was nicely rounded off when the 13 young children in the village playgroup, along with their teachers, came along to school to eat up what was left of the buns.... I think I shall remember for a very long time to come".

In July both HM and Mrs Cox attended the funeral of Mr Sam Hood, who had been a member of the Board of Governors up to 1979 and a popular local figure in Aberford – "the church was full to overflowing".

In September, with 95 children enrolled, HM recorded that three former pupils were to be in school for a term as part of their Community Service Course. They were to help generally in school and where required in specific classes. The Schools Psychology Service was accessed to help with a pupil – playground markings were repainted – Miss Michelle Lean, a former pupil, began to rehearse with the children for the forthcoming Harvest Festival. She went on to give a very great deal of musical service to the school.

There was a nasty accident when a boy (Benjamin Armstrong) broke a toe in the playground at lunchtime: "he had dropped a very heavy stone, believed to be the original foundation stone to the school, on his foot".

In November HM referred to the booklet 'Aberford in Times Past' which was published at this time and to which he had contributed

222

text to accompany the many photographs. A reporter and photographer from the Yorkshire Post came to school to take details. Within the Log Book is a letter from the Director of Education for Leeds congratulating HM on the booklet, a copy of which was to be lodged with the Education Library. Occasionally there are now letters stapled within this Log Book – mostly from grateful parents. During this month the children planted many bulbs at the base of the wall in school lane and these continue to bloom in spring to the present time.

In December all the children went to see a puppet show at Barwick school: "heavy rains of the last few days had resulted in Cock Beck bursting its banks and flooding surrounding fields, thereby providing spectacular views from the top of the bus". There was heavy snowfall to accompany the Christmas productions this year and the residential visit to Ingleborough Hall was repeated for class J3.

Hurricane winds were experienced in early January, doing a lot of damage in the area and slates were blown off the main school roof – the damage was repaired with the usual speed such things seem to take .... it was late February before completion. Heavy snowfalls came again this month and HM describes a delightful scene – "the school ... looked like a scene from a Christmas card.... we arranged a snowman building competition and each class built its own individual snowman. Each one was different – there were traditional imaginative and funny ones dotted around the playground and we invited the parents in to have a look at them".

Several parents went to see HM about 'paired reading' – a new system to be tried out for the term and a new after-school craft club began under the guidance of Mrs Cox and Mrs Fowler. The skills of knitting, sewing and crocheting were to be developed – skills which the girls of many years ago were taught as a matter of course – HM did not say whether any boys joined the group!

There was a visit from an HMI who was generally satisfied but "was critical of the lack of sand and water and stimulating display in reception class". Following similar comments from the LEA's

Primary Advisor in February, and his talk after school at a staff meeting about current educational trends and how they could be applied in Aberford School, HM agreed with Miss Tyler that certain changes would be made to classroom organisation, furniture arrangement and teaching method.   HM decided to help with creative activities lessons.

In March HM and Miss Tyler visited two other schools to look at infant methodology and organisation in the classroom. HM received a projection concerning future numbers of pupils to be expected over the coming years – this showed a likely fall to 86 by 1990 with an obvious effect on staffing levels.

The Lord Mayor of Leeds, accompanied by the Sergeant at Mace, visited Aberford School on February 8th – the old place should not have felt overawed, given its ancient history and connection to a venerable Oxford College!   HM recorded that the Mayor, Martin Dogson J.P. "had a down-to-earth manner which created a good relationship with the children". A 'thank you' letter from the Mayor was inserted in the Log Book.

There were various educational visitors to school throughout the year but one in March deserves special mention: "Havergal College Choir from Canada, who have been staying at homes in and around Aberford whilst singing at York Minster, 55 girls 13-19 years of age, under the conductor Mrs Muir, sang for us a lovely arrangement of "Sing a Song of Sixpence" and we sang for them our special "Welcome to our School" song. ... lovely group of girls they were and we said many a tearful goodbye ... we went to the bottom of School Lane to wave them off. What a lovely, lovely start to our day in school... we here ... will long remember".

The School Psychologist began to make termly visits to discuss children with special needs "as designated under the 1980 Education Act".

There was a big effort made to ensure a successful Spring Fayre in school on a Saturday in April: "school was crowded with parents, children and village residents. We had a visit from Jackie Merrick from the T.V. programme "Emmerdale Farm" and he was a great hit as he signed autographs for the children. The Fayre raised £290 – a splendid effort indeed".

Easter this year was the hottest and sunniest for 40 years and the school photographer must have had many suntanned faces to shoot on his annual visit.

In early May class J2 went with Mrs Cox, Mrs Knowles and two male students from Leeds Polytechnic College of Education to Haworth for a three day residential visit.

In late June there was a difficult incident with a boy who had exhibited some challenging behaviour previously. Whilst HM was with a class visiting Hazlewood Castle, the boy initially struck a girl on the head with a ruler. Subsequently he became very agitated and ran from the room. During the rest of the afternoon there were various incidents in and around the school – stone throwing, threats to burn a classroom, damage to a fire door and other more serious behaviour with the two teachers unable to contact the boy's mother and attempting to keep order and calm amongst the frightened children. Eventually, when HM returned, he was able to come upon the boy in the churchyard and caught him, disarming him of a knife which he had taken from school kitchen. The damage to one classroom was quite severe and HM contacted both the Psychology and Advisory Divisions of the local authority to discuss how to proceed – the boy was suspended and it was eventually agreed that it would not be appropriate for him to return to Aberford School. A very sad and disturbing incident for everyone involved.

The school's float in the Gala this year was on the theme of 'Los Angeles 1984' (Olympic Games) with all the decorations made by the children. When the float won first prize the money was used to buy lollipops with one for every child in school. These days it might have to be apples on the grounds of healthy eating or possible allergic reactions or tooth decay – but we can be sure those lollipops sure tasted good! The annual family outing was to Sandsend and Whitby with 100 children and parents taking part: "we were rewarded with a lovely sunny afternoon and the visit proved most enjoyable".

Sports Day races included skipping, potato, hoop and egg and spoon races in addition to the running races. No doubt there were the usual tumbles, tears and triumphs!

At the school year-end 17 pupils left to continue their education at Boston Spa, as did Mrs Fowler who moved to East Garforth Infant School – Mrs Jones was to join in September on a part-time basis .

The new school year saw the threat resurrected of removal of one of the mobile classrooms and a special Governors' meeting was held to discuss a consultative paper on local school closures and amalgamations. It was decided to send a letter to the Director of Education setting out the reasons why Aberford school should not be considered as a candidate for closure. The Vicar also wrote a letter to the Director of Education. We may suppose the letters were something along the lines of 'not in this life'!

A beginners group of guitar players was started with Mrs Timms giving tuition in a private capacity. The guitar players were not recorded as playing at the Harvest Festival this year but the programme is of interest: Class 1 – The Dingle Dangle Scarecrow (poem), Class 2 – Preserving the Harvest (wine, jam etc), Colours of Autumn, Class 3 – Harvest of the Sea, Class 4 – The Meaning of the Harvest.   The collection this year was for the Martin House Children's Hospice Appeal. A little later in the month the Venerable Richard Seed, Archdeacon of York, came to talk to children about the Hospice Appeal – this was to be for terminally ill children and sited at Boston Spa. Richard Seed was one of the prime movers in bringing this Hospice to fruition – it was to be only the second one opened in the UK, dedicated to caring for children with life-limiting illness and their families.   Generous Yorkshire folk had the satisfaction of seeing it opened in 1987.

Lighting was installed along School Lane – a first in 268 years! – an indoor fireworks display was held to celebrate Guy Fawkes Night – a successful jumble sale was held with funds going towards the recently installed lighting.

Mrs Knowles left at Christmas as she was having a baby and HM recorded: "sadly we said goodbye to Mrs Knowles who will be sorely missed. She has been a most hardworking, sympathetic and helpful member of staff whose talents, not only in the classroom but also in the areas of netball and music, will be difficult to replace".

The usual Christmas festivities and concerts were held; Mrs Pringle was appointed to replace Mrs Knowles and she started in charge of Class 3 in January 1985. During that month there were periods of heavy snow and a staff meeting was held "to discuss the use of GRIDS self-evaluation material for internal school development" – one more pebble in the mountain of such initiatives being introduced more and more during Mr Hewitt's time. HM began to write of his appreciation of the rare occasions when he was able to spend longer periods of time with a class than just one lesson. Attendance at external courses of one sort and another began to eat into the time of all teachers.

In February of 1985 a few children were absent with slightly unusual illnesses: "scarletina, shingles and scabies". Five trainee teachers from Bramley Grange College spent a day in school, split between two classes: "they observed classroom practice and said how much they had enjoyed their morning with us".

Computers were being introduced into schools and equipment continued to be purchased to enhance the one in school – a trolley was obtained to move it around the classrooms. Some spotlights and a control panel were purchased with the proceeds from the sale of the book on 'Aberford in Times Past'. HM recorded: "1000 copies have been sold, a remarkable achievement in a village where there are only some 300 houses, and I know that many copies have been sent all over the world. A total of £510 has been raised for school funds". A sponsored spell raised almost £300 for a Famine Appeal.

A german measles epidemic affected attendance during Spring. The flu bug also struck in March. Later in the month came some good news about Mrs Knowles who'd had a baby girl 'Hannah Lucy'. Further good news in April was that Mrs Jones was to be made a permanent member of staff.

In May HM attended a Leeds City Boys under 11 football match: "David Brooker had been selected to play ... this was a great honour for him especially as the game itself was a trophy final match.... it was an enjoyable occasion and David did himself and his school proud".

A few days later "A former teacher at this school, Mr Pickles, came to talk to the children in Assembly about the Maundy Money he received on Maundy Thursday last from the Queen at Ripon Cathedral. It was most interesting to see the silver coins at first hand and to hear about Mr Pickles' experience which reflected honour and credit on him for the service he had given to the communities of Garforth, where he now lives, and Aberford where he taught for so long".

Gymnastics Club re-formed for more able pupils and Mrs Knowles informed HM that she would not be returning to work after having her baby – he framed an advertisement for her replacement to start from September.

Aberford School took part in creating a little piece of history, though HM did not record just what exactly the children did, when the BBC did a 'Domesday Project'. "The new survey, to mark the 900th anniversary of the original ....will survey the Aberford area for amenities, land cover and an overall picture of life in the area in the year 1985. The results will be recorded on computer disc and some 10,000 national surveys will be stored for posterity on two laser video discs. We shall in fact be making a little bit of history – quite a responsibility". Over a million people co-operated in this Project which included virtual reality tours of landmarks and datasets like the 1981 census. In 2002, when advances in computing began to mean that the discs would become unreadable, a further project was undertaken jointly between the University of Leeds and University of Michigan to reformat the discs and it is now possible c2008 to download this information into personal computers. (Ref: Wikipedia.org.)

The trend of families to have a holiday abroad as easily as they once simply journeyed to the British seaside, was highlighted by several children describing their experiences in Assembly immediately after Spring break. Destinations such as Holland, France, Austria and Yugoslavia were mentioned. This trend had been growing since the 1960s. However, it was still possible to enjoy an educational visit to Scarborough in June "a glorious June Day .. no visit would be complete without a paddle, have a donkey ride and enjoy an ice cream".

The introduction of a new initiative , 'The Primary Needs Programme' was to give some help in additional teaching and resources from September which would mean a teacher would be appointed to be responsible for the development of science and special educational needs throughout the school – Miss Carolyn Capps was appointed in place of Mrs Knowles.

Four baby guinea pigs were born in July, to the delight of the children. Class 4 with Mr Hewitt spent a week at Ingleborough Hall – arriving home on the Friday "happy but exhausted". The P.S.G. outing this year was to Chester Zoo with 87 parents, children and staff taking part.

In September there were 79 children enrolled, Miss Capps commenced in charge of class 3 and a Mrs Bowles joined for a term under the Primary Needs Programme. Some small monetary prizes and certificates were presented to some children who had won classes in handwriting and painting at the village Horticultural Society Show. The inclusion of these children's classes was an annual occurrence. A representative of the Primary Needs Programme called: "to ask what might be spent on the building to provide the sort of richer environment the programme is aiming for. I asked for (a) water to be provided in the 2 mobiles and one infant classroom and painting sinks in the boys, girls and infants cloakrooms, (b) external painting, (c) lowering of display boards, (d) renovation of the Hall floor and (e) window boxes and tubs for the entrance facing school lane. It will be interesting to see just which, if any, of these features will be provided".

A P.S.G Barn Dance was held; each teacher spent £40 on books for their class library; a new caretaker, Mrs Ingle, began duties. A

Halloween disco was held and HM wrote: "Due to the late withdrawal of the D.J. I had to don the mantle of the D.J. – a rather harrowing role". These few words open up a real world of pain for HM with so many 'hyped-up' children raring to show off their dancing prowess! He continued: "However, the children danced and seemed to enjoy themselves and the evening could, I think, be termed a success".

In November the school hosted a seminar for York Diocesan C of E Schools and Mrs Knowles kindly: "spent a day in school painting a large backcloth for this year's concert". This depicted a Christmas fireside scene.

HM mentioned the first meeting of the newly reconstituted Governing Body: " Rev. B. Harris (Vicar and Chairman), Mr A Bell (Vice-Chairman) and Mrs S. Cox – Church Representatives, Mr G. Tait and Mr R. Richmond – Parent Representatives, Mr D. Stainton – Parish Council Representative, Mr H. Thompson and Mr J. Hey – Political Representatives, Mrs E. Picken – Teacher Representative and myself. The enlarged body elected Mr D. Stainton as Clerk and I hope this new body will prove to be a supportive and effective unit".

Children in Class 4 helped to bake mince pies for the after-concert refreshments, aided by two parents. The first afternoon performance of two plays, 'The Tailor of Gloucester' and 'The Night Before Christmas' was seen by around 60 family members. The evening performance was seen by around 90 with mince pies and rum punch served afterwards. The final performance was attended by around 100. It seems little wonder that the following day: "the children seemed very quiet .. probably because of the two late nights of concert performances". Some 50 children, parents and staff went around the village carolling and: "were refreshed by hot mince pies and sausage rolls from one of our parents en route. £30 was collected for the C of E Children's Society".

In mid-January 1986 an Authority Dance Co-ordinator spoke to staff about introducing the subject of dance to children and staff. She began working with each class later in the month.

In February Classes 3 and 4 visited a car museum and Metro transport control centre. A Mrs Dimmock replaced Mrs Bowles as P.N.P. teacher. Two classes were involved in Shrove Tuesday: ".. the aroma of pancakes permeated school with two classes preparing the seasonal dish to be heartily devoured with sugar and lemon. In front of the assembled school, Mrs Cox and I tossed pancakes, much to the amusement and delight of the children".

In March HM expressed to Governors his concern about lunchtime supervision – he felt that if this task was to be done by unqualified staff it would mean greater danger from minor accidents and greater indiscipline amongst children. The Governors agreed to write to the Chairman of the Education Committee and the Director of Education stating their concerns.

Later in March, school was closed from lunchtime: "in support of the National Association of Headteachers' campaign for a satisfactory lunchtime supervision scheme, which would include teachers as well as ancilliaries".

In a new initiative, the children attending the Aberford Play Group were brought to school to watch a cartoon and a comedy short film and enjoyed a drink of orange juice and biscuits: "As a way of introducing these future customers to school it was a great success". The following evening a family film night was held.

In mid April, despite the extremely cold and windy weather, Class 4 enjoyed their residential visit to Cloughton, staying at Cober Hill Guest House. Visits were made to Hutton le Hole, Goathland, Scarborough, Whitby and Robin Hood's Bay. Follow up work was done by the children back at school and parents were invited to see the results which showed them what sort of work could spring from such a visit. Later in the month the usual school photographs were taken: "The children had come to school especially tidy, many wearing best dresses, jumpers, shirt and tie etc. and a number of parents brought their younger children, not yet old enough to come to school, to take part in family photos". This was before the introduction of a school uniform.

Infants had a very wet visit to Beamish Museum in May – some forty children and five staff enjoyed their day: "the rest of the school with only one class in the main building was very quiet!".

During the Spring break, 13 pupils took the Cycling Proficiency Course with the Schools Road Safety officer, P.C. Temple. 11 passed: "but all hopefully will be safer on the road as a result of their course". Later, in June, several pupils gained gymnastics badges and certificates. The elderly people who attended the village Tuesday Club were entertained to a musical concert one afternoon: "the children's efforts were much appreciated and we promised to make a return visit at some time in the future". A parent who was a professional weather forecaster talked to Class 2 about his job.

School summer 'Fayre' was held in early July – an idyllic description is given by HM: "....various stalls .... plants, cakes, bottles, white elephant, books and toys and jewellery stalls. There was also a barbecue and an exotic cocktail bar run by Mrs Cox and Mrs Jones. There were scones and coffee for refreshment and several games for the children. Everything was set out in the playground and all the stalls with the garden umbrellas and tables made a colourful sight indeed. There was a fancy dress competition for the best dressed waiter and waitress and 25 children entered with prizes going to Charlotte Turner, Nicholas Coplowe, Andrew Green and Alison Davis. A profit of approx. £280 was very pleasing and part of this will go towards providing a Royal Wedding party on July 23rd".

There were two celebratory occasions in late July – Miss Tyler completed 25 years of service and was presented with a silver tray to mark the occasion – a 'street party' was held in School Lane to mark the wedding of Prince Andrew to Miss Sarah Ferguson. The street party was another 'mammoth event' which Aberford School teachers and children and their parents put on so well – the lane was strewn with banners, posters, streamers, balloons and bunting and tables to accommodate all 84 children were set out. Buns and cakes had been baked with a royal theme and there was a splendid three tier wedding cake. All were dressed in red, white and blue with tiaras, crowns, medals and sashes and a 'replica' Prince Andrew and

Sarah Ferguson played their parts. Even the bout of heavy rain with thunder and lightening didn't spoil the occasion despite making some of the buns soggy! Some film of the proceedings was taken by a Yorkshire TV cameraman to be shown on the local news programme that evening. HM recorded that it was a very memorable day.

19 children left to transfer to Boston Spa school with Mrs Dimmock leaving to move to Baildon in Essex. Miss Capps was presented with a cut glass bowl as she was getting married in the summer holidays and would return as 'Mrs Walker'.

In September there were 72 children enrolled and Mrs Ingram joined as a P.N.P. Co-ordinator in place of Mrs Dimmock. 16 of the boys were in the football team and 25 girls in the netball team. Mrs Jones left at Christmas as her husband had obtained employment in America. HM felt it most unlikely she would be replaced. A new after-school club started for crafts – with HM and Mrs Cox offering clay, papier mache, sewing, knitting and corn dolly making. The R.N.I.B. was to be the school's charity for the year.

The Christmas production this year was decided upon in early November: 'Christmas Around the world'. The younger children to perform 'Babushka' and the older ones the pantomime of 'Red Riding Hood'. A huge backcloth was put up in the Hall for the forthcoming concert: "every class has contributed a mural on the theme of Christmas scenes and messages from Denmark, Holland, Sweden, Australia, Russia, Italy and Germany". The Christmas Tree lights were switched on early December: "as always by the youngest child in school – this year four year-old Hannah Hinton". All went well at the concerts and there were the usual carol concert, parties and fun and games for the children as term drew to a close. After Christmas dinner on the 18th, there was a visit from Waldo the Clown. For the first time children were able to watch a video recording of themselves performing the Concert: "frozen in time to view in years hence".

January 1987 brought a wind from Siberia with the lowest temperatures ever recorded. Children enjoyed heavy snow for a few days. A 'Roman Centurion' visited and enthralled the children with tales of his lifestyle and they all learned a tremendous amount about the Romans in Britain – some of whom had passed along the village road just a few hundred yards away! Later a Roman assembly was held at which children showed the follow-up work they had done.

Staff continued to attend various courses: "Mrs Walker attended a course in Leeds on the festival of Easter and its multicultural implications". As Mrs Jones had informed HM she was to resign to go to America with her husband, a replacement was appointed – Mrs Cliff who was to commence in April.

HM attended a seminar in Leeds concerning the AIDS illness which was recognised at this time as a deadly virus having no known cure. He recorded: "a greater concentration on general hygiene and on extreme care when there are blood spillages will be necessary if the effects of this potentially deadly illness are to be avoided". A month later P.C. Temple spoke to children about possible dangers of abduction by strangers and left the children with the message always say no to strangers. HM recorded: "it is a sad reflection on our times that children should not talk to strangers no matter how friendly".

There was a visit – in Victorian dress – to Armley Mills Museum in Leeds to live for a school day as Victorian children would have lived. The children found the day "both strict and somewhat tedious" The younger children had a delightful visit to Home Farm up Becca Lane when Mr Richmond "showed them round the farm and the children saw the new-born Spring lambs, the pigs and piglets, the hens and the bulls".

The Governors decided to "ask the Authority .. whether there was to be nursery provision at Aberford ... falling rolls situation .... viability of this small school ...presently with 76 pupils". Despite this small number, the quality and breadth of education being delivered was reflected in a group of 20 children giving a concert to elderly residents of the Tuesday Club in March. "There were old time songs and instrumental pieces on recorder, flute, clarinet and folk guitar which were enjoyed by those present".

Expenditure was authorised by the P.S.G. to enable each class to be equipped with a computer system. School said goodbye to Mrs Jones in early April: "Her departure .. will be a considerable loss to the school for she was a talented teacher, a hard worker and a most pleasant and co-operative colleague".

The usual residential was held for the children of Class 4 at Cloughton – very enjoyable for all concerned and HM recorded: "the children will have increased their sense of independence at this young age of 10 and 11 years". In late April the school held two open mornings as the L.E.A. had designated the week a 'School and Community Festival', with about 50 parents and Governors attending: "as we attempted to show our visitors what we are trying to achieve with their children at school".

The country dancing group reformed under Mrs Ingram and a computer and hardware was acquired for the mobile classroom housing Class 2. Miss Tyler attended a course on the use of word processing with computers and a printer was purchased.

There was interest in eating healthily at this time – as there has been again in the early years of this new century. In May a questionnaire showed: "children would like more salad, fewer chips and more sweets such as yoghurt. Clearly the palates of this generation of children are more educated than in the past as the trend towards more healthy eating is apparent. It is to be hoped that those running the school meals service take notice of their customers' views".

At this time there was a two week holiday at Spring Bank. Immediately after, HM attended a course on 'Sexism and Racism Awareness' and Governors decided to press for Aberford School to be a given a higher priority to have a nursery class attached to school. The Governors also wanted children in the fourth year to continue to be taught French – inexplicably the French Adviser for the L.E.A. had requested that this should be stopped despite the fact that children would be taught French in their first year at senior school!

The Village Gala was quite a large and well-attended event even at this time and Mrs Ingram and Mrs Cliff decorated the school float with the theme of 'The Garden Gang'. "The decorated float looks splendidly colourful. We took all the children down to Mr Dennis's barn where the float is stored to see it". The converted farmhouse and cottages of this large ex-working farm are opposite the village garage. The Gala Queen was Vicky Crook this year and she and her attendants toured the village in a pony and trap.

There was a new innovation in late June: "Despatched annual report to parents prepared by the Governing body and required by the 1986 Act of Parliament". A few days later, as required, parents were invited to an annual meeting with the Governors: "the main issue raised was that of the long-term future of the school".

HM recorded on 3rd July that the previous Headmaster, Mr Cowell, had died after only a few days of illness. A few days later: "I attended the funeral service in St Ricarius Church .. a large congregation containing many former colleagues and pupils and in his sermon the Vicar outlined the value of Mr Cowell's 31 years of Headship .... great contribution to the life of the village".

Children raised almost £600 by doing a sponsored spell and were rewarded with a puppet and magic show, a class visited Canal Gardens and saw tropical fish and Class 2 visited Templenewsam House with Miss Tyler in formidable form driving the self-drive minibus! Those who knew Miss Tyler would know it was highly unlikely that she would have experienced any trouble from her charges!

Leavers' outing was to Wetherby Baths when HM was enticed into the water and this was followed by a lunch of fish and chips and a call at Lotherton Hall with a conducted tour of the house. HM recorded the names of all 14 leavers this year saying that they had been a delightful class all the way through school.

The number of children fell to 76 from September but four more children started by Christmas. Only three children needed treatment following a visit from the school dentist. Wheatfields Hospice was chosen to be the recipient of funds to be raised during the year. HM recorded his disquiet when badges, posters and cards arrived to be displayed in school "to bolster the number (of children) taking school dinners. Is this the first example of how in the coming years we are to commercially 'market' education?"

Harvest Festival this year saw Class 1 giving a poem; Class 2 told the story of Little Red Hen and gave a dramatised documentary on the value of fish; Class 3 acted out the story of the blackberry and illustrated harvest in other lands. "The recorder players and folk guitarists were also in fine form". £53 was collected for Wheatfields Hospice.

Staff were obliged to consider the L.E.A's Special Needs Policy with HM and Mrs Ingram attending a meeting at Boston Spa School. In October the Parents Social Group organised a 'beetle and bingo evening' which was well supported: "an evening of simple and unsophisticated, may we say, old-fashioned family fun".

In November there was an unusual event when an actor gave a narrative performance as Guy Fawkes one evening. 140 parents and children crowded into the Hall and were enthralled by the: "dramatic and realistic reconstruction of the events of November 5th 1605". A supper and rum punch rounded off the evening. Sadly there was some minor vandalism committed on Mischief Night in and around the school and HM used a morning assembly to stress to children: "the anti-social and vandalistic associations of the night and that the best place for them on November 4th was indoors at home". Class 2 visited Yeadon Airport as they were doing a topic on flight.

This year's Christmas production was 'A Christmas Carol' and festivities started with the traditional dressing of the tree in the Hall. A stall at the Village Hall Christmas Fayre raised £11.50 for funds. Guitar and recorder group presented a concert in the Village Hall for the Tuesday Club. There was the usual massive attendance at the Concert performances with light refreshments provided, including mince pies baked by top class children. The well-supported carolling around the village raised over £109 for Wheatfields Hospice.

The first snow fell towards the end of January 1988. HM had a preliminary talk to four mums about their helping with baking and sewing and some children visited Mr Freeman's workshop in the village – he was a wrought iron worker. The extra hands were very welcome during sessions of baking and sewing "which are very demanding in terms of teacher time".

The first national 'Comic Relief Day' was held in early February: "to help starving people in drought-hit areas like Sudan and Ethiopia". Red plastic noses were sold, various events were held in school and £73 was raised. "An extremely colourful day, the like of which Aberford School has never seen before and may well never see again. Comic Relief Day was tremendous fun and a great fund-raising success both locally and nationally".

The tree in the playground was inspected following violent winds which had blown down small branches but it was found to be healthy. Very warm weather was to follow during the half term break. Later the school lime tree was found to be approximately 150 years old and a bore showed it to be well but lopping of a large beech in Vicarage Drive was recommended.

Children visited Skipton Castle and Jorvik Exhibition in York.

In March HM and Mrs Cox visited the Multicultural Centre in Leeds to look at information "on how to promote greater awareness of other cultures within our society for our own children, all of whom are 'white' and C of E". Discussions about the crumbling boundary wall were held with Mr Tate and the Road Safety Officer was contacted about the speed and volume of traffic passing through main street which the crossing patrol person had to cope with. The wall was subsequently pointed and a beech tree overhanging the playground from the Vicarage Drive side was lopped.

The science and technology aspects of classwork were extended as was parental involvement. On May 13th: " .. we now have parents working in classes throughout the school on Thursday and Friday mornings".

When children returned after the Spring break: "a sign of a 'shrinking' world in modern times. Some of our pupils had been to such locations as Corfu, Spain, Tunisia and America!"Teachers continued to attend various external meetings and eight fourth year children visited Boston Spa school for a morning so that it would not be so strange when they transferred to senior school.

Sports Day this year was won by 'Green team', after 'Blue team' had been in the lead for most of the afternoon. Two days later there were fierce storms and torrential rain overnight – lucky that Sports Day had been held when it was! The first summer evening barbeque and disco was held this year – this was to become a yearly event. Held in the school playground, there was a colourful scene with entertainment for children and 140 parents plus children attended. "... it was so successful that I like to think we may repeat it next year. In addition a profit of £120 was made for school and Parent Social Group funds". Later, in July, a P.S.G. trip was made to Whitby and Sandsend with two coaches of parents, children and staff enjoying their day.

The Governors' report was presented to a small gathering of parents with the main concerns being the dangers of crossing the main road at the bottom of school lane, the proposed provision of a nursery unit within a 10 year period and the appalling state of the external woodwork and paintwork. The Governors began to press for nursery provision and the Authority Primary Advisor visited school in October to assess the premises.

This year there were eight fourth year juniors who left to go to Boston Spa and HM stated that they had been a pleasure to teach. There were just six new infants and the total numbers continued to fall at this time with the classes from September arranged as follows:

Class 1 (Miss Tyler)   -   15
Class 2 (Mrs Cox/Mrs Cliff)   -   25
Class 3 (Mrs Walker)   -   18
Class 4 (Mr Hewitt/Mrs Picken) -   18

The school year proceeded much as usual with swimming, football and netball resuming. An Advisory teacher recommended some changes in Class 1 to give more progressive and challenging work for the older age group. The Harvest Festival collection went this year to 'Give for Life' appeal. Teachers attended various courses including HM in October: "... the implication of the National Curriculum and the testing thereof. This major reform in education is going to create a great deal of extra work for Leeds and staff with this stipulated curriculum content. It will be introduced in September 1989 for 5+ children with the first testing in 1992". The flexibility that Aberford children had enjoyed in their lessons for the previous 273 years was now to be curtailed.

The long-serving school secretary, Mrs Glenville, left after 18 years service and was replaced in November by a rather nervous Mrs Malloch – replacing someone after such a length of service was not easy! Also in November HM attended a meeting of Head Teachers to learn about one of the main elements of the 1988 Education Reform Act concerning: "... financial delegation to schools which will create major changes in school and give all of us a lot of extra work!"

The Christmas production this year was a variation on the Nativity called 'The Smallest Angel' and the older children presented 'Jack Frost'. The Leeds Wind Quintet played for the children and they were entertained by a theatre company. Michelle Lean was specially thanked for playing the piano at the Christmas concerts – she was to continue to give tremendous service to the school certainly to the time this history ceases.

When school re-opened in January 1989, HM was away for the first six weeks on secondment at the Headship Unit at Woolley Hall. The course was entitled 'The Management of Change' Indeed there were to be huge changes for teachers, brought about by Central Government, during the approach to the new century. Mrs Cox took charge of school and a temporary teacher came to work with Class 4 during HM's absence.

The P.S.G. held a successful barn dance. Staff visited Collingham School: "to see the results of an in-service day on materials, particularly weaving". A member of the Authority's Computer Team came to give some training which was to be an ongoing occurrence as computers began to play a bigger part in school life –

not only for the children but for administrative purposes. In March Cllr. Wakefield gave £100 towards a computer concept keyboard.

In February a video recorder and £250 were presented to school by the licensees of The Arabian Horse – proceeds of fund raising events in the pub. HM had to 'hang tough' with the Authority's Caretaking Section: "no relief Caretaker has been found – no cleaning has been done". A few days later: "Mrs Ingle in school, very upset that the office had asked her to return from leave to duty. I was very angry too and again spoke to Mr B, Head of Caretaking Section, about an unacceptable situation. I sent Mrs Ingle home". Eventually a relief Caretaker was provided.

A day of fun in March for Comic Relief raised £100 and in April Mrs Whyte joined the staff as School Assistant to work every afternoon in classes and around school generally helping out – she was to stay for many years and became the school Secretary later in the year. A successful week's visit was made by fourth year pupils to Bewerley Park Outdoor Centre at Pateley Bridge and staff attended a training day on how to identify and deal with child abuse.

A special Governors' meeting was held in April: "to consider a written response to the L.E.A on its proposals for a scheme of formula funding as financial delegation of budgets under the Government 1988 Education Reform Act". Classes 3 and 4 made visits to the National Museum of Photography at Bradford.

In May a well-known Aberford figure – Mr Bennett (who was a local shopkeeper for many years and had the kind of hardware shop where one could buy almost anything from fuse wire to a scrubbing brush) – gave a talk to children which sounded very interesting: " .... history of cycles and cycling. He brought with him a penny-farthing bicycle and demonstrated the rather precarious riding technique, much to the amusement of the children". Staff were advised that their number had to be reduced by one as from September: " ... we shall have to reduce from a four class to a three class school, not an attractive prospect, but nevertheless a situation we shall have to face".

Miss Tyler enquired about early retirement with a view to going at the end of July – HM heard in mid-July that her application had been granted.

A heatwave in June made conditions in the mobile classrooms very difficult. During this month a parent offered to install a burglar alarm system free of charge as a thank you for all that had been done for his children. Though it is not clear that this offer was taken up, a system was installed in late July to protect the school's valuable equipment. The good weather made for a delightful family barbeque this year which raised £315 for the school and P.S.G. funds and the weather also favoured the village Gala when Anna Stainton was Queen. On the 27th however: " we had 60 unexpected visitors this afternoon as a torrential downpour caught a Garforth school on a visit to Aberford unawares and we gave them shelter".

Recycling of aluminium cans began with any money raised to go towards a free disco for everyone. Although little money was raised for the large amounts collected, "a major part of the exercise is to convey the importance of conservation of resources to our children". A fire drill was held during the lunchtime period to test the supervisory assistants who all coped well in getting the children out of school safely and quickly. Governors requested that the L.E.A. survey the external walls and roof which, in places, were deteriorating badly. At a later meeting it was decided to question parents about adopting a school uniform. A ballot was held in October: "84% of parents replied and of them 77% are in favour ... a sizeable majority clearly supporting the idea".

There was a new trophy for the winning Green team on Sports Day – given by parents of two pupils who were leaving this year: " ... presented to the Captain of Green team by John Hey, one of our School Governors".

The treats for children at the end of school year included Classes 2 and 3 having separate picnics in school field, with Class 3 eating all the things they had baked that morning. Class 4 went to Lotherton Hall by horse-drawn charabanc and had a tour of the house followed by a game of rounders.

The last week of the school year was a momentous one in the life of Aberford School for Miss Tyler retired after 28 years of service. She had been a teacher many Aberfordians thought of as 'of the old school' – her departure marking the end of an era. These are extracts of HM's Log entry: "We presented her with a School 'Book of Memories', happy retirement cards and gifts from children and staff comprising luggage, music cassettes, books and a Bonsai tree.......We sang our special school song for Miss Tyler ... I hope she will have many memories, hopefully mostly happy ones, to take away with her into retirement... .. we hope that she will pop in to see us from time to time".

There were 19 pupils who left this year and Mrs Cox was to be loaned for a term to Garforth Infant School as Head so there were to be changes in teaching personnel for the new school year. During this year it is interesting to know about the many meetings staff attended which arose from the forthcoming educational changes. Subjects covered were:

New Role in Reception Class
Maths Course
Use of Clay in School
Management of the National curriculum
Use of concept keyboard
National Curriculum for 5 year-olds from September 1989

Two days training on National curriculum – including new forms of record keeping, schemes of work, classroom organisation

Aberford School's response to the challenge of the National curriculum which was to operate in all schools from September 1989.

There were just 69 pupils enrolled from September and Mrs Ingram took over Reception class with 15 children: "which has a new bright and interesting feel to it". There were four classes with Mrs Cliff working fulltime with a class of 19 whilst Mrs Cox was away. Mrs Walker had 15 children and Mr Hewitt/Mrs Picken had 20 children. Just before Christmas, Mrs Cliff was appointed to her post permanently against stiff competition.

HM took about 20 children to help a long-time resident of Aberford – Mrs Hills – celebrate her 100th birthday: " ... the Parish Council paid for the erection of a seat, suitably inscribed, in Beech View, behind the new Bowling Green..... we all sang 'Happy Birthday to You' ... a sprightly 100 year-old indeed".

Two police horses visited school to the delight of the children. At this time the naming policy for these horses was to call them after villages in the West Yorkshire Force area and Aberford was, of course, the first chosen. P.C .Barrowclough rode 'our' horse and about a month later another visit was paid together with three other horses: "... to present to Mr Frank Watson of Aberford Parish Council a large framed photograph of the horse. The Parish Council meets in school and so presented the photograph to us to hang in school". The occasion was reported in the Evening Post and an item appeared on Yorkshire T.V's Calendar News programme.

Despite the piano tuner doing his best with the instrument in mid October: " [It] is tuneless and needs replacing but the L.E.A. appear to have no funds for replacement". A Halloween disco, with HM donning the D.J. hat, went very well and a pre-Bonfire Night event was held: "firework display, parkin, gingerbread men and toffee". Yummy! A preliminary visit was held to discuss the forthcoming residential visit of Class 4 to Cloughton.

Mr Richmond and Mrs Coplowe were elected to the Governing body and they soon had a lengthy meeting to attend: "from 7 to 10p.m. – surely the longest ever recorded with a mountain of paperwork to deal with – an indication of the volume and pace of change being thrust upon schools at present".

The Christmas production began to take shape and this year was 'Sing a Song of Christmas'. It was 'fingers crossed' for a flu virus was sweeping schools across the Country and HM recorded: " if it were not for the concert this week, I suspect many more children would be absent". A number of children did miss the last performance meaning several last-minute changes of cast. Mrs Walker left after four years popular service: "she takes up her new appointment at Yeadon Southview after the holiday".

The new decade of 1990 ushered in a school uniform – a new departure unless one counted the very early days, during the 1700s, when a rudimentary uniform look prevailed with the boys wearing caps and girls aprons! The colours chosen were red and grey with sweatshirts bearing the school logo. Photograph 6 shows the children in uniform at this time. Mrs Cox returned to Class 2 and Mrs Knowles in a supply capacity taking Class 3 until Mrs Cliff took up her appointment after Easter this year. Later Mrs Knowles became temporary part-time teacher for Special Needs provision within school. A pantomime visit was made by children, parents and teachers to see 'Goody Two Shoes' – much enjoyed. HM attended the first this year of continuing meetings about the National Curriculum. In February a few parents attended a meeting to been given information about the changes.

Class 3 paid a visit to the Yorkshire Mining Museum near Wakefield: "... including a one hour tour underground – the first time any of the children had been down a mine and so it was a unique and exciting experience". How the times had changed for these children of the late 20th century, for had they lived in the village in earlier times, many of their fathers/older brothers etc. would have had first-hand experience of the hardships of being a collier. Indeed many of the boys would have gone on to become colliers themselves.

HM began to occasionally mention unseasonable weather as when it was very warm in February and storm force winds blew down one of the old beech trees in Vicarage Drive, blocking it for a short time. March 1st brought heavy snow but glorious spring weather was enjoyed on the Juniors' residential visit at the end of the month to the Hutton-le-Hole area.

HM recorded his sad feelings about some of the changes being brought in: "I began the first day of a 3-day course... to prepare schools and Head Teachers for the 'burden' of Extended Financial Management which will allocate a budget directly to the school and Governing Body, the budget to be administered by them instead of the L.E.A. as in the past. This will clearly be a complex and time-consuming task, not welcomed by me certainly at this time of great pressure and change in schools. Head Teachers are now becoming 'managers' rather than Head Teachers of schools. I'm not sure I really want to be an educational bureaucrat!"

HM was disappointed when the L.E.A. declined to allow Mrs Picken to have two weeks leave of absence to visit Australia which meant that her employment would technically cease in early April but she agreed to remain in a supply capacity to the end of the summer term. Mrs Ingle, Caretaker for five years, was to leave at the end of the summer term.

At this time, Wetherby still had an active cattle market right in the middle of town and Class 2 paid a visit. They also visited Mr Richmond's Becca Farm, had a picnic and a ride on one of the farm carts.

Early May saw temperatures of 25 degrees Celsius and all the children visited West Yorkshire Playhouse Theatre as part of the International Children's Theatre Week. At the end of the month HM recorded: "Mrs Cox ... was successful in her application (for the post of Head Teacher of Roundhay St John's C.E. Aided School) ... will leave in September and after such a long and happy association I shall be very sorry to see her go.." HM was very unhappy to be told that no deputy Head Teacher would be granted to replace Mrs Cox due to overall numbers of children in school. He recorded: "I am really upset at the news and feel that, in the current educational climate, we are being asked to do more and more in terms of management and administration with fewer and fewer resources. A sad day for this school".

Mrs Ingle had a period of illness during the time leading up to her finishing work at Aberford School and this caused difficulties for HM, meaning he had to unlock and lock up school and there were evening meetings to cover. HM attended a Governors' meeting in July and a few days later, the Chairman of the Governors resigned as a result of a heated disagreement which had occurred at that meeting. In November the Chair was taken up by Rev Harris.

Sports Day this year was won by Green team with Captain Mark Horan receiving the shield from Parent Governor Mrs Coplowe.

Only six parents attended the annual parents evening: "due to .. England v. West Germany was being live televised in the semi-finals of the 1990 World Cup. England lost the match on a penalty shoot out...".

There was a preliminary visit of new starters who numbered fourteen from September. A 'pre-painting' inspection of the exterior of school was made – HM waited to see if this would really happen!

The family barbeque was enjoyed by everyone with 170 parents and children present and over £300 profit was made for school and P.S.G. funds. It was a sad occasion when both Mrs Cox and Mrs Picken left the school – Mrs Cox was presented with a cut glass decanter and Mrs Picken with a silver tray. The treat for the twenty Class 4 pupils was a visit to the swimming baths: "which was refreshingly cooling considering the 90 degree heat today". HM had found the year 'trying', particularly with the implementation of new and time-consuming initiatives and he hoped for calmer waters for the forthcoming school year.

HM hoped the higher intake of 13 pupils represented a trend to reverse the falls of previous years. Mrs Ingram now had 26 pupils, Mrs Cliff 19, Mrs Picken/Mrs Knowles 15 and HM himself ceased to have a class teaching commitment: "In many ways I shall miss it but the administrative and curriculum demands have become so great in recent years that a half-time class teaching commitment has simply become too heavy a burden to carry any longer – a sad reflection of these constantly changing times in Education".

How astonished the earlier Headmasters would have been if they had been able to look into the future and see highly trained teachers becoming unable to do the very thing that attracted them into their vocation. What greater pleasure could a teacher experience than to guide and inform the minds of future generations – interesting times in education indeed!

Staff began as usual to attend various courses throughout the year, with the following being just during the first half of the school year:

Mrs Cliff   2 days at Bramley Grange on the role of the curriculum co-ordinator
            Classroom organisation course
            ½ day on Technology

HM   1 day book-binding course followed by a meeting of the Pyramid
            Group at Boston Spa School – subsequently all staff had a go at this
            skill by attending after-school sessions
            1 day course covering data bases and data handling for Key Stage 1
            1 day course on maths policies and schemes
            1 day course, use of SATs

Mrs Ingram   1 day on "making music" at Elmete Primary Centre
            Half day music course
            ½ day assessment course at Elemete
            1 day course – ditto –
            1 day course 'use of materials'
            1 day course, use of SATs
            1 day course at Elmete – evaluation of SATs.
Mrs Knowles   'L.I.S.S.E.N.'course - Mrs Knowles became Special Needs Coordinator

The charity chosen for the school to support this school year was Wheatfields Hospice. Mrs Janet Booth was selected to take charge of Class 3 as of January 1991. She had previously worked part-time at Woodlesford School. A 'Children in Need Day' sponsored by B.B.C. television saw Mrs Foxcroft, the crossing patrol lady, raise over £50 from 'passes' and children raise over £42.

This year's Christmas production was 'The Night Before Christmas'. As the time drew near HM was a bit apprehensive as many children had coughs, colds and chest infections. At the first afternoon performance, one little shepherd found it all too much and made a run to his mum in the audience! However, first time nerves seem to have been conquered and the rest of the performances went very well as usual. The carol singing around the village raised £92 for Wheatfields Hospice. The folk guitar group with Mrs Timms – their teacher – and HM, played for the residents of Parlington House in the evening on the 19th December. The whole school were able to see themselves performing their Christmas concert via a video recording and were much amused!

In January 1991, two Boston Spa pupils began a term's work experience within school and another pupil undertook three days work experience later in the month. HM mentioned the nearby Fairburn Ings Bird Sanctuary when Class 2 visited: "in connection with their topic on flight".

Councillor Wakefield gave a cheque for £400 to school to use "to purchase external seating, window boxes and an animal cage". New steps were completed to the outside classroom, replacing wooden ones. A "new generation Archimedes A300 computer was delivered to supplement the 3 B.B.C. Master computers". The first heavy snow for nearly four years prompted HM to let the children play in it during the morning "many of our youngest children have never actually experienced snowfall and snow play". School had to close the following day with Mrs Cliff and Mrs Ingram unable to get in, Mrs Booth arriving late and a foot of snow in the playground.

An improvement to the large mobile classroom was made in February when a sink unit for both hot and cold water was installed, meaning children and staff no longer had to go to the main building in order to get water, clean paint equipment etc.

In common with the other members of staff, Mrs Booth began to attend various courses from time to time, starting with a two day course on curriculum leadership at Elmete Centre. HM enjoyed his brief return to class teaching.

Comic Relief Day raised the sum of £70 for this good cause with HM dressing up as a judge complete with long curly wig which must have greatly amused the children. A P.S.G. event with the theme of a 'Western Evening' raised over £200 for funds.

In March HM recorded the school budget for 1991/1992 which was £110,000 being £99,000 for staffing costs and was approximately the previous year's budget with 9% for inflation.

HM recorded his feelings about the introduction of Standard Assessment Tasks: "We started the National Curriculum testing of seven year-olds today ... In all they will take at least two weeks to administer to the 6 .. in Class 1. These SATs are extremely controversial and many teachers (including myself) believe that the danger of branding children as 'failures' at an early and tender age is great. Children will be allocated level 1, 2 or 3 with the vast majority of them expected to achieve level 2. They are also very time-consuming to deliver and it is difficult to give the required attention to the other children in the class at the same time. The administration is a legal requirement so we shall have to get on with the job. I feel that this is a retrograde step in educational 'progress' though". The results were recorded as: "1 child achieving level one, 5 level two and 1 a high level 3 in reading".

Falling numbers of children meant that there were just 8 juniors who went on the five day residential visit to Cober Hill in April with HM taking them in a minibus. Lovely weather was enjoyed and the children were well behaved. The photographer this year completed his work by the morning break with less numbers to photograph.

During 'National Environment Week' the children collected litter in and around the school and "we have had a splendid new animal cage installed, new window boxes and seating around the playground which all improves the overall external appearance of the building". The boxes were planted up with summer bedding plants.

In June: "set up a display of children's arts and crafts in St Ricarius Church as part of the annual Craft Fayre ... paintings, sewing, weaving, woodwork, clay, ... bookbinding by pupils from Classes 1, 2, and 3 were attractively set out".

An L.E.A. Adviser called to talk about a possible nursery unit for the school but prospects were not felt to be good at this time due to unsuitable premises and low numbers. The family barbeque evening was 'touch and go' due to showery weather but proved successful as always and raised £270 for school and P.S.G. funds. Class 3 visited the office and printing works of the nearby Bradford Telegraph and Argus newspaper. Eight pupils had a look around Boston Spa School and met their prospective tutors. A classical guitar concert was given to the rest of the school by four pupils with their peripatetic teacher Mr Schofield. The children involved were Vicky Roberts, Sally Coplowe, Rebecca Lock and Charlotte Roberts.

HM recorded his feelings that the Governors Meeting, as required under the 1986 Education Act, was somewhat of a waste of time with only 5 parents and 7 of the 9 Governors present. A few days later some 20 parents attended an open morning to see all classes as they were in normal operation working on a variety of activities.

The unpredictable weather caused a last minute cancellation of Sports Day after all the children had arrived in the field – it was held three days later on a glorious day! Yellow team were the winners this year with Captains Sally Coplowe and David Nicholson receiving the Sports Shield.

The parents consultation evening had a high attendance: "the new style reports issued for the first time to children in years 1, 2 and 3 and reception".

The Village Gala was blessed with pleasant weather and Vicky Roberts was the Queen with attendants Caroline Hardaker, Shelly Green, Zoe Piper and Rachel Lee. There was a P.S.G. family outing to Haworth with 60 parents and children going by bus to Keighley and then on the Worth Valley Steam train to Haworth.

On 17th July: "Went with Mrs Cliff and Class 2 to the Leeds Schools Technology Exhibition at Beckett Park College in Leeds. Eighty schools were exhibiting and Class 2's entry featured work on their Middle Ages topic. They showed plans for a siege machine, armour, catapults etc. as well as the models themselves. Ours was a good standard of work and presentation, certainly compatible with other schools showing work of children in the same 8/9 year group".

Eight children joined Reception class in September. Mr and Mrs Powell generously donated a new hifi system to school incorporating a compact disc player. HM was delighted with this as: "a valuable addition to our range of equipment". Staff had to familiarise themselves with changing technology – the new Archimedes computer was rather different to the B.B.C. machine.

The P.S.G. planned a lively programme: "and the group was enthusiastic about larger-scale fund raising later in the year to provide a completely new library and reception area in the room currently used by class 3".

Dental health continued to improve – reflecting the improvements in knowledge and practice of dentistry. Only three out of sixty-six children required treatment. Fear of the dentist was very much becoming a thing of the past.

The L.E.A. Adviser informed HM that he and another Adviser would visit in November to inspect and give an overview of the school's work. Their report was overall complimentary and positive.

In October Rev Harris made a farewell visit to school and was presented with a card and pen and pencil set. He had been in the village for about 13 years and was to take a new post as Vicar of Hemingborough near Selby. Just a few days later the usual Harvest Festival was held with a collection going to the Church of England Children's Society but HM did not say whether Rev. Harris officiated.

The P.S.G. disco held in the Village Hall raised a profit of £128 for funds. Buildings Division began to show some interest in school – a pre-painting survey was talked about!

Two student teachers made a preliminary visit and a lady came to talk to children in Classes 2 and 3 about the Jewish faith. A few days later they visited the synagogue in Harrogate Road, Leeds. Class 3 also visited the Victorian schoolroom at Armley Mills wearing Victorian dress and they had the type of lessons with which Victorian children would have been familiar.

In November: "one of our parents, Mr Hardaker, presented a cheque for £315 to school from a fundraising event he had organised in the Village Hall. The money will go towards the provision of the new library". Preparations for the Christmas concert began with the junior children planning 'Red Riding Hood' this year.

In late November HM recorded the death of an Aberford man who was well-known to all in the community: "I attended the funeral service for Alf Bennett, who used to have Bennett's shop and who was always very supportive of school and generous especially at Christmas time when he provided the presents for the infants on a non-profit making basis. I also collaborated closely with him when we wrote the 'Aberford in Times Past' book. He was a most kind, helpful and community-minded man whose death is a loss to the village".

Freezing fog in early December meant the Hall and Class 3's room were extremely cold all day. However, a few days later the Christmas concert went well as usual with mince pies and hot punch after the performances. There were Santas galore on the 17th: "I was Santa at Barwick School this morning and then, at our infants party this afternoon, Mrs Booth's husband did the honours for us".

New gas convector heaters were installed in the Hall, Class 3 and Resources over the winter break. HM recorded that all staff were very glad for the two week break as the preceding four weeks had been very hectic as always at this time.

When the National and Leeds Authority results of SATs were published, HM was very pleased that the group of top infants at Aberford performed better than the national average. "Subjects tested were English, Reading, Maths and Science".

The P.S.G began to organise some large fund-raising events for a new library. A fashion show raised £125.30. Councillor Wakefield gave a cheque for £250 towards the library in March.

The football team was mentioned from time to time, with mixed fortunes, but HM recorded in February: "Rachel Lee, who played very well, became the first girl to represent the School's football team". On this occasion the team lost 3 – 1 to a much bigger Harewood School side. Some central Government funding allowed the purchase of a new Archimedes A3000 computer with printer and monitor.

March saw work to prepare the external woodwork for painting. It was eventually completed in colours of burgundy and white in the middle of June: "what a dramatic improvement to the outside of the building!"

HM recorded his personal pleasure at becoming a grandfather. His daughter Alison gave birth to a son on the 18th March which made him feel rather old despite being only 48 at this time!

Following a visit by two coaching staff from Leeds United football club, a party of children went to Elland Road ground: " ... to have a conducted tour.... and to watch the first team players train. As Leeds United are currently top of the First Division this proved to be an exciting visit indeed". Oh happy days and how are the mighty fallen at this time in 2009!

A bit of fun in school for April Fool's day: ".. the children .. told of a pet kangaroo called 'Bounce' having escaped in the village with a reward for its recapture. The older children soon realised they were being April-fooled but the infants frequently reported sightings of the missing pet throughout the day".

The annual residential this year had just six children participating with HM helping out teaching the remainder of Class 3 once or twice during the week. He thoroughly enjoyed this opportunity to actually teach.

During the Easter holidays, in an effort to raise funds HM "and other staff members went to Safeways supermarket at Garforth to sell raffle tickets in aid of our new library appeal. Over a period of two days £950 worth of tickets was sold". Eventually the raffle raised £3000. The Spring Fayre enjoyed glorious weather and raised a huge sum of £1000 for the library appeal.

A few weeks later, the total sum raised proved to be a massive £6000 which was a magnificent achievement for a small community and school.

In mid-May HM and the Vice Chair of Governors attended a meeting to discuss the Council's proposal to devolve the whole of the education budget to schools.

The family barbeque in mid-June raised over £400 for P.S.G. funds with a record number of 170 people attending.

Sports Day saw Red team triumph after an interval of 13 years! Photograph No: 7 shows the Team Captains, Ben Piper and Vicky Roberts, holding the shield aloft. Ben remembers giving a little speech (entirely unrehearsed and much to the amazement and pride of his mother) and that Mr Hewitt did a little bit of coaching of Team Captains in future years to prepare them in case their team won. The six pupils who would transfer to Boston Spa School went there for a familiarisation morning and the prospective twelve pupils and parents coming to Aberford School had a morning visit which went well.

In July Class 3 moved: "from their traditional home in the small classroom at the front of the main building to the small mobile so that we can begin the decoration of that room which is to become the new Library". Later the room was painted as was the Hall with new curtains being added.

An end of term staff training day saw each teacher preparing a resource pack: "of photographs, video, street plans etc., to use in the geography element of the National curriculum".

The new school year from September 1992 saw twelve new reception children and two others join school which was a net gain of seven and made 74 pupils enrolled. HM was very pleased with redecoration: "overall appearance splendid and subtle blue/peach colouring (in library) provides a very restful atmosphere. Corridor flooring also completed replacing the awful yellow gloss colour with magnolia and rust red contrast. What a pleasing effect overall in the Hall, corridor and Library – it has given this lovely old building a real lift".

This term the charity 'Help the Aged' was chosen to receive money collected at the Harvest Festival celebration (£41.78) and from concerts/carolling at Christmas (£154.00). The Methodist Minister, John Barnett, spoke to children: "about the legendary Sammy Hick .... famous in the late 18th and early 19th centuries". New football and netball kit had the school and sponsor's logo on it – Swan Hotel.

HM attended courses on 'preparing job descriptions' and 'personnel management'. A further course on 'Teacher appraisal' was attended the following January. P.S.G. continued to be very active organising a Quiz Night, a children's Beetle Drive and a Fashion Show, this latter raising £197 for school and P.S.G. funds. The national fund-raising day for Children in Need raised £77.

The Christmas concert this year was 'The Best Gift of All' from Class 1 and Classes 2 and 3 combined to present 'An Old Time Music Hall'. There was plenty of audience participation in the Old Time Music Hall part of the production! As usual, the recorder and folk guitar players entertained the older folk of the Tuesday Club in the Village Hall and a few days later the residents of Parlington House.

In January of 1993, two students joined school for a five week teaching practice session. HM was pleased that two more children enrolled: "now 78 maintaining the gradual rise throughout the year and which will trigger extra funding in the school budget in the near future".

The P.S.G. agreed to fund a replacement piano plus some other small items and agreed to hold a children's Valentine Disco and an Easter 'hop' for parents. An extra toilet was provided in the Class 1 entrance as the single unit was not adequate for 23 children.

During February HM recorded: "Headteacher Appraisal Day! Another Government initiative means that Headteachers have to be appraised by two appraisers every two years. .... this involved one of my appraisers... observing me negotiating a draft job description with Mrs Ingram..... he and the other appraiser also interviewed each member of staff about their perceptions of how well, or otherwise, I manage them as a team. I shall receive more feedback after half term".

At this point in early February 1993 HM came to the end of one Log Book and began another and reproduced here is what he wrote:

"To begin writing a new School Log Book is a rare event indeed and yet, writing today, Thursday February 11th 1993, it makes me realise that it does not seem long at all since I began the previous log on September 25th 1981. During that period of 12 years, the changes that took place were considerable – two generations of children passed through school, all the staff with the exception of myself has changed, the number of pupils on roll has fallen from 108 to 78 and the building itself has changed considerably albeit in cosmetic ways. I have no doubt that by the time the next new Log Book is started more changes will have taken place, but let us hope that they will all have been changes for the better and that there will have been plenty of good teaching and learning, good friendship and good humour along the way."

The new piano arrived in March and HM recorded his mixed feelings: "... the old Hilton.. has been in school for some fifty years or more.... sad to see it go though as it has featured in so many singing lessons, assemblies and concerts and been the tuneful partner to the voices of thousands of children. I suppose it's a sign of the times too that the replacement, a Reid Sohn, although German-sounding, was actually made in Korea". A few days later a Mr Gott visited to give a concert of music on the new instrument – he had previously been employed direct by the L.E.A. to visit schools and had been many times previously to Aberford school. HM recorded that "this sort of enrichment service has been lost to schools with the advent of school budgets".

There were two bits of good news in March – the children had won three first prizes in a Road Safety competition and the 1993/1994 school budget had been set at £156,872 with a planned expenditure of £141,064.00 which would give a healthy looking projected surplus. The upbeat mood was continued when the football team beat Bramham 4 – 2 after being behind by 2 – 0 early in the game. Later, in May, this success was followed by another victory over Harewood with a 6 – 1 score. In March there was a presentation to the children who had won prizes and this was filmed by Yorkshire Television and an article appeared in the Yorkshire Post.

Towards the end of April HM and Mrs Booth took a party of 23 children to Cober Hill for their residential week. Mrs Booth used her car and HM drove a mini bus and there was good weather for the many activities. However, HM recorded that it was a poor spring and early summer.

June 7th marked HM's 50th birthday and staff and children had gifts and cards for him. A staff birthday party was held at lunchtime and he enjoyed his day. The next day 'our' police horse 'Aberford' visited with his rider P.C. Smith who talked to the children about his work and HM got to ride the horse as a birthday treat, as did some of the children.

As usual the Gala Queen and attendants were chosen 'by lot' and this year the Queen was Rachel Lock with Jessica Bradley, Rebecca Dawson, Sarah Cowling and Lucy Jackson as attendants.

Yellow team won the Sports day competitions and a few days later a temporary addition to pupil numbers when a little American girl, who was visiting a family in the village, began to attend school for a few weeks to the end of term. Another visitor was Rev. Douglas Moore and newly appointed Vicar. At a Governors' meeting, Mrs Ingram was appointed 'acting Deputy Head' to be reviewed annually. The annual family barbeque raised over £450 for funds.

HM attended yet another course: 'Managing the Primary Curriculum' – a wide-ranging challenging course raising issues right across the primary sector. A few days later he attended an OFSTED course on school inspections.

Twelve children with parents visited school and spent a morning in Class 1 and year 5 pupils went to Boston Spa School. Parents consultation evening went well as usual with a number of verbal compliments paid to the school and staff.

HM recorded his sadness that the classical guitar lessons would no longer be funded in the coming year because of cuts in music expenditure and the small group at Aberford would have to be disbanded. The seven mums who had been helping various classes during the year were invited to have a buffet lunch with staff. This year there were eleven children leaving.

There was a note of weariness when HM recorded: " Personally, I have found it a very tiring year with more new schemes, systems and initiatives thought up by central and local Government and other quangos such as Ofsted and the National Curriculum Council. All these new initiatives mean extra work as, although they are no doubt intended to improve education and raise standards, they in fact drain the physical and mental resources of teachers and Headteachers and leave them with less energy to devote to the pupils in their care!"

In September there were 79 pupils enrolled, divided into three classes. Class 3 had three year groups and Mrs Knowles began to help Mrs Booth with that class. During the first few days there was heavy rain which prevented outdoor play and the noisy lunchtimes upset one or two of the new little children: "who cried and asked when mum was coming to collect them".

The Harvest Festival collection raised £77.20 for the charity Royal National Institute for the Blind. Rev Moore started taking a morning assembly in school on Thursdays and HM reported he had a good rapport with the children. After half-term the long-promised second toilet was finally installed for the infants.

HM attended two Ofsted courses; 'inspection process in P.E.' and ' the quality and range of the curriculum' In November a lengthy Governors' meeting was held: " .. a long agenda and a lot of correspondence which is symptomatic and indicative of the increasingly bureaucratic world we live in. ...... agreed to write to Lane Fox and Partners about the possibility of school obtaining a piece of ground area adjacent to the school playground for recreational purposes".

The Christmas production this year was 'The Snow Robin' from Class 1 and 'A Christmas Carol' by Classes 2 and 3. There were two evening and one afternoon performances with over 110 attending each of the evening ones and 60 the afternoon concert. A total of £92.67 was raised for the R.N.I.B.

In mid-March there was a visit from the Havergal College Girls Choir: "The 40 strong choir sang for the school and we returned the compliment singing 'Colours of the Day'. This was a repeat of the visit a previous Havergal Choir made in March 1984 and which I remember well. ... the girls went on to York to sing on Radio York and in York Minster".

The budget for the year 1994/95 was set at £152.490 so that, with a surplus carried forward of £20,000 HM felt there would be no difficulty with operating costs: "but in the medium to long term savings are clearly going to have to be made".

In April the P.S.G. met to organise the social programme for the summer and agreed to fund the purchase of an electric clay kiln so that the children's artwork could be fired. The Spring Fayre actually raised £1056 towards this kiln. Unusually for HM he was absent ill from April 18th to 27th.

In early May HM mentioned the new Key Stage 2 pilot tests for 11 year-olds "The results of these trial tests will not be reported this year".

The amount of vehicle movements over School Lane and in the area where it joined Main Street started to be of concern. The crossing lady, Mrs Foxcroft, raised the matter with HM. At this time there was a car repair business operating from premises along School Lane and HM asked the owner if his customers could refrain from using the lane when children were going to and from school. In addition the Governors' meeting agreed to several measures including: "contact the Church to seek their views on stopping parking on the church apron at the bottom of School Lane, erect two signs in School Lane to warn car drivers of the dangers of children... write to parents asking them for their co-operation in not parking near the bottom of School Lane". HM had to reinforce the request to parents by sending out a further letter a few weeks later.

In June the L.E.A. Security Adviser came to discuss the general security measures "to help to keep out unwelcome strangers". Later in the year, security handles were fitted to external doors and signs directed visitors to the one door which now gave access into school with other doors being exits only. The local community constable P.C. Norman attended the area at the bottom of School Lane at home time to help discourage parents from parking in that area.

Computers began to play a much larger part in the administration of school. In mid July: "Along with the School Secretary, Mrs Whyte, I went to the M.I.S. Centre at West Park to have an introductory meeting concerning the planned installation in Sept/Oct. of a SIMS computer system which incorporates a word processor. This will computerise all our data on pupil records etc., as well as putting onto computer disc the ordering and accounting procedures, all of which are currently undertaken manually. Certainly, in the short term, it will involve a lot of work to establish the system, learn the procedures and enter all the initial data".

Later in July interviews for two non-teaching posts were held. One was a temporary 15 hours per week post in Class 1 and one for a Special Needs Assistant 'to work with two statemented pupils' in Class 3. Nine children moved on to senior school this year and another two children left to go into private education.

The September term opened with 80 children enrolled, 13 of them were in reception class and HM recorded that everyone was in school colours and/or uniform. The new Teaching Assistants began work – Mrs Sanders and Mrs Barratt. The new L.E.A. peripatetic pianist began to come to school every Tuesday morning – Michelle Lean had played in school for a long time and was well known to all. Later in the month HM recorded that, following a freak accident when a large tree branch fell onto a walker in Parlington Park killing him and injuring others, HM asked for the lime tree in the playground to be inspected together with the large trees in Vicarage Drive. Following inspection the lime tree was pronounced as healthy but some of the old trees in Vicarage Drive required attention and the owner was contacted.

The SIMS computer system was installed in school and HM and Mrs Whyte had to attend several training courses over the rest of the school year.

Children had a visit from a 'corn dolly' maker and a talk about hedgehogs and animal welfare in general. Classes 1 and 3 had a session on making computer-linked music.

Teacher appraisals were mentioned in November: "... All appraisals and reviews were completed on time for July 1994 and the new two year cycle began in September 1994". November also saw the launch of a national campaign to immunise all children between the ages of 5 and 16 against measles and almost all the Aberford pupils had the injection. The midday supervisor, Mrs Turner, left and was replaced by Mrs Dorothy Foxcroft. The National Grid [electricity] office, which was housed at Becca Hall, donated £300 to school funds which was used to refurbish the outdoor playground furniture. Personal pupil data was entered into the SIMS system.

The Christmas concert this year was Class 1 performing 'The Smallest Angel' and Classes 2 and 3 a mixture of carols, songs and comedy called 'All the Fun of Christmas'. There were the usual festivities which always resulted in quite tired children and staff at this time of the year.

The new year of 1995 was to herald a change of leadership for Aberford School. HM had a period of absence due to illness for two weeks. The weather was very cold with snow at times and children having to be kept indoors at playtime.

The Chair of Governors must have been rather surprised when HM informed him in early February that he intended to take early retirement at the end of the school year. HM told him that he had not felt well for over a year and: "I am also tired of the constant changes and new schemes and initiatives which seem to appear almost daily. It is like operating on shifting sands and working in this way I believe eventually takes its toll and has left me mentally, if not physically, exhausted. For these reasons and after sixteen years as Headteacher, I think that now is the best time for both myself and the school for a change". HM informed staff and sent a letter to parents and received numerous good wishes and sentiments of regret in return. Indeed many of the children seemed genuinely upset when they heard the news.

However, the life of the school continued as normally as possible throughout the rest of the school year with arrangements being made to find a new Headmaster. There were initially 29 applicants and interviews took place after Easter with Mr B. Young, the Deputy Headteacher of St. Chad's School in Headingley being appointed.

As HM's time drew to a close he was very pleased that negotiations were concluded with the owners of a piece of land next to the schoolyard, to enable school to lease the land for a 'soft' play area. The lease was signed in April: "I have to admit to a feeling of satisfaction and great pleasure".

In June a major repair of the Hall ceiling was undertaken which caused much disruption and dirt within school. The Hall floor became ankle deep in dust and rubble! Cleaning was a major operation after the repairs were completed but eventually by early July all was restored.

HM was a guest of the Lord Mayor at a reception for retiring Headteachers in July and recorded the occasion as being quite 'genteel' and 'old fashioned' but very enjoyable: "no gold watch or cut glass decanter, more a cup of tea, a sandwich and a 'pat on the head'.

On July 18th a retirement party was held in school with over a hundred parents, Governors, L.E.A. Officers, staff past and present and family and friends. The Director of Education attended: "I was given two splendid gifts – an inscribed carriage clock from Governors and staff and a camping fridge to use on our caravan holidays by the parents. The whole evening was, for me, totally memorable. The atmosphere was warm and supportive, the Hall looked marvellous, the food and drink of the highest standard, the music was great and the company even better. I had a truly fantastic send off and it was a night I think I shall never forget".

There followed an afternoon surprise party with the children and two police horses made an appearance – one of them 'our Aberford'. HM must have been particularly thrilled: "The horses were ridden by two policewomen ......I taught Melanie Smith at my first school, Methley Junior in 1969, I taught Elisabeth Pharoah at my second school, Woodlesford Langdale, in 1977 and around me were the pupils both young and old from here at Aberford C of E – the three generations of children I have taught – a very moving experience for me personally".

On HM's last day he recorded his final words, some of which are given here: "I shall finish with the words I always say to the Year 6 leavers and which I shall say this afternoon at the closing assembly. 'I hope that, when you leave Aberford School, you will be able to say you worked hard and played hard and remember that you will leave a little bit of yourselves behind and take a little bit of this school with you wherever you go in the future'. I hope it's true for the children and I hope it's true for me too. Keith Hewitt. July 21st 1995

Chapter Nineteen
THE YOUNG YEARS

Mr Bob Young began his time as Headmaster on the 4th of September 1995 and here is what he first wrote in the most beautiful handwriting of all the Headteachers: "It is with a deep sense of history that I begin my tenure as Headteacher of Aberford C of E Primary School. I look forward to leading the school into the 21st Century and the challenges ahead".

There were 82 children enrolled at this time. Computerisation of paperwork continued: "Great satisfaction was had when we were able to produce Class lists from the computer for the first time at Aberford Primary". As usual with a new HM, there were lots of meetings with various L.E.A. departments and individuals: induction meetings for Head Teachers, someone from the Finance Office to go through ordering and reconciliation with HM and Mrs Davies, a visit from the School Link Advisor and a parents and friends association meeting with 15 parents and 5 members of staff. SIMS computer training continued for Mrs Davies and there were several more sessions for both her and HM on financial and budget matters.

HM was told an OFSTED inspection would take place beginning on the 6th November and thought it very short notice as some schools had received a term's notice: "amount of work to do before then is staggering". An insight into what such an inspection involved can be gained from the Log starting 19th October: "Lead

Inspector arrived... He spent the morning in school, first talking to me, then to Mrs Sanders and Mr Moore (Governors) and finally to staff. He left with the completed paperwork and two large files containing Policy Documents and other school procedures and details". On 6th Nov: "2 Inspectors in from Monday noon until Thursday p.m. The Lay Inspector was in all day Tuesday, while the Section 13 person attended 4 assemblies. They observed 43 lessons and interviewed the Chair of Governors and then each subject co-ordinator. The whole week was very stressful but the children were excellent while the staff performed magnificently. Everyone worked for each other and a good sense of teamwork developed". On the 10th Nov: "sighs of relief all round".

A few days later there was good feedback from the inspection: "This was a verbal report back but it was very pleasing. It begins with the words 'Aberford C.E. School is a good school which serves its pupils well.....' All that hard work was rewarded".

Towards the end of November there was a non-uniform day in aid of the Children in Need appeal. Mrs Foxcroft joined in and £100 was raised. To encourage children to consider the wider world, HM attended a meeting concerning multi-national links between primary schools. "Class 3 have this term written to Class 4/5C at Hagabersskolen in Lindesberg, Sweden. We are waiting for our first reply. Class 1 are also to write to some younger children at the same school".

The Christmas concert this year was 'Why Choose the Angel' with: "lovely special costumes made by 2 mums – Mrs Sanders and Mrs Dyson". As there had only been three weeks to plan and rehearse for this year it was a real team effort involving parents, staff and children. The usual busy parties and carol concerts took place and HM played 'Santa' at Barwick Primary School: "another first!"

There were one or two burst pipes in school over the Christmas break of 1995 which saw very low temperatures of minus 7 degrees Centigrade. However the normal routine of school was soon resumed and a group of children and parents went to see a pantomime – 'Mother Goose' in Castleford. HM recorded: "had an enjoyable evening – Oh yes we did!"

There were visits from two different Reading Scheme Representatives "as we are considering the introduction (phased) of a new scheme". HM attended a meeting to discuss links with Europe and talked about the links developing with a Swedish primary school with the exchange of information, pictures etc. regarding customs and traditions. Mrs Cliff attended a 'preparation for KS1 SATS' and reported more changes! Staff development meetings were held to set priorities for the year. Parents of Class 1 children came into school to see their assembly and appreciated the invitation. Later, parents of Class 2 children repeated the exercise.

It was pleasing to everyone that the school featured in the Yorkshire Evening Post towards the end of February: 'Small School makes Big Impression' following the OFSTED Report. The Director of Education wrote to School to praise the result.

HM recorded a budget cut for 1996/97: "Even with a carry forward of £14,000, we have to make cuts of £5,000. After much thought and discussions ..... all temporary contracts are to be cut. These were – Deputy Head, 11 hrs Admin Assistant and 14 hrs Classroom Assistant. Not a happy situation and next year could be worse, when the likelihood is we will have to lose a teacher". The school had been funded for pupil numbers from January 1996 of 84 but there were only 79 enrolled.

In late April HM found, after attending a computer course, that it was possible to produce all sorts of "wonderful items on the office computer – or rather Mrs Davies is able!"

HM and Mr B. Hogg (Governor) carried out a Health and Safety Risk Assessment around school which had been highlighted by the OFSTED Report and found there was much flaking paint and mould internally. The assessment would be presented to the Governors' Meeting and a copy to Building Division with the hope of getting some major repairs done to the fabric of the building especially to roof which HM thought needed replacing.

SATS examinations were held during two weeks in May causing a huge amount of work for the class teacher Mrs Cliff. The Spring Fayre was again a great success with £1070 raised. This money was spent on a computer with CD ROM and some new benches for the playground. HM attended a driving test for a minibus so as to be able to take children in Wetherby Community Bus.

There were two staff training days for report writing: "the very detailed reports to parents are extremely time-consuming for staff to prepare".

Governors were informed of the proposed budget and the implications that staff would need to be reduced: "it was decided that a Staff/Governors meeting/social would be arranged to discuss various issues". This, the first meeting of its kind, was held in early July with discussions covering many school issues.

The children who would be moving to senior school were given the opportunity to talk to a member of staff from, or to visit, their chosen school. Unlike in most previous years, where all went to Boston Spa School, the choice was mostly split between that school and Garforth Community College which had been rising in its examination performance ratings.

HM attended a residential weekend at Ripon St Johns on 'the Church School Ethos' but it was interrupted by the urgent need to view the Euro'96 England v Spain match which England won on penalties, only to lose to Germany in the semi-final!

Children from Swarcliffe Primary School visited in late June: "as part of their village study...... the third school this term.... The Swarcliffe children were amazed by the smallness of our Hall but loved our school field and playground".

At the end of June Mrs Booth secured a new appointment as Seconded Advisory Teacher for I.T. to start from September for at least a year, possibly two. HM recorded his appreciation of her and that her class would be taught jointly by Mrs Knowles and himself, with Mrs Knowles teaching fulltime. The budget savings would be most welcome.

A final canoe session was held at Yeadon Tarn for Class 6 with all of the children ending up in the water. Surely by design! "3 very successful sessions to be repeated next year". The family barbeque saw over 180 adults and children attending with straw bales and barbecues loaned by Bob Richmond. Reference to the 'beef scare' was made with pork burgers instead of beef being used. At this time there was apprehension about a fatal neurological disease being transmitted to humans through the consumption of certain beef products and many people wanted to minimise risk by avoiding beef products.

An Evening Post photographer came to school to take a picture of Luke Sanders who had never had a day off school in his seven years. "Luke puts it down to always being ill during holidays and at weekends". Was there a note of regret in Luke's words? The photo and article appeared in the paper dated 10th July. In mid July two teachers from a school on Crete came to visit: ".... were in Leeds on a European project with older children...   Hara and Sifis talked to the children, answered many questions and finally taught them some Greek dancing". Mrs Timms was still holding a guitar group which gave a concert for the school on the 12th July with Mrs Whyte and Miss Wilkinson taking part in an excellent performance. In the afternoon Classes 3 and 2 went to Sherburn Primary to watch: "a very polished exhibition of movement to music". There was very hot weather at the end of this month and Class 1 enjoyed a Teddy Bears Picnic type party in the playground, Class 2 had a Pirates Party with games led by 'Captain Cliff' and Class 3 had a party with lots of silly games.

When School re-opened in September there were 83 children enrolled arranged in 3 Classes. The P.F.A. meeting decided on social events for the term and "agreed that we could spend around £800 on books in order to set up our own fiction library". The chosen charity for the year was the N.S.P.C.C.

In October two students from L.M.U. visited: "both seem very young". They were to be in School for a year under the new 'mentoring system' with school receiving a small amount of money (£250 per student) and Mrs Cliff overseeing their 'hands-on training'. Mrs Cliff had to attend a student mentoring course at L.M.U. Harvest Festival collection resulted in £93 being given to the N.S.P.C.C. There was a sad personal record in late October when HM's father died and he had to leave school just after the start of the day.

In early November four members of staff went to Morley Books and spent £1000 on library books, obtaining 248 books "which will be covered and catalogued for us (£800 from P.F.A.)". In late November the Librarian attended school and told stories to each class with books available to buy after school on two evenings. In a sign of the times, some 40 parents and staff attended a 'Drugs Awareness Evening'.

There was a Swedish visitor in school for a day in early December "she talked to class 3 and baked Swedish bread and cake with them". The concert this year was 'Hosanna Rock' with the usual 'full houses' and favourable comments from parents. Around £100 was collected from the carolling around the village and went to the N.S.P.C.C. Some children performed songs from the concert for the residents of Parlington House and to the Tuesday Club in the Village Hall. A visiting Theatre Group performed a play for the children in the afternoon of the last day of the term.

The first entry for January 1997 recorded that Mrs Knowles was to attend a 10 day LEA-funded course: "for co-ordinators of R.E. to write a policy/scheme of work and define the School's ideas about R.E." HM and Mrs Davies only took an hour to complete the computer data entry for all 84 children enrolled. HM attended a meeting about Government legislation for Assessment of Reception children.

A 'Family of Schools' was set up in the area – HM had to attend several meetings – the grouping consisted of two high schools (Wetherby and Boston Spa) and twenty-five primaries. The group was "looking to pool resources and co-operate in several ways e.g. to purchase PCs and link up via the Internet".

A new style family service started in Church which the new Vicar, Douglas Moore, had been promoting in school during the week.

Later in February Mrs Cox, who was a Governor, went into school to get to know the old place again – it will be remembered that her father Mr Cowell had been HM for very many years; she had attended school as a child and had taught for many years there herself before moving to a Head Teacher post elsewhere. She began to take the occasional assembly which was a welcome change.

In March HM discussed with the owner's agent the renewing of the lease for the land on which a mobile classroom stood: "we talked about turning the overgrown patch into an environmental area with a pond, wild flowers etc....... since houses were planned for the old farm ... might not be appropriate. ... to get back to me".

In April the LEA schools security officer called to discuss with HM how the site could be made safer. This was difficult to achieve with its open nature. Also in this month Mrs Cliff began the Key Stage 1 SATs with Year 2 which were to take about a month to complete – "extremely time consuming". In May K.S.2 SATs were held which had taken on more importance since the publication of results in newspapers.

Class 3 visited Becca Hall which was the Northern H.Q. of the National Grid for electricity at this time before the industry was privatised. "Very impressive visit and the last school to see it working before it closes". Subsequently this large property reverted to a private house.

HM visited the Records Office in Kew, London whilst on a course in the capital and he searched for any Trust Deeds about Aberford School but found none. In mid May he attended a meeting of some 200 Head Teachers in London: "the idea being to involve successful primary schools in the training of student teachers. This did not receive much enthusiasm from the gathering of Heads".

The annual residential for class 3 was to Cober Hill with exciting visits to Scarborough Sealife Centre, a Shire Horse Farm, Boggle Hole to fossil hunt, rock pooling etc., Much work followed back at school as usual from this visit.

In June there was a visitor from a company which rented out brass instruments and encouraged lessons in schools. There was a demonstration and talk to children and parents. This resulted in 4 children wanting to learn saxophone, 2 cornet, 1 flute and 1 clarinet starting in September.

There was a new initiative by parents from the PFA when an evening spring clean took place: "cleaning cookers, weeding, clearing cupboard and painting. A parent provided a tractor and trailer which was quickly filled". This effort was repeated in subsequent years.

Late in June a parent – Mr Robinson – completed 'The 3 Peaks Walk' and raised over £300 for school in sponsorship. Mrs Ingram went on a course about the 'Baseline Assessment': "which is being introduced .... for all children starting school. A part of the D.F.E. policy to assess how much children improve between starting school and being tested at age 7".

Also in June HM went on a course: "which brought together 25 Italian and 25 Yorkshire Teachers ... to find partners .... to bid for 'Comenins' money in order to visit and plan joint curriculum projects. Funded by the E.U. in order to spread understanding of other cultures and lifestyles. ...... this will make the links more formal and allow Teachers to visit our partner schools. Maria Peliti in Rome and Gunilla Akerlind in Lindesberg, Sweden".

There was a memorable day for HM on 16th July: "I was invited by H.R.H. Prince of Wales to a reception at High Grove House. This was, the letter said, in order that Prince Charles could give his support and encouragement to schools which reflect a particularly high standard of teaching. Since only six Leeds schools were invited it was indeed an honour. I went as a representative of the school and feel it reflects well on all at Aberford Primary School, Teachers, non-Teaching staff, parents, Governors and of course the children. It was an interesting reception with drinks in a marquee on the lawn in front of the house. Prince Charles mingled with the 200 Headteachers, gave a short speech, followed by David Blunkett (Sec. of State for Education). We were then given a tour of the gardens, which were all environmentally friendly in design and construction".

The new year which started in September saw pupil numbers increase to 85 with 2 more expected in October and HM recorded: "I am not accepting any more children into Class 3 as, when the children are all together in the afternoons and all day Friday, there are 34 and very little space".

The nearby tennis courts were cleared of vegetation by some Community Service people and the L.E.A. promised to refurbish them after April. The school had a Netball pitch marked on them at this time. The lease for the land on which the classroom for class 3 stood, together with the playground field, was renewed.

In October Mrs Sanders was re-elected as a Parent Govenor. HM began a one evening a fortnight training course on staff development. A month later he had discussions with each member of staff about 'personal development' which were to become yearly meetings "although much informal discussion also takes place". The children's fancy dress disco attracted 90+ children and all teaching staff with many classroom assistants: "reflecting the staff commitment to the school".

Early in November a Park Lane College student began a two week block practice in Class 1. HM recorded that she was just one of many young people on 'work experience' who were now passing through the School. Often these were older pupils from local high schools and an Induction Booklet was specially written for them to introduce them to school and its routines and expectations.

The school cleaning team of Mr and Mrs Gothard retired together with Alice Nicholson who had been a dinner lady for many years. Increased pupil numbers made future school budgets look better in the short-term. "Planning for more than one year at a time is difficult in a small school like ours – slight increases/decreases in pupil numbers make substantial changes in the overall budget".

Seating had to be limited to 120 for the Christmas concerts – still an incredible number to be packed into the school Hall when one considers the space the children needed to perform! In mid-December Mrs Book, who had been on secondment, learned she was to be appointed to Deputy Head of East Garforth Junior School starting from January.

In January 1998 an incubator and twenty-four eggs arrived from Meanwood Valley Farm. HM did not record how successful this venture was. Year 5/6 children had a coaching session organised through Yorkshire Cricket Club. Class 3 visited nearby York Minster. Later in the month HM and Mrs Knowles visited Rome: "we met Maria (Italian teacher), Birgitta and Maud (Swedish teachers) and planned activities for 1998/99 as well as filling in the forms necessary". The visit was funded by the Central Board for Educational Visits and Exchanges.

More paperwork for teachers in February: "Staff meeting to discuss our newly introduced Curriculum Support Diaries. Each Subject Co-ordinator to record anything undertaken for their subject". In early March HM attended a course: "Target Setting, another Government initiative. Targets have to be set for year 6 pupils June 2000 (Maths and English)".

March had plenty of variety: a family quiz was organised by Mr and Mrs Cliff, there was a book fair week with books for sale and story telling sessions and a Canadian Choir sang for the children as they were staying in Aberford as part of their tour of the U.K. Although HM did not say who they were, they were surely our 'friends' the Havergal Choir from Toronto! The 'Investors in People' award scheme was discussed and how to prepare/apply for it.

In April there were training sessions for staff covering First Aid, IT training for Mrs Ingram in English, Mrs Cliff in Science, HM in Maths. There was the annual spring clean with many parents and staff doing various jobs around school. Netball teams A and B had mixed fortunes against Barwick and consisted of both girls and boys.

A National Grid for Leaning briefing session was held in early May: "Government plan to link all schools to the Internet". Interviews were held for the part-time teaching post for 1998/99: "the idea being to create a fourth class to be taught by myself and the new appointment. Helena Angstmann was successful". The Spring Fayre was a great success: "again ably co-ordinated by Mrs Eades (parent of David Y6)" and raised over £1000 despite poor weather. A group of children had their Church of England 'Confirmation ceremony' conducted in York Minster: "a wonderful setting".

The appointment of Mrs Ingram to Deputy Head of Great & Little Preston Primary School meant that there was a vacancy for a KS1 teacher. Mrs Liza Curtis was appointed to start from September and she was a newly qualified teacher. There was a 'leaving event' for Mrs Ingram with a presentation.

In mid July, HM Mrs Cliff and Mrs Knowles attended a two day session on 'literacy training': "Government introducing a 'literacy hour' every day for all children. Funding for books seems quite generous".

Sadly the school had suffered some vandalism during the summer break but not much damage was done. Pupil numbers had increased although the figure was not given and there were now four classes with Mrs Curtis taking Reception and Year 1, Mrs Cliff Years 2/3, Mrs Knowles Years 4/5, HM and Mrs Angstmann Years 5/6. In addition Mrs Whyte continued as a fulltime non-teaching assistant, Mrs Walton was in Class 1 in the afternoons and there were three other SNAs working a variety of part-time hours – Mrs Phelan, Mrs Walker and Mrs Moore. Mrs Davis was in the office and more chairs had to be purchased for the staffroom.

Swimming lessons re-commenced for Class 2: "very few ... fail to learn to swim after 2 years". The P.F.A. meeting was attended by 10 parents and 4 staff and a committee was set up "for the first time, although this was not terribly formal. Mrs J Hills – Chair, Mrs D. Kirby and Mrs L Tiffany – Secretary".

Mrs Curtis attended a Baseline Assessment course and later in the month an induction course for newly qualified Teachers and discussed a series of courses to be attended throughout the year. She also discussed Baseline Assessment of the Reception Children with the 2 Class Assistants.

In late October HM met with a representative of 'Network Connections': "the company chosen to install the computer network. The cost, which will be met through the Government NGFL grant, will be the region of £8000". Mrs Knowles the Special Needs Co-ordinator met with parents of all children on the Special Needs Register to discuss individual progress.

In December a 'shared review' took place. "The LEA plan these to be a yearly event which reviews progress, results SDP etc. The meeting lasted 3 hours and was very searching – but useful in the light of our being notified of another OFSTED Inspection in the summer term 1999".

The carolling around the village raised over £90 for the 'Children's Heart Foundation' at St James Hospital in Leeds this year. 'Sheik Rattle and Roll' was the Christmas production this year with tickets restricted. Staff had a night out at L.A. Bowl in Leeds with a meal afterwards but HM does not record who won the bowling!

After a well-earned break, one of the first things to be tackled on the HM's return in January 1999 was to meet several publishers' representatives concerning the 'literacy hour' materials they were able to provide. "We eventually invested some £2000 in the Heinemann scheme to run alongside our reading scheme". Later in the month: "We have finally finished our video for our European Project and received the Swedish and Italian effort. All 3 are to be combined professionally by a local firm. Ours lasts 14 minutes but took 2 hours to edit. It shows our preparations for Christmas – Christingle making, chocolate log making, concert rehearsals and Father Christmas' visit to Class 1. The final video is very impressive and shows wonderfully the similarities and differences between the 3 Countries".

A month later Mrs Cliff and Mrs Knowles visited Sweden and met up with Mrs Peliti from Rome. Many plans were made and: "they returned tired but full of enthusiasm for the project, having stayed with the Swedish staff and been extremely well looked after".

Mrs Angstmann was proving to be an enthusiastic and well-organised Teacher but found the sharing of a class with HM hard work due to his non-teaching commitments. She did a 'singing slot' at the Easter Bonnet festivities later in the year.

HM began to attend the many meetings required of him throughout the rest of the school year and one Governor went into school concerning design and technology and another to observe the literacy hour in operation. A supply teacher took year 5 children for a few Wednesdays so that HM could concentrate on year 6 children: "paid for by Government 'Booster Class money'. The idea being to boost the SAT results of the Year 6 pupils".

This next entry surely indicates that statistics can often be made to mean anything! A chap from the Assessment and Achievement Unit visited to discuss the PANDA (Performance and Assessment) Report. "This analyses our Test Results for the last 3 years and compares our children's performances with those in like schools. He agreed that we were broadly in line with comparable schools but, because of our small year group numbers, fluctuations were common and so analysis of results had to be taken with a pinch of salt".

Preparations started for the forthcoming OFSTED inspection with questionnaires being sent out to parents to get their views about the school.

HM recorded in April that the school was being used for various meetings by villagers at this time: Neighbourhood Watch, Parish Council and the Yorkshire Country Women's Association.

In May HM mentioned the plan to celebrate the forthcoming Millenium. "Mrs Cliff introduced the idea ....to produce a large plaque made up of children's claywork .... placed outside on a wall and be constructed by a local artist. Funding has been applied for ... from the National Lottery".

KS1 SATs began mid-May and KS2 children took the national tests in Maths, English and Science: "also this year we are undertaking the voluntary SATs for Years 3/4 & 5 in order to track children's progress more closely and identify any general areas of weakness and to target individual children". Eight large folders of documents were collected by the Lead Inspector having taken a considerable time to put together and he met with the Chair of Governors, two parents and staff and took the parents questionnaires. HM had a visit from a nearby Headteacher whose school had been inspected by the same team which was to inspect Aberford and he made some reassuring comments. The anxious feelings and workload such inspections engender certainly 'come off the page' to a reader of the Log. Mrs Cliff had to put on hold her 50th birthday celebrations!

14th June – inspection week. "... they would watch 46 lessons, assemblies, registrations, playtimes, lunchtimes etc. ..... meetings with curriculum co-ordinators, followed by close examination of the children's work samples which continued into Tuesday. .. talked to parents, Govenors, staff ... children were questioned closely and really did themselves proud. The feedback.... extremely positive with some 10 items listed as things the school does well and just 3 weaknesses. . minute observation".

HM praised everyone for their efforts when Friday finally arrived and bought flowers for staff and sweets for the children. Lunch was sandwiches from the Arabian Horse pub nearby, eaten on the school field and he recorded "What difference a day makes!". The Inspection Report was, as might be expected by those who know the school, a very good one.

In late June six Swedish teachers visited school: "staying in a small Hotel in north Leeds" and they visited Mr and Mrs Cliff's home for an enjoyable meal. These ladies sang at an assembly and visited every classroom. They were taken to a production at the West Yorkshire Playhouse Theatre in the evening. On a further occasion visits were made to the city centre, Art Gallery and Civic Theatre with Classes 3 and 4. A buffet meal was put on in school with all staff and many partners attending along with Governors and some parents.

More training in late June: "3 days of Numeracy Training with all staff attending for at least 1 day......much better than last years Literacy Days .... the idea being to introduce a 'Numeracy Hour' for all children..".

In these 'glory days' of the local football team Leeds United, Classes 3 and 4 visited their stadium: "The children particularly enjoyed sitting in the Dressing Room which had many of the famous players' shirts hanging up".

In July there was a second canoeing session for the Year 6 children: "Never had so many fall in accidently – emptying the canoes proved difficult as I was on my own on this occasion". Maybe some of the fallers went in more by design than accident if the day was a hot one!

A Governors' meeting discussed 'Home/School Agreement'. "Another new Government initiative to encourage Home/School contact. Not really needed in our school ...." Obviously at Aberford School there is ongoing contact and involvement with parents.

Class 1 loved their visit to Becca Hall Farm where Mr and Mrs Richmond made sure they had a very enjoyable visit "the children talked and talked about the animals they had seen on their return...." At the Class 4 Assembly the children dressed as Teachers: "Andrew Hogg was me in a bright shirt and sunglasses singing 'Do You Want to be in My Gang' (as per Gary Glitter)".

Mrs Angstmann left at the end of the school year, her part-time post being taken by Mrs Alison Wall, a newly qualified Teacher. A lunch was held for those mothers who had helped in school throughout the year and there were many tearful goodbyes from the children leaving this year.

When the new school year started in September 1999 the staff comprised Mrs Curtis in charge of Reception and Year 1, Mrs Cliff with years 2/3, Mrs Knowles with years 4/5 and Mrs Wall and HM sharing years 5/6. Mrs Whyte had mornings in Class 1, afternoons in the other classes. Mrs McNally was in Class 1 as a special needs assistant due to the numbers of children requiring extra help and 3 other ladies continuing to work part-time as SEN assistants on temporary contracts of varying hours.

There were difficulties with a new child in Class 2 who was being fostered by a family in the village. "He has proved extremely disruptive, displaying unheard of behaviour at this school". There followed discussions, telephone calls and visits from various 'agencies' involved with the child which took up a huge amount of staff time. "Mrs Cliff is trying various strategies but very little improvement in behaviour seen. Luckily she is a very experienced and dedicated teacher. A SEN Assistant has had to be diverted from several other children in order to remove the child from the classroom at times".

An assessment took place to see if the school could obtain 'Investors in People' status. "Feedback at 5.00p.m. confirmed we had achieved the required standard in staff development, training etc., An excellent achievement". Later in September: "Lyndele Fozard (artist) attended our weekly staff meeting to discuss our 'Millenium Project' – a clay plaque for the front of the school." The artist was to later work with each class during the course of a week. Each child would have a piece of claywork placed within a large 'church window' shaped plaque and the finished piece greets the visitor to the school at the present time. A grant of £1700 was obtained to pay for the work.

In October the Early Years Advisor called to work with Mrs Curtis – "the first of several visits to give advice on organisation, planning etc." HM spent two hours with Mrs Knowles writing a SEN report on the child with behavioural problems. Another course was attended by HM: "update on the latest Government Initiative – 'Appraisal and Performance Management'. This looks to involve considerable administration!"

Staff discussed their first European Education Project task for the year. A booklet was to be produced and the British contribution was to be the legend of Robin Hood. "The older children will précis the story into 14/15 sentences, one for each page with a picture. ..... The Swedish plan is to do Thor and Italians Romulus and Remus".

An internal audit proved satisfactory but Mrs Davies had been "extremely busy producing paperwork, mostly computer generated". Mrs Knowles and HM attended a training day in mid-November concerning 'Booster Class ideas'. "A Government Initiative to increase standard of children who are unlikely to achieve Level 4 at Key Stage 2 (11 year-olds). The Government has sent targets for these children – 80% in English, 75% in Maths".

A well-known figure about the school, Mrs Trayford who was a lunchtime supervisor for 25 years, retired at her 65th birthday. "A presentation was made and the children sang Happy Birthday at lunchtime".

The concert this year was 'a Victorian Music Hall' which played to the usual packed audiences . A meeting was held abut the design of a school website to be funded from the European Project grant. All the computers were shut down for the Christmas break at this significant year end for there was worldwide worry that they might be affected by the time change to the new millenium. (The so-called 'Millenium Bug'). However, these fears proved to be groundless.

So the school passed another milestone in its history as it continued into the new year of 2000 and though this volume ceases at the date of 2000, Mr Young was to continue until December 2007. It seemed only fair to reproduce what he had to say upon his slightly early retirement:

"21st December 2007 – Final assembly led by Mrs Cliff with the Hall packed with children, staff and parents, with my wife and son and daughter as surprise guests. Lots of kind wishes, thoughts and fantastic presents – most notably a signed Berwick Rangers shirt! After 12 years and a term I am leaving a fantastic school with an excellent staff and wonderful children. As the Chair of Governors commented recently 'we have secured a new Headteacher who will sustain the wonderful ethos Mr Young has nurtured and take the work of our school forward with the same values and spirit very much in mind'. Bob Young Dec 2007."

Postscript:

Mr Young recalled that one of his proudest moments during his time at Aberford school was when he went to Highgrove House to meet Prince Charles when the school was recognised for the high standard of teaching.   He also remembered being called out to the playground one lunchtime to find the children enthralled at the sight of a cow giving birth in the field next door. A great cheer went up when the calf appeared and struggled to its feet! Over the history of the school this was probably a sight seen by many children.

APPENDIX I
LADY ELIZABETH HASTINGS
(AND QUEENS COLLEGE)

During these early years Aberford School was one of many such institutions to benefit from the charity of Lady Elizabeth Hastings. Leeds Central Library has a copy of a book written about her life which is extremely interesting (Medhurst, Reverend C.E: "Life and Work of Lady Elizabeth Hastings" published 1914, R. Jackson.) The following information was extracted from this little book.

Lady Elizabeth was the daughter of Theophilus Hastings, 7th Earl of Huntingdon and her mother was the daughter of a very wealthy East India merchant with vast estates including the Manor of Ledstone which was bought from the son of Lord Strafford. She lived in various places in her early life but did not marry and settled at Ledstone. She was a very pious and charitable lady and gave away a fortune during her lifetime to very many good causes:

List of Charitable Acts by LEH:

1 Orphanage founded and maintained
1 Orphanage part-maintained
10 Elementary or Charity Schools (as they were called then) and Masters' houses
14 such schools on the Isle of Man
12 Scholarships at Queens College, Oxford
10 Churches being rebuilt or restoration + silver communion vessels and funding for bread and wine
2 Almshouses for men and women
30 Benefices endowed with land and tithes
Funding for 2 Infirmaries – Leeds and York

Many Church Societies benefited such as those for the propagation of the Gospel.

Just before she died in 1739, Lady Elizabeth prepared a Trust Deed which was extremely detailed and stipulated how the income from the property held in trust was to be distributed. At this time

Aberford School would have been in existence for just over 20 years. Within this Deed was a stipulation "the charity school at Aberford the yearly sum of £5.5s.0d to be paid to the Vicar for the time being".

In addition Aberford was mentioned twice more: " Vicarage House at Abbeford – to Rev Mr Bentham or his successor in trust to be by him employed towards rebuilding the Vicarage House the sum of £30 .... Plate – Ferry Fryston, Abbeford, Thorner and Castleford for providing the Parish Churches a silver chalice, paten and flagon – the plate for each Church weighing with the change of old plate now used in the said Church, 66ozs – there to be used at the celebration of the Holy Sacrament for ever."

An extract from the Charities Commission Report of 1897 showed that Lady Elizabeth's bequest to Aberford School had grown:

"Lady Betty Hastings charity:

In pursuance of her directions the sum of £10.10s.0d per year is paid by her trustees to the Master of the school at Aberford, appointed by the Vicar, to instruct the children of the poorer inhabitants in reading and writing and he teaches accordingly about 30 children as free scholars and with other children, paid for by their parents, in a room built by a subscription of the inhabitants. The sum of 40/- per annum is also paid by the trustees to the Churchwardens to find bread and wine for Communion and the surplus if any to be given to the poor and it is duly applied for those purposes."

Not only does Aberford School have a connection to Oriel College, Oxford but the village of Aberford has, in fact, a connection to Queen's College, Oxford via Lady Hastings Trust and this is as follows.

Lady Elizabeth had corresponded with Provost Smith of Queens College, Oxford and she went on to fund some Scholarships there – again she stipulated in great detail how the scholars should be chosen and, as this involved Aberford, the terms are given here for their interest.

Scholarships were to be awarded every five years. Originally for five poor scholars who were to receive £20p.a. to enable them to be maintained at Oxford. By 1914 the Scholarships had risen to 20 scholars each receiving £100p.a. Full details were given by Lady Elizabeth as to how the scholars were to be tested and chosen.

1 poor scholar each from the principal schools in Leeds, Wakefield, Bradford, Beverley, Skipton, Sedborough, Ripon and Sherborne – from Westmorland St Bees and from Cumberland Penrith. These scholars were to be brought to the best Inn in Aberford (Abbeford or Abbeforth) to be tested by seven Vicars from named Parishes – they had to do a translation into Latin of part of an oration by Tulley, 2/3 verses in Latin testament into Greek. In the afternoon 2 subjects – practical divinity out of Church catechism – each boy to give his thoughts in Latin on 8/12 lines, distinguished sentence of a classic author – each boy to give two distichs of verse.

Some 330 boys were helped with Scholarships between 1764 and 1912. Many of them went on to have distinguished careers of various sorts – the majority in the fields of the Church and Education.

A striking picture is brought to mind when one reads about the young applicants being brought to Aberford to be tested by the clergymen and it would be interesting to find out if this indeed happened and how long the practice continued. Perhaps they stayed at the White Swan Inn for it was probably the principal inn. In fact the Queens College Archivist has found no actual evidence that this did occur, but he stated that he had no reason to suppose it did not. In 1860 the situation changed when much of Oxford was being reformed and the Archivist gave this information: "the ordinances were rewritten to state that candidates were to come to Oxford to be examined there instead. The system of closed schools has been long abolished but the Exhibitions live on. When a student (already part of the College) is elected to a Scholarship or Exhibition if he or she is an alumnus of one of the Hastings schools, then they are called a Hastings Scholar. However, the Hastings schools no longer have a head-start in applying to the College".

APPENDIX II
TYTHE BARN/SUBSCRIBERS AND COSTS

The following was amongst papers given to the author by Mr Bob Young, Headmaster of Aberford School and appears to be a copy (typed) of an original letter (not traced). To be lodged with Borthwick Library, University of York 2008.

"To the Reverend Master and Fellows of Oriel College, Oxford

Whereas the Gentlemen, Freeholders and Inhabitants in and about the Parish of Aberford in the County of York, have by their liberal contributions, advanced a considerable sum of money to be paid yearly for and towards the setting up of a charity school in the Town of Aberford to teach poor children to read and write and instructing them in the Knowledge and Practice of the Christian (faith) as it is profest and taught in the Church of England.

Whereby nothing is left undone to ... the benefit of the Town of Aberford (wherein there is abundance of very poor ... Familys where parents are unable to pay for any learning for their children) but the want of a convenient school for the master and children.

And whereas, upon a meeting of the trustees... they found that the master and children could not assemble together with any tolerable case or convenience without creating a new building ... and through many of the .. contributors did again subscribe towards building a school house yet the money... is not sufficient to defray the charge of such a building ...

And whereas there is an ancient decayed Tythe Barn upon the Rectory in the Town of Aberford belonging to Oriel College in Oxford which has been useless to the Farmer of the Tythe for a great many years by reason of another Barn being built upon the said Rectory....

The Farmer of the ... Rectory is willing that (the Tythe Barn)should be applied to the building of the school ... provided the Reverend Masters and Fellows agreed and consent to the same.

Therefore, we whose names are subscribed... do most humbly beseech that you would (instruct) your Tenant to take down the decayed barn and apply the materials towards building such a school... as ... will be, by the blessing of God, a lasting good... to the poor town of Aberford.."

Signed by: J Gascoigne Esq., J Plant, Tenant to ye Rectory, R Potter, Vicar , G. Rhodes, S Duffield, J Cox.

Consent must indeed have been given and the new school was erected using some of the materials of the old Tythe Barn but a great deal of new material was used. The names of subscribers and their subscriptions are listed below:

	£	s	d
Thomas Sampson		5	0
Geo Heptonstall		10	0
Thos Tomlinson		5	0
Jno Brown		5	0
Mr Cox	1	0	0
Rev Mr Dawson	1	0	0
Mr Rhodes	1	0	0
Jno Gascoigne by Val	5	0	0
Valentine Priestman	1	0	0
Mr Appleby	1	0	0
Wm Abbay		2	6
Geo Longley	10	0	
Jno Kay		5	0
Edwd Jackson by Val	10	0	
Mr Akid		5	0
Geo Longley in field	6	3	
Also received by Rev Dawson:			
Mr Appleby	2	0	0
Rev Mr Richardson	1	0	0
Mr Clapham		10	0
Mr Midgeley	10	0	
Rev Mr Mappletoft	1	0	0
Mr Appleby by Wm Akid	1	0	0

287

	£	s	d
Thos Bloome (the SM)		10	0
Mr Appleby by Miles Lowly	1	0	0

The list of costs for building the School are shown below:

	£	s	d
Sparling (Carpenter)			
In earnest of his bargain	1	0	
Ben Lassey the Mason			
And Sparling laying the			
foundation	1	6	
Sparling for the Woodwork	4	0	0
Also for other work not			
in the bargain	1	10	0
The Mason 25roods,5yds			
at 3.6d	4	10	0
Also them for other work	6	6	
Nettletons, their bill of slating,			
Rigging, range stones			
and hearth	6	3	3
Spent when the school			
was reared	1	5	0
In drink at other times	1	6	
Brayfoot about the Plainster	5	10	
Expenses upon the Boon			
Draughts	1	8	8
Math Bucktrout for 8 loads			
Of stone leading		2	6
Wm Abbay 10 deals		15	0
3 sacks of coals to air ye school	1	10	
Matt Laystow setting ye ranges			
2 days		2	0
2 man a day dressing and			
Laying on tabling		2	0
Wm Shires his bill of			
nails,glue etc		13	6
23 bricks to set the ranges			3
Thos Johnson a day's work		1	0
Ed Tarberton ye Glazier his bill	1	1	6

R Nicholson ye Blacksmith			
his bill	2	14	0
Joseph Hague his bill of lime	1	12	3
Lime and Leading Sand		14	0
Latts, carriage	1	0	3
2 Locks		1	8
13 Sacks of Moss		2	2
Wm Akid leading a Load of Slate		3	0
Rob't Akid for a Chair		2	0
Mr Veves for 7 Bush (?) of Hair		3	6
Jno Sparling for a Table		5	0
Boards, Workmanship & Gemmers			
For Window Shuts		11	8
Oil and Ocker to Paint Doors			
Windows and Shutts		5	4
The Plaisterer his Bill	1	15	0
Brayfoot's Daughter an errand			2

To materials wood and stone given to the building valued at £15.0s.0d

Other wood stone and brick and most of the leading given valued at £5.0s.0d

There was quite a large gap in the subscriptions raised and the total cost but how this gap was dealt with is not known. Oriel College retained some form of ownership over the school through the position of it and use of the old Tythe Barn.

Indeed, as late as 1914, when the school and land were conveyed to the Archdeacon of York, the link to Oriel College still existed for the signatories to the conveyance (see Appendix V) were the Archbishop of York, Cosmo Gordon, the Vicar of Aberford, Reverend Shepheard-Walwyn and it stated it was with the consent of the Provost and Fellows of Oriel College whose seal was affixed (presumably to show proof of their assent).

This transfer – at no cost – was perhaps to 'tidy up' the situation with regard to 'ownership' of the school and the land it stood on.

Early Regular Subscribers

There were 45 persons who paid the first of the regular contributions given to the school in 1716.Many of the old Aberford family names were represented including Akid, Hick, Cullingworth, Addey, Priestman, Bachus and Lady Vavasor (Vavasour). The following year Lady Hastings and Col Sidney were notable names supporting the school.

In 1720 the Archbishop of York contributed £10.10s.0d – a considerable sum, In later years, before the National Society became involved, it seemed as if money was loaned out to produce interest income and the number of subscribers became far fewer.

From the start some income was produced by a collection being taken up at a special church service when a visiting Minister – sometimes just a gentleman – took the service. Many Ministers from surrounding Parishes appeared but one unusual one was in May of 1792 when 'Mr Crowe, Publick Orator at Oxford' was listed. This practice continued with just a short gap between 1814 and 1825 until the end of the book in 1848.

(Starting in 1818 and continuing until 1883 and the end of the Account Book, Oriel College contributed £5.5s.0d every year to the school. Perhaps they started this practice after the National Society became involved in extending the school and the building of the cottages c1815).

Little Houses

During March and April of 1717 workmen were busy: 'Charges of building the Little Houses to all adjoining; the Steps and Seats in the Church'. What these Little Houses were and where they were exactly situated is not known but they must have had a close connection to the school itself, There is a list of the work and costs in the Account Book and the total cost came to £8.2s.7d and included such items as: Matthew Bucktrout leading a load of wood for the roof of the little houses and seats in the church; 18 yards of matting; wood given by Mr Moor out of Hazlewood and tile by Sir Peter Vavasor (Vavasour)'.

GettingThings Started

There seems to have been some teaching going on just prior to the school building being opened – perhaps it was slightly delayed in construction. An entry dated February 8th 1715 stated: 'Paid Master Wilson 15 weeks for teaching the boys. On April the 27th that year: Moses Settle 3 weeks ditto'. In July of 1715: 'Mr Wilson setting up the benches when the boys went to Mr Sampson's house'.

All sorts of matters must have been dealt with as the school came into being for instance on the 17th March 1716: 'a messenger going to Hull to enquire after a Mistress'. In that same month there was postage on a letter for Mr Oats the Attorney.

It appeared that paper was used for writing from the first – 'quires' being ordered regularly. In 1752 there was a list showing clearly the restricted reading materials of the times: 'Common Prayers, Spelling Books, Lewis's cat (echism), Prayers for Charity Schools, Prayers for Apprentices'. In 1755 'Advice after Confirmation' made an appearance, In 1763 'Watts Songs for Children' was added. Two years later 'Exercise against Lying' and 'Young Man's Duty' were listed.

Reference:Account Book dating from 1716 – Aberford Church Vestry document – consulted 2009. Deposited with the Borthwick Inst. Of Historical Research, York University

APPENDIX III
TEACHER TRAINING COLLEGES

From the middle of the 19th century, teaching became more recognised as a valuable and worthwhile profession and more formal training was introduced. The Committee of Council (for Education) of c1846 began to issue Certificates aimed at improving the qualifications of Teachers. These Certificates entitled the teacher to a larger salary and a Pupil Teacher system was designed to bridge the gap between leaving school and entering a Training College by subsidising the pupils for some years to gain practical experience of teaching and to carrying on studying.

Selected scholars would remain in school for five years being apprenticed to the School Managers. They would receive some payment, serve as Teachers during the school day and receive instruction from the Master after school hours and be checked by Inspectors on a yearly basis. The instruction was to be for 1 ½ hours a day for 5 days a week and a syllabus was laid down for each year. In the case of girl pupils the syllabus was somewhat modified but they were expected to be proficient in sewing. If the School Managers applied to have Pupil Teachers then the school had to fulfil certain criteria like being well-organised and with a Master or Mistress who was qualified to carry out the further education of the Pupil.

A school could have one pupil for every twenty-five scholars and the Master received payment for instructing pupils at the rate of £5 for one, £9 for two, £12 for three and £3 for each one above three. The Master could also receive more if boy pupils were instructed in gardening or some craftwork suitable for Schools of Industry or if girl pupils were instructed in sewing, cooking, baking and washing. Pupils were to be paid on a scale of £10 in the first year, rising by yearly increments to £20 in the final year.

Pupils were not bound to continue to become Teachers, the Certificate that was granted to them could be used simply as an educational qualification but the hope was obviously that they would continue. Sometimes pupils were able to immediately take up posts as Masters or Mistresses but Scholarships were awarded annually which carried a grant, although this was insufficient to meet the whole expense of attending a Training College.

There were annual examinations at Training Colleges and upon the results of these the Certificates were granted, a First Class for those completing the first year, a Second Class for the second year and so on. The examinations were open to Teachers not trained in College and if they were successful they would receive higher salaries. The School Managers would usually provide a house rent-free and an equal sum by way of salary.

The scale of increase in salary was – First Class Certificate £15 or £20, Second Class Certificate £20 or £25, Third Class Certificate £25 or £30. Women would receive two thirds of these amounts. This meant that a male Teacher who had completed 3 years successful training might receive a salary of £60 per annum with a house.

By 1850 when Pupil Teachers who had completed their apprenticeship were presenting themselves for the first time for Queens's Scholarships, they were asked to select the Training College they wished to attend so that they would sit the examination for that College. The examination would follow these lines:

Scripture (if Church of England), English history, Geography, Arithmetic, Grammar and Composition and lesson notes. For qualifications in an extra subject there would be an increase of £5 in the value of the Scholarship. The number of Scholarships was limited to 25% of the students and it was limited to 1 year but was to be renewable for another year at the Training College.

Pupils could also sit for a Certificate if they had served for three years as an Assistant in an Inspected Elementary School. Ex Pupil Teachers could be appointed as Assistants to Certificated Teachers at £25 a year (£20 for women) and one Assistant was considered to be equal to two Pupil Teachers. It became common for students from Training Colleges to become Assistants before taking on the Headship.

In 1854 provision was made for the certification of 'Teachers of Infants' when Training Colleges were authorised to provide a one year course and they could sit for a special Certificate of two Classes which would lead to their salary being increased. Those who obtained a First Class Certificate would be allowed to have Pupil Teachers and the examinations would be open to all teaching in Infants Schools. Gradually, in order to fill Colleges, the limits on Queen's Scholarships was abolished and extended and pupils could apply to Colleges after they received their results. Drawing became compulsory. For established Teachers aged over 35, a new class of "Registered Teacher" was established with a requirement to pass an examination with questions on Scripture, English history, Geography, Arithmetic, English Grammar and Composition and the Theory and Practice of Teaching.

After a while, the trainees were encouraged to stay for the full three years in Training Colleges, which received higher grants for those who stayed on and around 1856 Queen's Scholarships were made available to all those recommended by the Colleges, even if they had not previously been Pupil Teachers, provided they were over 18, and that no more then 10% non Pupil Teachers were admitted. This also applied to Infant School Teachers.

The Church of England set up Training Colleges for both men and women and a smaller number of Colleges were set up by the Roman Catholics, Wesleyans, Congregationalists and a Non-denominational College was set up with the help of the British and Foreign Society at Bangor. Lecturing was the staple method of instruction and students studied together, took meals together, used a common room for recreation and had little privacy. Discipline was strict and emphasis was put on morality. In women's Colleges attention was given to training in domestic matters which was often an excuse for making the students do most of the housework!

In these early days, the quality of Teachers turned out by the Colleges varied wildly with many having too much irrelevant information causing their teaching to be over-elaborate whilst they neglected the dull routine work in the lower classes of their schools. Training in actual teaching eventually came to be done in ordinary schools under everyday conditions with schools local to the Training College being used. The Liverpool College prepared the student for non-teaching duties such as how to complete Registers and Log Books and it was commended by Inspectors. 'Date and fact' teaching was the order of the day – there was much mechanical teaching. Young bright 'working class' men (and some women) began to see becoming a Teacher would allow them to rise up the social ladder and achieve a higher standard of living than they could otherwise have had. A typical example is that of an ancestor of the writer which may be of interest and is set out in Appendix IV.

APPENDIX IV
A BOY WHO MADE GOOD!

Walter was born c1858 the 3rd son of John Blackburn and Elizabeth Maude. There were two older brothers and one younger and five younger sisters.

Walter's father was described in the 1871 census as a Card Setting Machine Tenter – a textile job. The two eldest boys, age 19 and 17, were similarly described at this time and Walter – age 13 – as a "Worsted Spinner" as were his two sisters age 11 and 8. Clara age 7 and Sarah age 4 and Robert age 2 were also listed. They lived at 88 Hunsworth Moor, Cleckheaton.

It would have been quite usual in those days for children to be working – probably half time and attending school for part of the time. The 1870 Education Act had established limited compulsory schooling for children. However, there had previously been a good deal of literacy amongst working class people – often education was delivered by the Churches and privately for those who could pay. Increasing industrialisation was fueling a demand for a workforce which had basic literacy and numeracy skills. There were also very many Mechanics Institute- type movements bringing education to the masses.

It is speculation that Walter was a bright boy, perhaps taken under the wing of someone. It was common for brighter pupils to stay on at school and begin teacher training under the supervision of the Headmaster. They had to sit a formal examination in July of each year and could sit for a Scholarship which would allow the pupil to go on and attend a Training College to study to become a Certificated Teacher. What is certain is that Walter went from working (at least part-time) in 1871to some 10 years later, listed on the 1881 census, age 24, a "Second Master" at a Methodist school called Prospect College in a small village called Shebbear in Devon! Perhaps this establishment was a Training College but more likely Walter had secured an actual teaching position .

Shebbear College began its life in 1829. A group calling itself the Bible Christians had been meeting near Lake Farm in the North Devon parish of Shebbear since October 1815 under the leadership of James Thorner, a local farmer. A Chapel had been built in 1817 and, in 1829, Thorne's two sons John and Samuel began a Christian school for 20 boys called Prospect College after the name of the house built to accommodate the school.

The school saw many changes until it was re-founded by the Bible Christian Church in 1841 as Shebbear College. Eventually the Bible Christians became part of the Methodist Church and today Shebbear College is one of a series of Independent Boarding Schools which form part of the Methodist Church's involvement in education.

It seems astonishing that someone from such a humble background in Yorkshire should travel all the way to Devon and rise to such a position but indicative of the route many such bright young men were to take.

APPENDIX V
EXTRACTS FROM CONVEYANCE

From copy Conveyance provided to author by Archivist of Oriel College, Oxford 2007. This Conveyance was dated 26th May 1914. To be lodged with Borthwick Library, University of York 2008:

"All that plot of land situated at Aberford .. containing by admeasurement One thousand four hundred square yards ... also all that messuage, or School, with the outbuilding and conveniences thereto adjoining and belonging erected on the said plot ...to hold the same unto and to the use of the said Archdeacon of York and his successors for ever ... upon trust ... used as and for a School for the education of children or adults or children only of the labouring, manufacturing and other poorer classes in the Parish of Aberford aforesaid and for no other purpose such school to be always in union with and conducted upon the principles ... of the Incorporated National Society for promoting the education of the Poor in the principles of the Established Church ....

... said Archdeacon of York....may consent .. at the request of the National Society...grant or convey for educational purposes but not otherwise to any body, corporation or bodies corporate or person ... the estate or interest herby vested in them or any smaller interest in the said School ..."

APPENDIX VI
VILLAGE PEOPLE/CHILDREN
MR FREEBORN WOULD HAVE KNOWN

From "The Village of Aberford" unpublished manuscript by Tomlinson. At the beginning of the account it says the time referred to was 75 years ago and the preface said it was written in the 1950s – so this makes the period described c1880/1890. The writer stated that his father was G. Tomlinson a coachman and that the family lived in the bungalow below present-day Aberford Pine, opposite the Almshouses (Priory Park). The author's first name was not given but he was probably George Tomlinson and some information about this family has been found through searching the Census records.

The preface said that it was written at the request of Mr Hudson-Watson the Agent for the Parlington Estate at that time and discovered in the estate office when the office was cleared out. It was given to a lady in Aberford. Some time later a Mr Sparks of Garforth borrowed it and made a copy. From that copy the one in the Leeds Central Library was typed up – the original having disappeared. The Library's copy was typed up and donated by Mr G.S. Hudson with an address in Hythe Kent. [The writer also has a copy which was with papers from Aberford School]

From 1871 Census a George Tomlinson Snr aged 34 was living at Hicklam Lodge and his occupation was given as Groom/Domestic Servant. His wife Elizabeth was also 34 and there were four children at this time: Mary aged 8, Annie aged 6, Fanny aged 4 and Sarah aged 1.

By the 1881 Census the family had moved and the father had become a Grocer. With him on that date were his wife and Mary described as a Kitchen Maid, Fanny a Scholar and two sons had been born – George aged 9 and William aged 6 both scholars. George must have been born in 1872 and William in 1875 and might be expected to have started at Aberford school therefore in

299

1877 and 1880 respectively. At Hicklam Lodge there was Alfred Morrell a Coachman and his wife and son aged 3 months.

By 1891 Census Tomlinson Snr was continuing as a Grocer and at home with him on that date were his wife and Sarah, George a Joiner's Apprentice and William a Grocer's Apprentice. On the 1901 Census George was still at home but his father had died.

"The school consisted of one large room for Standards 3,4,5 & 6 with the Headmaster Mr Freeborn and two Assistants, a classroom for Standard 2 and Infants' room with Headmistress and Pupil Teacher. A Sewing Mistress, Mrs Robinson, attended every Wednesday to teach sewing to the girls. Mr Freeborn was a great man, strict but fair, and had no favourites. He turned out some great scholars, later to be Bank Managers, Accountants and business people in general. Parents paid 2d per week and the school grant allowed only on the report of the Government Inspector thus making Teachers responsible for the result of his or her respective classes. The school yard was a long narrow yard with only a swing pole in the centre. No playing fields, football or tennis courts or weekly baths as now. No pampering, just learning and everyone was happy and contented. Two half-timber cottages – one for the Headmaster and the other for Mr J Moor, Grave Digger and his wife who was the Church cleaner."

From the account, at the north end of the village where there was once a quarry and Nut Green cottages: "The first cottage was a bungalow in which lived Mrs Spencer, a widow with two sons. Both sons, Joe a joiner and Fred a painter, worked on the estate". In the 1881 census Joseph (Joe) was aged 19 and a joiner's apprentice and Fred was aged 16 and a gardener's labourer. These young men would have been nine and six years respectively older than George but he would have known them as older boys at the school.

"Becca Hall estate .. the farm Bailiff George Lindley had a son Jack, very swift of foot. He once raced a hare in a harvest field downhill and caught it within a hundred yards". John (Jack) was aged 20 in 1881 so would have only been known as an older boy but his younger siblings would have been grouped around George in age –

Sarah aged 15, Charles aged 13, Henry aged 11, Fred aged 9 and Ann aged 8.

In an area somewhere near Green Hill: "Mr Bulmer had a son Dick, a Pupil Teacher at the village school". On the 1881 census Thomas Bulmer was a Mole Catcher and lived with his wife Ann and children William aged 20 an agricultural labourer, Richard aged 17 a Pupil Teacher, Emma aged 11 and Thomas aged 8, both scholars. Certainly George would have known Richard Bulmer who was seven years older than him and perhaps would have been taught by him at times.

In the area known as Beckside Cottages just off Cock Beck: "The cottages on the riverside were called 'Rotten Row' [because they were flooded from time to time]. One tenant, Sam Perkin, was another with a horse and cart, coal leading and carting jobs kept him busy. He had a son Tom who went to America and did well". On the 1881 census Sam Perkin was a coal miner and lived with his wife Ann and son Thomas aged 18, a butcher's apprentice and daughter Jane aged 14, a scholar. Thomas was some 8 years older than George but would have been known to him as an older boy at school.

"At the Post Office, William Cathercole was Postmaster and his wife baked bread and helped in the shop. They always supplied buns and oranges for the Aberford school children at Whitsuntide to the order of Miss Cathercole. Mr Cathercole was killed later while riding a horse that threw him into the sunken area of the houses that were built below street level". The Cathercole family had two small children in 1881 – Harry aged 3 and Sarah Ann aged just 1. No doubt George would have known the children following on behind him at school.

Close to the old Rose & Crown Inn: "Joe Nettleton's shop .... and his son William. Two daughters kept house for him". Joseph Nettleton, listed in 1881 as a Draper and Tailor, lived with his wife Ellen and children Mary aged 18 a Teacher of Music, Sarah aged 16 a Dressmaker, Annie aged 14, William aged 12 and Florence aged 9 all Scholars. The three younger children were close in age to George and he may well have played with them.

At the Rose & Crown Inn: "William Wood the Landlord was also a farmer. His son, Sampson, kept hunters and was a rider at point-to-point and the local race meetings". William Wood was indeed a farmer of 100 acres according to the 1881 census and had two daughters, Elizabeth aged 21 and Mary aged 19 with no occupation given for them. Sampson was aged 17 and, again, no occupation was listed but he would have been known to George being some seven years older.

At the bottom of Bunkers Hill/Lotherton Lane junction: "Tom Naylor had a son Charlie, a good bass singer and a daughter Nellie". Tom Naylor was a Grocer in 1881 and he lived with his wife Elizabeth and children Charles aged 19 a grocer's assistant, John Thomas aged 18 a clerk, Harry aged 3 and Eleanor Jane aged 2. The younger children would have been a little close in age to George and 'Nellie' is most probably Eleanor Jane.

APPENDIX VII
GLIMPSES FROM MR RAYSON'S TIME

Some information has been obtained from an Aberford resident who was at school at this time. One of Mr Rayson's old pupils – Mr Walton - who lives in what was Mr Rayson's old house in School Lane – talked to the writer about his old Headmaster.

He could not recall there being any presentation or ceremony to mark Mr Rayson's departure and believed that he simply retired upon reaching retirement age. Mr Rayson was a good teacher and well-respected and he was quite a sportsman, especially involved in cricket. He was also Choirmaster of the Church choir and Mr Walton was chosen to be in the Choir which used to practice on Wednesday evenings and he was given 3d a week to sing. The Church services during the War years were certainly packed, with the congregation swollen by the servicemen and women from the nearby 'Camp'. [Where Parlington Villas now stands.] Mr Walton thought they were Royal Engineers who were servicing vehicles. The vehicles were painted in the colours for desert service as in the Africa/Italian campaign.

One day an old pupil called Bob Kemp was passing through the village with his Army unit and brought a 'scout car' up School Lane to show to the children at his old school. No doubt the boys were all envious! It may be that this man was the brother or a relative of Leslie Richard Kemp who had been killed in 1943.

Mr Walton spoke about Mr Pickles and remembered his science lessons when an embalmed cat was brought out and Mr Pickles explained all about it's 'inner workings'. Mr Pickles cycled to work from Garforth and was very well liked.

There were coal fires in school during Mr Walton's time with one in every room and one at each end of the Hall which was divided by a folding screen. Lighting was by gas and at Christmas time the children would make paper lanterns and streamers to be hung from and in-between the gaslights. Happy Christmas parties were recalled but no concerts at this time within the school.

The school bell at this time was hand-wrung but Mr Walton recalled that there had been a dome on the roof which was 'leaded' and within it hung the original bell. There was a rope from it which came down through the roof so that it could be wrung.

The toilets were in two blocks outside of the main building – one block was immediately on the left as one enters school yard at the present time and this was for girls, the other was at the back of the school yard for boys.

The school yard extended around the rear of the school and covered the area where the mobile classroom now stands in 2008. The garden area was in full use, where there is now a large detached house and the children had gardening as part of their mainstream lessons but Mr Walton does not know what happened to the produce. Certainly he does not recall any of it being used in school which seems strange.

Here are some recollections by another pupil a bit older than Mr Walton: "Now then I am going to tell you a bit about Aberford School. I would like to tell the children to enjoy their years at school because it is the best time – best part of your life and don't be frightened to ask the Teachers if you want to know anything as they are there to help you and they will help you. They aren't Teachers like we used to have. Today the teachers are more understanding and they don't give you the cane or hit your knuckles with a ruler or blackboard rubber or pull your hair – they don't do that nowadays.

Well, the Headmaster – he was a Headmaster – and a really bad-tempered Headmaster. He'd sooner give you cane than look at you. He were a different kettle of fish 'cause all he thought about were cane and that was where he came in! I agree sometimes we deserved the cane but sometimes he gave you a cane for nothing.

Now Aberford School is a real good school and, on a Monday morning when I went, it was always the Vicar who used to come down to say prayers on a Monday morning. Once he'd been away for a week and, when he came down, he said "my Policemen were on duty while I've been away". What he meant was, he had an orchard with some apple trees and one boy went to get some apples and fell down a tree and landed on a wasp nest and he got stung. In them days your mothers used to dab you with "dolly blue" and the boy were like a spotted dog by the time she'd finished !

Now I'll tell you what we used to do for us own entertainment. We used to get an old bicycle wheel and take the spokes out and get a stick and run up and down the street making the wheel go round fast. Then there used to be whipping top, shuttlecock and battledore and there used to be skittles for both boys and girls and jumping and all them kinds of things. We were never angels but we never did no wilful damage and the best days of everybody's life is their days at school so, if I were you children, I would try hard. We couldn't afford no toys as money were very short in them days. Now then at School there's everything to look forward to, so you children enjoy it while you get chance". (iii)

APPENDIX VIII
THE ABERFORD SPITFIRE

Early in WWII Lord Beaverbrook came up with the idea of 'Presentation Aircraft'. A person, organisation, town or village could donate the funds for an airframe and the cost was set at £5000. The aircraft would bear the name of the donor on the fuselage. There were more Spitfires 'presented' than any other aircraft type and around 11% of the total production of Marks I, II and V Spitfires were funded in this way. This is the story of the Spitfire which bore our village name and some of her adventures. Many events were held to raise the money and it was a large amount for a village with such a small population, but somehow it was achieved.

Aberford was a Mark V model with the serial number P8640 and she was 'taken on charge' at Brize Norton on the 2nd June 1941. Her first assignment was from the 26th of June when she was allocated to the 609 (West Riding) Squadron at Biggin Hill which was engaged on sweeps and bomber escort operations. At this time there were many Belgians who had joined this Squadron and perhaps one of them flew Aberford, necessitating her learning the first of the foreign languages she would come to need!

Whilst at Biggin Hill she was transferred on 6th September to 92 (East India) Squadron. Though only with this Squadron for 2 months she would have seen plenty of action. The motto of the 92 was 'Either Fight or Die' and it had seen intense action during the Battle of Britain during 1940. By the end of that year the Squadron had claimed 127 enemy aircraft destroyed. During the summer of 1941 Aberford must have been scrambled many times to intercept Luftwaffe raids.

On the 15th November 1941 Aberford was sent to 610 (County of Chester) Squadron for convoy patrols. This Squadron had been formed pre-war and it's motto was 'Ceres Rising in a Winged Chariot' – a very appropriate one for a plane! Aberford suffered an unfortunate accident on the 26th March 1942 when she collided with a stationary lorry on a narrow taxiway. Apparently this happened quite a lot with Spitfires for they were very 'nose up' and when on the ground the pilot had to 'weave about a bit' in order to see what was in front. On a narrow track this would have been impossible so it was expected that other things would keep well out of the Spitfire's way but someone must not have been looking! In any event she was sent for repair and did not return to active service until 12th September 1942.

A new experience for 'our lass' for she now had to learn a second foreign language. She was allocated to 308 (Polish) Squadron based at Heston in the suburbs of London. However, since this Squadron was away at armament practice camp, she actually joined 302 (Polish) Squadron who were also based at Heston. The 302 called itself 'City of Poznan Squadron'.

It was formed on July 10th 1940 at RAF Leconfield – under W/Cdr. L.G. Nixon. Its official RAF name was '302 Polish Fighter Squadron'. Continuing the Polish Air Force pre-war tradition, where fighter Squadrons were given names of the cities in which they were stationed, the 302 became known as City of Poznan. (Bomber units bore names of Poland's provinces). The Squadron's badge was a raven on a tri-coloured background, the assigned code letters were WX and pilots wore dark brown silk scarves.

Nearly all the personnel were veterans of the Polish and French campaigns. These included pilots with combat experience gained there. The vast majority of Poles knew no English or very little and a number of British officers (11) and NCO's (33) were posted to the unit. In the beginning the Polish personnel numbered 163.

During 1942, under the command of S/Ldr. Lapka, the Squadron made many offensive sorties over France and Belgium. On May 19th, during the Dieppe operation, the unit took off 4 times in a full strength of 12 aircraft but recorded no losses or victories.

Until the end of the year the 302 flew mostly bomber escorts either individually or with the Wing. At that time the 2 Polish Fighter Wing consisted of 4 Squadrons (rather than the usual 3) of which numbers 306 and 315 were stationed at Northolt, whilst numbers 302 and 308 were at Heston. Both these locations were at that time

Polish airfields, W/Cdr. Mumler commanding at RAF Northolt and W/Cdr. Janus at Heston.

Aberford had a flying accident whilst in the hands of this Squadron – perhaps whilst engaged in 'dogfighting' or perhaps whilst flying too close to another Spitfire when flying in formation. The brief details are that she was being flown by Flg. Off. E. Horbaczewski when she was hit by the propeller of another Spitfire being flown by Plt. Off. M. Muszynski. Luckily both aircraft were able to return to base safely.

Research turned up some interesting information about Eugeniusz Horbaczewski which said that he took command of Polish 315 Squadron during 1944 flying the new Mustang Mk.III.

Further research on www.elknet.pl/horba/horba/htm. revealed photographs and details of this man's war record. Sadly he was killed in August 1944 whilst leading some Mustangs against the enemy near to Beauvais. His plane crashed close to the village of Vellenes. He was just 26 when he died, having been awarded the D.S.O. and D.F.C. Research failed to find whether Plt. Off. M. Muszynski survived the war.

Here is part of what G/C Douglas Bader had to say about the Polish pilots: 'They were gallant and dedicated to destroying the enemy .... forever loyal .... it was a privilege to know them, fight with them and live with them. ...'

After Aberford was repaired following her brush with another plane's propeller, she was sent to 15MU Squadron at Wroughton on the 20th February 1943. This was a maintenance unit and 3 months later she went to Vickers for a fuel system modification. Eventually on the 7th July 1943 she joined the 416 (Canadian) Squadron at Digby, no doubt having to 'get her ear in' so far as the Canadian accents were concerned!

This Squadron was formed on 18th November 1941 at Peterhead in Scotland as one of the Squadrons of the Royal Canadian Air Force. The motto of the Squadron was 'Ready for the Leap'. It was equipped with Spitfire Mark IIs and became operational on January

11th 1942. The Squadron took part in many active duties including defence patrols, convoy protection, bomber escort, anti-shipping operations and armed reconnaissance. It was disbanded in March 1946.

In November of 1943 Aberford joined No. 2 Tactical Exercise Unit which seems to have been a training unit for pilots and at some point an engine failure caused a forced landing for 'our lass' but she was a tough old bird and survived this trouble.

The next record, perhaps after repairs, was on the 10th February 1944 when she was transferred to 186 Squadron at Tain in Rosshire – thence renamed as 130 (Punjab) Squadron at Lympne on April 3rd. Perhaps yet another language had to be learned by 'our lass'. The motto of this Squadron was 'Strong to Serve' and whilst with them Aberford sustained some damage on landing but it was repaired on site.

On the 8th June 1944 Aberford went to Scottish Aviation at Prestwick, thence to 8MU at Little Rissington. Little Rissington was an airfield near Burford in Gloucestershire and had three runways and is used to the present day (2007) for gliders/instruction of air cadets. There were to be a few frequent moves – to Brize Norton on the 2nd May, to Pembrey Air Gunnery School 2 days later, to Lyneham 33MU on 15th June and to Portsmouth Aviation on the 4th September.

Finally Aberford was 'struck off charge' on the 10th September 1945 and presumably scrapped. There was no glorious end in mortal combat for 'our lass' but she had carried her pilots safely home from every mission, despite being wounded on more than one occasion. She'd had a hard life with plenty of knocks and came to her end in an unremarkable way having given a lifetime of steadfast service. The motto of the RAF is a fitting one for her 'Per Ardua Ad Astra' - through adversity to the stars.

Note:
Research was helped by a photograph and short text in 'Aberford in Times Past' by A.G Bennett, T. Hayton & K. Hewitt: Published 1983 by Countryside Publications Ltd., page 29 ISBN 0 86157 115

0. A paper was found at school with notations on it which hinted at the 'life' of Aberford and I was helped by Mr Steve Graham the 'webmaster' of the Spitfire Society who managed to interpret the notations. Further research expanded his information.

REFERENCES

(i) No listed Author : (1712) An Account of Charity Schools in G.B. and Ireland etc. :   Various Extracts, Printed and sold by Joseph Downing of Bartholomew Close, Near West Smithfield Google Book Search: Reproduction of Original from Goldsmiths Library, University of London. (Accessed online 2008).

(ii) Papers being extracts from the early Account Book (book subsequently traced to Church) given to the author by Mr Bob Young, Headmaster of Aberford School.

(iii) Cressida Annesley & Philippa Hoskin (1997) "Archbishop Drummond's Visitation Returns 1764 : volume I Yorkshire A – G", pp 1 and 2.   University of York, Borthwick Institute of Historical Research.

(iv) Aberford Town Book at University of York Borthwick Institute of Historical Research, Parish Records ABE11.

(v) Rev. Charles Page Eden: Notebook, (c1861) University of York Borthwick Institute of Historical research, Parish records ABE44.

(vi) Rev. Barnes-Lawrence: (c1886 – early 1900s) Notes given to author by Mr Petre, Archivist of Oriel College, Oxford, (Lodged with Borthwick Institute of Historical Research library, York University 2008)

(vii) Rev James Landon, Account Book (c1807 – c1850) University of York, Borthwick Institute of Historical Research, Parish records ABE34.

(viii) An Account : University of York, Borthwick Institute of Historical Research, Parish records ABE80.

(ix) Bogg E. (1904) "The Old Kingdom of Elmet" Reprint 1987. p 164.

(x) Bantoft A. (1999) "Barwick School: Education in a Yorkshire Village" pp 16 and 17 Wendel Books

(xi) Papers given to author by Mr Bob Young, Headmaster of Aberford School, being photocopy from "Ecclesiae Leodiensis" (Churches of Leeds). No date/no author (Lodged with Borthwick Institute of Historical Research library, York University 2008)

(xii) Tomlinson G. Unpublished account of Aberford Village c1880/1890: various extracts – From copy given to author by Mr Bob Young, Headmaster of Aberford School. Also Leeds Central Library, Family History Section, Reference Aberford.

(xiii) Banks, 'Dick': unpublished account of 'A Walk Through Aberfor' c1930. Edited by M.R. Piper and published on www.aberford.net in 2008 under 'People and Places'.

(xiv) Aberford School Minute Book 1904 - 1933: Borthwick Institute of Historical Research, University of York Record ABE133

(xv) Morris, D: www.tadcaster-wwI-memorials.com

(xvi) Commonwealth War Graves Commission: www.cwgc.org

(xvii) Fifield, C (2005): 'Ibbs and Tillett: The Rise and Fall of a Musical Empire', page 200. Ashgate Publishing Ltd., Gower House, Croft Road, Aldershott. Google Booksearch accessed online 2008.

(xviii) Gilleghan, J (1994): 'Highways and Byways from Leeds': The Kingsway Press, Leeds. Page 266

ACKNOWLEDGEMENTS

Thanks must go to many people and organisations who gave their support and help with this updated book. Amongst them were some who helped in specific ways:

Mr Rob Petre	Archivist of Oriel College, Oxford University
Archivist	Queens College, Oxford
Archivist	Church of England Record Centre
Borthwick Institute of Historical Research, University of York	
Mr Bob Young	Loan of various School records/Log Books/Registers and photograph
Mrs Jo Heggie	For support and encouragement
Mrs Norma Kaczmar	For loan of helpful book and guide to correct referencing
Mr Norman Sutcliffe	For discovering and making available the old Account Book
Mr & Mrs Kilner	Photographs of Oriel Cottages/Mr Freeborn and stories about Mr Freeborn
Mr E. Pickles	Photograph and stories
Mr Walton	Stories of Mr Rayson's time
Mrs Cox	Photograph
Mr K. Hewitt	Photograph
Mr S. Piper	Computer help
Ms Z Piper	Proof reading